Castro's Cuba, Cuba's Fidel

There is nothing more difficult to carry out,
more perilous to conduct,
or more uncertain of success,
than the initiation of a new order of things.
        —NICCOLÒ MACHIAVELLI,
                THE PRINCE

De l'audace, encore de l'audace,
et toujours de l'audace.
        —DANTON

D0910719

Castro's Cuba, Cuba's Fidel by Lee Lockwood

AN AMERICAN JOURNALIST'S
INSIDE LOOK AT TODAY'S CUBA
—IN TEXT AND PICTURE

with a new Afterword
by the author

VINTAGE BOOKS

A DIVISION OF RANDOM HOUSE

NEW YORK

VINTAGE EDITION, April 1969
Copyright © 1967, 1969 by Lee Lockwood

All rights reserved under International and Pan-American Copyright Conventions.
Published in the United States by Alfred A. Knopf, Inc., New York, and
Random House, Inc., New York. Distributed in Canada by Random House of
Canada Limited, Toronto. By arrangement with The Macmillan Company
Manufactured in the United States of America

PHOTOGRAPHS BY THE AUTHOR
A Black Star Project

Acknowledgments

I would like to express my gratitude to Howard Chapnick of Black Star, Inc., whose patient generosity in large part made this book possible. Thanks are due also to Alan Rinzler for his valuable editorial guidance. I am grateful, too, to The Macmillan Company for having accorded me complete editorial freedom in writing this book. Despite its sensitive subject, they have never, at any time, attempted either to modify what I had to say or to suggest what I ought not to say. I also owe a deep and unrepayable debt of gratitude to Joan Lamm of Random House, whose devotion and care in supervising the production of the Vintage edition far exceeded the bounds of normal professional obligation, and whose efforts are mainly responsible for the success of this edition. Finally, a word of appreciation to my many friends in Cuba who helped make the preparation of this book such a rich experience.

To Joyce: it is your book too

Contents

PREFACE TO THE VINTAGE EDITION XI

INTRODUCTION XIII

ONE: A TRIP TO UVERO 1

TWO: WITH CASTRO ON THE ISLE OF PINES 55

THREE: CASTRO'S CUBA (INTERVIEW—PART ONE) 87

FOUR: FIDEL'S FIDEL (INTERVIEW—PART TWO) 147

FIVE: CASTRO LOOKS AT THE WORLD (INTERVIEW—
PART THREE) 211

SIX: POLITICAL PRISONERS 247

SEVEN: CAMARIOCA AND THE EXODUS 283

EIGHT: PHOTOGRAPHIC PORTFOLIO: IMAGES OF CUBA 303

NINE: CONCLUSIONS 325

TEN: APPENDIX: CHE GUEVARA'S DISAPPEARANCE 342

ELEVEN: AFTERWORD 349

A SELECTED BIBLIOGRAPHY OF BOOKS ABOUT
CUBA 359

INDEX 361

El deber de todo revolucionario
es hacer la Revolución.

Fidel Castro

Preface to the Vintage edition

I am pleased that Random House has decided to publish this book in a Vintage edition, at a price that now makes it available to students, young people of the left, and others generally interested in Cuba. They are the real audience for whom the book was always intended.

The photographs constitute an important and integral element of the book. They are intended to play a mediating and objectifying role between the subjective discourse of Fidel Castro and the first-person observations and judgments of the author, which, together, make up the text portion. Although, for reasons of economy, both the quantity and the size of the pictures have been somewhat reduced from the original hardcover edition, it is my feeling that the necessary balance has been maintained and that nothing significant has been sacrificed in this edition.

Three years have passed since the original manuscript was completed—a long time in the frenetic history of the Cuban Revolution. For this edition, I have revised the Introduction and inserted footnotes where necessary, and have added an Afterword that brings the book up to date through 1968. I have also included a Bibliography and an Index, which the original book did not contain.

LEE LOCKWOOD

Boston, Massachusetts
January 2, 1969

January 1, 1959: "Batista Flees!"

Introduction

It was my extremely good fortune to be in Cuba on the very day the Cuban Revolution took power. I can take no credit for this; it came about solely through the insistence of a friend and fellow journalist, Bob Henriques. In late December, 1958, we were together at Cape Canaveral (now Cape Kennedy), Florida, when he received an assignment from his editor to proceed immediately to Cuba. There were reports on the wires of heavy fighting around Santa Clara, and the editor correctly surmised that a "big story" might be about to break. I personally did not think so, but my friend argued with me so long and insistently that at last, with great reluctance, I agreed to accompany him to Havana.

So it was that my first visit to Cuba began, quite by accident, on New Year's Eve of 1958. In the early hours of the following morning dictator Fulgencio Batista fled to Santo Domingo, and Cuba unexpectedly found itself in the hands of Fidel Castro's rebel army. The city of Havana, which had exhibited its opposition to Batista by passing a sober and uncelebrant New Year's, erupted in joyous pandemonium which lasted for eight days. Mingled with the sounds of rejoicing the reports of firearms were frequently heard as the vanguard of Castro's rebel army, aided by the citizenry of Havana (nearly everybody seemed to have a gun or rifle), went about cleaning up pro-Batista pockets of resistance, sometimes in extended pitched battles. After three tumultuous days in Havana my friend and I commandeered a car, and after an arduous and dangerous journey down island, caught up with Fidel Castro in the town of Ciego de Avila, several hundred miles eastward. From there we followed him down the central highway on the remainder of his slow, triumphal progress from the Sierra Maestra to Havana.

No one who was in Cuba then, whether Cuban or foreigner, and regardless of his present opinion of Castro, could ever forget the spirit of exaltation and hope that permeated the island during the first days of the Revolution. The central highway was a 500-mile-long parade route lined an entire day in advance with Cubans waiting to catch a glimpse of Fidel as he passed. In each provincial capital Castro made a speech that lasted four, five, even six hours; some of them did not begin until after midnight, yet hundreds of thousands of *cubanos* listened to the end, cheering with delirium. During a speech in Santa Clara somebody released a flock of white pigeons; one spiraled upward through the spotlight beams to the high balcony where Castro was standing, lit upon his shoulder and perched there comfortably while he spoke. Days later, entering Havana, Fidel addressed a crowd

January 1, 1959: Liberated prisoners in Havana street

of 500,000 gathered in front of the Presidential Palace. Then he walked down the stairs, and, completely unescorted, passed through the entire assemblage, which chanted his name, *"Fi-del! Fi-del!"*— parting before him and closing behind him, like Moses passing through the Red Sea. It was a fabulous time, one of those rare, magical moments of history when cynics are transformed into romantics and romantics into fanatics, and everything seems possible. For Cubans, and for much of the onlooking world, Fidel Castro seemed a modern incarnation of the legendary savior-hero, a bearded Parsifal who had brought miraculous deliverance to an ailing Cuba.

It all seems a very long time ago—much longer than the seven years that have transpired since Fidel Castro came to power. Since that day almost everybody and everything Cuban have undergone great change, Castro himself not least of all. In retrospect, it is now clear that the true Cuban Revolution began *after* January, 1959, and that it is still going on. Like all revolutions, it has sacrificed the well-being of the few for that of the many and has brought with it violent controversy and division. Many thousands of those who jammed the sun-swept plaza in Havana that January afternoon, and cheered Fidel as he passed through them with the fever of prophecy in his eyes, now loiter in exile on the stoops of Manhattan and in the dark poolhalls of Miami's Flagler Street, embittered, dreaming with diminishing hope of the day when the United States will send its marines to liquidate Castro and restore them to their homeland. For the millions who remained in Cuba, those first euphoric days are an ever more distant memory, bearing scant relation to the years of economic hardships and political crises through which they have since struggled, or to the overwhelming sense of pressure beneath which they are now laboring to construct a Communist society within ninety miles of the American mainland.

In this process, the United States has played a significant and shameful role. Almost from the moment that Castro acceded to power, the U.S. government has done everything within its means, short of full-scale armed invasion (if one excludes the Bay of Pigs), to bring down his regime and replace it with a reactionary one representing the *status quo ante.* Except for differences of degree, the United States' policy toward Cuba has changed hardly at all through the administrations of Presidents Eisenhower, Kennedy and Johnson. Indeed, our policy of blockade, embargo, and infiltration has become so much a routine that the American public has largely forgotten Cuba. At this point in history, of course, Castro has his own very good tactical reasons for wishing to keep tensions with the United States tightly strung. But the fact is that neither the government nor the people of the United States have made more than a token effort to understand Cuba in terms of her cultural heritage, her ethnic temperament, and her national aspirations, all of which differ markedly from our own. We show little comprehension of what a revolution entails or of the forces that produce it. We are surprised that Cubans do not seem eager to adopt for themselves our political institutions (which we regard as sacred), and that they are outraged when we tell them that Cuba lies within "the United States' sphere of influence" and therefore must "sever its links with the international Communist movement," as was announced in a State Department White Paper on Cuba published a few days before the Bay of Pigs invasion.

I made three more journalistic trips to Cuba in 1959 and 1960. Then came the Bay of Pigs and the missile crisis, and nearly four years passed before I was again able to obtain a visa, in 1964, when Castro briefly opened the doors to the American press to cover the 26th of July celebration in Santiago de Cuba. After almost four weeks of traveling in every province of the island, including an exciting and hectic seven-day, cross-country trip taken in the company of Castro himself (it was unforeseen and came about through the slenderest of coincidences), I returned to my country amazed at the contradictions between the beliefs about Cuba popularly held in the United States (and reinforced by the reporting of the U.S. press) and what I had actually seen with my own eyes. There had been considerable changes during the four years, of course, not all of them salutary. But I could find little evidence of the standard image of Cuba so luridly painted by American newspapers, magazines, and television: a Cuba whose economy was crumbling, whose populace was in tatters and near starvation, and whose political regime had lost its popular support and maintained itself in power through terror and oppression and with the aid of Russian soldiers. Instead, I found that in spite of the American blockade, nearly everyone was working and had money; that in spite of rationing, people were well clothed and more than adequately fed (especially in the interior); that there were few Russian soldiers to be seen anywhere, and that, contrary to all pronouncements by the U.S. State Department, Castro still enjoyed the support—the enthusiastic and affectionate support—of a great majority of Cubans.

These preliminary revelations, together with my personal fascination with the singular character of Fidel Castro, were what prompted me to attempt this book-length study. Taking advantage of Fidel's offhand invitation to "come back whenever you like," I returned to Cuba in May, 1965, and stayed three and a half months. During that time I traveled widely, without supervision or restriction, photographing freely and talking with hundreds of Cubans. I also made three separate trips with Castro. A promised interview with him,

January 5, 1959: Fidel Castro enroute from the Sierra Maestra to Havana

which almost did not take place, materialized suddenly at the last moment and grew into a marathon seven-day conversation in a secluded house on the Isle of Pines. I finally left Cuba at the end of August, returning for three weeks in October to cover the exodus of refugees from Camarioca (for *Life* magazine) and returning again in May, 1966. On both of these occasions I spent several hours with Castro and was able to make corrections of and additions to the original interview.

Of all the political leaders of the contemporary world, Fidel Castro is one of the most influential and easily the most interesting. Few would question this assertion, I think. Yet, inevitably, there will be many who criticize this book because it grants Castro so much space in which to set forth his views. (The interview, edited to less than half its original length, fills three chapters of the book.) However, I have provided Castro with such a forum precisely because, while our government and our press attack him virulently and unceasingly, we are allowed to hear nothing from the man himself. Officially, we don't like Fidel Castro; therefore, the entire American public must close its eyes and hold its ears (as if by so doing we could make him go away). Yet if he really is our enemy, as dangerous to us as we are told, then it seems obvious that we ought to know as much about him as possible. And if he is not—then that fact should be made known. Whether one agrees or disagrees with another, the best way to begin understanding him is by listening to what he has to say.

Finally, this book has an intentionally limited scope. It is neither a political analysis nor a sociological study of the Cuban Revolution, nor a psychological examination of its leader. All three kinds of studies are badly needed and other people should write them. This book is intended as an introduction to both Fidel Castro and revolutionary Cuba, nothing more. The title, *Castro's Cuba, Cuba's Fidel,* is meant to suggest that the focus is on both phenomena simultaneously —upon the interrelationship between the man and the society which he leads, an interrelationship so close as to border upon identity. To borrow a term from photography, the effect striven for is something like that of an intentional double exposure on one piece of film; that is, a double portrait of Cuba and Castro together, with Fidel's great image superimposed upon the foreground. Since contemporary Cuban society is dominated in every conceivable way by Castro's mind and personality, I believe that this is an accurate working image for an introduction to the Cuban Revolution.

LEE LOCKWOOD

New York City
July 26, 1966

one:

a
trip
to
Uvero

Thursday 4:30 A.M. I am picked up in front of my hotel in Havana by Korda, Castro's bearded photographer, in his immaculate white Porsche. In the trafficless predawn he does racing turns through the city streets, opening the throttle wide when we reach the highway to the airport. The motor, fitted with parts adapted from other cars, growls like an airplane engine. But it runs well. Cuban mechanics, perforce, are among the best in the world.

I ask Korda whether he knows where we are going or for how long. He laughs. From long experience he does not ask any more. Except for important national occasions, Fidel's movements and appearances are seldom announced in advance, not for security reasons alone, but also to allow him maximum mobility. Often Fidel himself doesn't know where his trips will lead him. We may be gone for two days, Korda says, or two weeks.

5:00 A.M. The sun isn't up yet, but Havana's airport is jam-packed with noisy travelers leaving on domestic flights, taking an early plane in order to spend a full working day somewhere. These days Cubans are in an unwonted hurry, trying to keep up with their accelerating revolution. We find Tamargo, an unshaven, paunchy man in rumpled green fatigues. He is Fidel's chief stenographer. Sleepily, he hands us our tickets. For the first time we learn that we are flying to Santiago de Cuba, Cuba's second largest city, at the eastern tip of the island. After that, who knows?

Our plane takes off an hour late. It is a new Soviet Ilyushin turbo-prop airliner, very fast. The plane is filled to capacity, its passengers about equally divided between Cubans in militia uniforms or *guayaberas* (a hip-length, cotton shirt-jacket with four pockets, worn outside the pants, traditionally Cuban) and Communist-bloc *técnicos* dressed in sport shirts and heavy slacks, conversing animatedly in Russian, Czech, and other eastern European tongues. In the morning paper there is a short official notice of a celebration that is to be held in Uvero, a small town in the mountains of Oriente, to commemorate a famous battle of the rebel army. "Aha!" says Korda, "that is where we are going to see Fidel, I am sure." The newspaper account does not mention whether Fidel will be there.

Five minutes later Korda is sleeping soundly. I watch him with affection. He is my oldest Cuban friend. I met him in 1959, in Havana, when we were fellow photographers covering the first mass celebration of the 26th of July, revolutionary Cuba's national holiday. At that time Americans were still fashionable in Cuba. In spite of the sour political animosity that has developed between our two countries since then, we have become good friends. I am proud of this, and I know he is too.

Korda is a genuine original. He is wearing a military fatigue uniform unlike any other to be seen in Cuba. The material is regulation GI olive drab, but the uniform is hand-tailored, with trousers tapered to an almost Italian slimness and a belted blouse like an African bush jacket; on his feet, a pair of sturdy half-boots, rather stylish, that he bought in Moscow. He wears a rakish tan cowboy sombrero, its brim pulled down low on his forehead to shield his eyes from the sun, which is now beaming through the airplane window.

Short, wiry, agile, and determined as a cock, Korda, with his fierce eyes, his rich basso voice, his dark, glossy, carefully curried beard, and his custom-made western clothes, is satanically appealing. The ladies adore him, and he reciprocates their tenderness with an enthusiasm that is notorious even in a country where multiple amours are a way of life. He once told me that he has only two abiding passions in life: making love and photographing Fidel. The first, he said, is his way of expressing himself as a human being: "as compulsive and as necessary as the act of breathing." The second is "the only thing that gives my life transcendence."

Like many another middle-class Cuban, Korda had been a happy-go-lucky bourgeois hedonist whom the victorious revolution struck with moral lightning. It bestowed upon him perhaps its greatest gift —a sense of identity and direction, of counting for something. His perspective changed, completely. For the first time in his life, he says, he became concerned about other people.

Although spiritually galvanized by the Revolution, Korda has managed to remain relatively untouched materially by the advent of Communism, unlike most other Cubans. He and his partner Luis, a genial, mad, old bear of a man with a Hemingway beard, still own one of the largest photography studios in Havana and operate it as a small capitalist enterprise. From this he gets enough money to support himself, his mother, and his three children by two ex-wives, as well as a smart balcony apartment by the sea in Miramar (a swank suburb of Havana); his snow-white Porsche; a Czechoslovakian motor scooter, which he keeps for tooling around town; and an expensively diversified love life.

Two things fascinate me most about Korda: completely counter to his tastes and inclinations, which are those of a voluptuary, he is passionately devoted to the Revolution and, I believe, capable of making any sacrifice whatever for it; and although far from being a Communist, he is accepted and trusted by Castro and by the innermost enclave of Cuba's Communist regime to a greater extent than any of his party-lining journalist colleagues. The solution to this anomaly is Fidel, who likes him, confides in him, and takes him everywhere. For example, Korda was the only photographer who accompanied Castro on his two trips to the Soviet Union.

7:30 A.M. The curvaceous Cubana Airlines stewardess serves us tiny paper cups of dark, sugary Cuban coffee. For this, Korda wakes up immediately. Lighting a Monte Cristo cigar, he tells me a story about one of his many trips with Cuba's Maximum Leader.

"One day in January of sixty-four Fidel called me up.

'Korda,' he said, 'are you busy this weekend?'

'No,' I said.

'Good,' he said, 'because I want to make a little hunting trip to the Pico Turquino [Cuba's highest mountain]. It will only be a short trip, maybe two or three days. Bring some warm clothes, because it's cold up there in the winter.'

So I thought, 'Pico Turquino—that will be a hiking and camping trip. I'll just take old clothes.'

The next morning when I get to the airport, I'm wearing a turtleneck sweater, some old U.S. dungarees, and my dirty old militia boots, with a rucksack on my back. The first thing I see is this big TU-114 Russian airplane. I say to myself, 'Wait a minute, that's too big for a trip to the Sierra.'

The next thing I see is Alexeiev, the Russian ambassador to Cuba, and it hits me: 'My god, we're going to Moscow!' And sure enough, two minutes later Fidel comes, very quickly. Bang! They close the door, and we take off for Russia.

Fidel looks at me and laughs, and he says 'Well, Korda, I'm glad to see you're all ready for a trip to Pico Turquino!'

Many, many hours later we land at the Moscow airport. The temperature is about twenty below zero. Snow everywhere, banks of it five feet high. And there on the runway waiting to greet us are Nikita, Mikoyan, and all the other top Russians. Naturally, I have to get out first to take pictures. Can you imagine the look on their faces when the first one out of the plane is this shivering beatnik photographer with a turtleneck sweater and dirty blue-jeans? Of course Fidel has a wonderful time telling Nikita the joke about how I thought I was going to the Sierra Maestra on a hunting trip."

9:00 A.M. We are met at Santiago airport by a party jeep and taken to a party guest house located on the Avenida Manduley, in a once-fashionable residential suburb on the heights overlooking the city. The Russian consulate is two blocks down the street. Except for the woman in charge and her husband, we are alone in the house. Having risen before dawn to get here early, we now spend the entire day waiting for word about our next move, alternately reading and dozing. Not until dinnertime do we finally learn, via a phone call that comes for Korda, that we will leave for Uvero tomorrow morning at four o'clock. Meanwhile we have been treated to three plain, albeit bountiful, meals and an unlimited supply of fine cigars.

In contrast to the breezy spring of Havana, here summer has arrived with suffocating heat. Santiago is not only seven hundred miles east of the capital but two hundred and fifty miles farther south, nearly on a parallel with Haiti and Santo Domingo, whose climate and vegetation it shares. The house yards and the center strips of the boulevards are thick with mimosa, bougainvillaea, flamboyant and other fragrant tropical growths. Their heady bouquets mingle and hang on the windless air, growing more pungent as the humidity rises. In the late afternoon a sudden thundershower brings momentary refreshment, then ceases abruptly, leaving the atmosphere more oppressive than before. Excited by the storm, a thousand crickets begin their chirping, harsh and metallic, as if their wings were of hollow steel.

9:00 P.M. Just lying on top of our beds in our undershorts, we are perspiring. Impossible to sleep. In another part of the house a loud, energetic, extraordinarily rapid conversation in Spanish is in progress, long speeches overlapping each other, punctuated by great shouts and guffaws. The people of Oriente are a breed apart from other Cubans; their energy, even in the heat, is unflagging. I am reminded that Fidel is an *Oriental*. Elsewhere somebody is watching television, the Cuban late show. Lots of gunfire. I can just catch a snatch of dialogue here and there. It is in English and unmistakable: a gangster movie with George Raft.

Friday 4:00 A.M. Off to Uvero in a Toyota, a Japanese copy of the British Land-Rover. The road climbs into the mountains, then descends steeply to the sea, the dawn sun and its reflection shining up into our eyes with a double glare. After about twenty miles the new road, which someday will girdle the entire southern coast of Oriente, begins to peter out. Macadam gives way to gravel, gravel to dirt gradings, gradings to a pair of tire tracks which themselves often disappear. At such times we simply drive through the water along the shore until the tracks appear again. We jounce through ruts and over rocks, slosh across small rivers. But the chief problem is the dust, fine as sifted flour, which is churned up by the front wheels and sucked in a stream through the windshield, bleaching our hair and clothes and parching our throats.

Such driving requires skillful coordination of gear-shift, clutch, and gas pedal. Our intrepid driver is Olga Guevara (no relation to Che Guevara), a short, pudgy young woman of about thirty dressed in green army fatigues with a first lieutenant's insignia on her collar. She has the jet-black hair of the women of Oriente, is endlessly vivacious, utterly good-natured. Called "Olguita" because of her tiny size, she was a famous guerrilla fighter during the war, head of Fidel's female forces in the Sierra Maestra. Now she lives in Santiago, spending all her time traveling around the Sierra in this same Toyota, helping, she says, to solve the "political and social questions" that arise in the mountain settlements. Over the Toyota's racket she chatters enthusiastically about her experiences with the *guajiros* and the things the Revolution is doing for them. Her obvious affection for the mountain people under her authority and the idealistic devotion to the Revolution which animates her voice are qualities I find extremely touching.

9:30 A.M. Our eyes streaming, our pores choked with silt, we arrive at Uvero behind a slow-moving caravan of trucks loaded with grinning *campesinos*. Many of them are sugar-cane cutters; they brandish their machetes proudly. I wonder that so many men can be spared from the fields for an entire day at the height of the harvest. In Cuba, it seems, political events take precedence over everything.

Uvero is hardly more than a tiny settlement. It is located in a spectacular setting on a small grassy plateau between the mountains, which rise in abrupt series to the north, and the Caribbean, which lies beneath a short, sheer cliff on the south. Uvero would probably still be little known even in Cuba if Batista's army had not maintained a small garrison there which Fidel Castro chose to make the site of the first battle—and victory—of his Revolutionary War.

The battle of Uvero was an engagement of small military consequence. As Che Guevara described it in his book *Passages from the Revolutionary War*, in an account written with authenticity and no little wit, its main value was psychological.

Castro and the other survivors of the *Granma** expedition had been

* Granma *was the name of the sixty-two-foot yacht in which Castro and*

in the mountains less than six months. Until then, their main objective had been simply to survive, to stay hidden from Batista's men, while gathering arms and acquiring and training more troops. Their greatest enemy at that time, says Che, was not Batista's army, whom they had seldom fought and rarely seen, but a certain kind of mountain horsefly that bit them incessantly and left wounds which became easily infected.

Since the Cuban Revolution is already passing into the annals of war mythology, it is sometimes forgotten that in a military sense the Revolution never really reached the magnitude of a true war. Batista capitulated and fled before this could happen, soundly whipped psychologically before he had hardly been engaged militarily. Uvero was the beginning of the end for the Cuban dictator.

According to Che Guevara, the rebels had done so little of note since landing in Oriente that the danger was growing that they would be either forgotten or given up for lost by the Cuban people. In fact, Castro himself had been presumed dead until only a month earlier, when Herbert Matthews' famous interview with him was published in *The New York Times*. Now they needed to do something dramatic in order to demonstrate their strength. They had a total force of 127 men, of whom eighty were well enough armed to attack. Che and Fidel discussed objectives.

Fidel proposed the idea of attacking the Uvero garrison. Che, more cautious, thought it would be quicker and easier to ambush one of the army's troop trucks which regularly went back and forth on the mountain highway. But Fidel, displaying even in the isolation of the mountains his grasp of what makes good newspaper copy, argued that the capture of a whole garrison in a military action would have much more reverberation in Havana. So the battle plans were laid. Che wrote:

"The garrison of Uvero was located on the edge of the sea in such a way that to surround it we needed only to attack from three directions. . . . Because of the surprise we had prepared we thought the fighting would be short-lived."

Shortly after dawn on the morning of May 28, 1957, Fidel Castro fired a shot from his telescopic rifle, signaling the beginning of the attack. The untested rebel army, eighty strong, advanced slowly on three sides, meeting heavy resistance. During the battle a man standing by Castro's side was shot through the head and died instantly. It

eighty-one followers sailed from Mexico to the eastern end of Cuba, where they landed December 2, 1956, launching the Cuban Revolution.

took two hours and forty-five minutes to subdue and capture the garrison. The losses on both sides were bloody.

Che Guevara, who had been a doctor in Argentina before becoming a revolutionary soldier-of-fortune, was responsible for attending to the wounded. Here is Che's account of the battle's aftermath:

"We arrived at the barracks, where we took prisoner two soldiers whom I had missed with my sub-machinegun, and also a doctor and his assistant. With this doctor, a peaceable, gray-haired man whose subsequent destiny I do not know (I don't know if he has been integrated into the Revolution or not) there happened a curious thing.

"My knowledge of medicine had never been very great. The number of wounded being brought in was enormous, and my vocation at that moment was not that of dedicating myself to health. However, when I went to turn over the wounded to the doctor, he asked me how old I was and how long I had had my medical diploma. I explained to him that it had been several years, and then he said to me frankly, 'Look, Chico—take charge of all of this, because I just got my diploma and I have very little experience.'

"Between his inexperience and his fright at finding himself taken prisoner, the man had forgotten every bit of medicine he ever knew. And so at that moment, I had once again to exchange my rifle for my doctor's uniform; which was for me actually nothing more than a washing of my hands."

Despite its high cost in casualties, the victory had the desired psychological reverberations in Havana and throughout the country. Reports of the attack were carried in the newspapers the next day. For many Cubans, this was the first news that there actually was a revolt going on somewhere in Cuba of potential significance. But its main importance was the boost it gave the rebel soldiers' morale to have attacked and captured a Batista fortress on their first attempt. In Che's words, it "marked our coming of age as guerrillas." At the end of his account he describes, with characteristic irony, the exultation in the rebel camp the night following the battle:

"Right up until dawn they continued to tell their tales of the combat. Practically nobody slept or else slept in short naps and everybody joined in the assembly, relating his exploits and those which he had seen done. Out of statistical curiosity I kept count of all the enemy killed by the narrators during the course of the combat, and it added up to more than the entire force that had opposed us. The fantasy of each one had embellished his own achievements."

11:00 A.M. It is a bright, sunswept day, a spanking breeze blowing off the sea. Trucks full of peasants are continuing to arrive, also groups on horseback. Reviewing stands are being erected and trimmed with pennants and bunting. In front of the grandstand a series of large photographs in frames shows the hierarchy of the heroes of the battle of Uvero. Che Guevara, who has recently mysteriously disappeared from public life, is still in third place, after Fidel and Raúl Castro and ahead of Camilo Cienfuegos, another revolutionary leader, who had vanished in 1960.* Further on is the garrison, now a school for scholarship students from the mountains. In front of it, schoolchildren are doing exercises in unison, drilled by a no-nonsense girl instructor keeping time with curt, shrill blasts on a whistle. Behind the school rise the steep slopes of the Sierra Maestra, the color of pistachio. Atop a near high hill two flags stand out stiffly in the breeze, marking the spot from which Fidel is supposed to have conducted the battle. Korda and I decide to climb it.

It is a difficult and precarious climb for our city legs. We stop often to get our breath. The three soldiers who are guiding us scramble for footing with the ease of mountain goats and cheerfully haul us up after them when we slip. It takes forty-five minutes to get to the top. I cannot imagine fighting a battle on such terrain. At the summit we encounter a squad of armed militia, sprawled in the sun under the whipping flags. They are studying from textbooks marked *Basic Education Course, Second Grade*. Two years ago, they tell us, they were all illiterate.

I inquire of the militiamen whether they remember the battle of Uvero. One of them answers apologetically that although they all live in the general vicinity, the battle happened eight years ago, when they were quite young, so they personally remember very little. "Of course, the story of the battle is very well known," he says.

A young *miliciano* jumps to his feet, dropping his rifle in the grass. He wears a steel helmet, painted green, and there is stubble on the chin of his handsome face.

"Do you want to hear how it happened?" he asks excitedly. "Right here is where Fidel stood, commanding the combat. He killed three *Batistianos* himself with his telescopic rifle. Down there," he says, pointing to the crest of a smaller hill considerably below us and closer to the garrison, "is where the army had their lookout. Raúl himself

* *In a small plane which apparently was blown off course and crashed into the sea, leaving no trace.*

8

came up from behind and killed him with his knife, like this." With a violent gesture, he pantomimes the movie version of a commando's clean, silent kill. "That was the signal for the battle to start."

I look around at the others. They are nodding their heads in assent: that is how it happened. The young *miliciano* continues, spinning a Homeric tale of great bloodshed and heroism. When he is finished, he gropes about in the grass and comes up with a handful of rifle shell cases. "Here," he says, proffering them to me with urgent generosity. "A treasure to take back to the United States—real bullets from the battle of Uvero!"

Now a third militiaman jumps up and offers me a cigarette. His grizzled face suggests he is a bit older than the rest. "You are a *norte-americano?*" he asks. His eyes search mine, not for an answer to the question, but for any evidence that I am already offended by what he is going to say. "I would like to ask you a question, but I don't want you to think I am discourteous. You are our guest here, and we welcome you, we honor you. So please do not think that I mean to be impolite. But can you explain this to me, please, so that I can understand it? Why is it that the government of your country has the policy of being the enemy of all the small nations of the world? Why are you the enemy of Cuba? Why do you intervene bloodily in Santo Domingo? Why do you bomb the people of Vietnam? We cannot understand that. We do not hate anyone. We love the people of America. We want to live in peace with all peoples. Can you explain that? Please do not think me rude."

He is standing there looking at me. The others are waiting, slightly embarrassed, but eager all the same to hear my answer. What to say? There is no answer to his question, only the start of a long, difficult, ultimately frustrating conversation. I glance at Korda, who smiles and shrugs his shoulders.

I have been asked the same question several times since I have been in Cuba, each time with a slight feeling of shock. It is not a question at all but a polite accusation, always put in the same words and phrases and delivered in the same slightly hurt tone of voice. At first, I would try to answer. I would say such things as, "The phrases you use are too extreme. You make everything too one-sided. There are no clear-cut answers. I don't agree with my government's policies in Santo Domingo and Vietnam. But I also don't think the wrong is only on their side. If you want, I'll tell you their point of view, and perhaps then you will understand, even if you still don't agree."

But it was no use, I learned. Cuban Revolutionaries, like all militants, are totally convinced of their own opinions and don't want to learn but only to argue. This peasant *miliciano* in front of me who is

9

waiting for his answer, courteous and sincere, won't understand a word I tell him. The thought of this fills me with immense frustration, and I search my mind for some polite way to demur.

The squad leader comes to my rescue. "No, Paco," he says sharply, shoving him away. "You must not annoy this *compañero* with your questions. He is our guest. He is not responsible for his government's actions." The tension is broken. The *miliciano* sits down sheepishly. Relieved, I bid them all good-by and, guided by the three soldiers, descend the hill with Korda, running and skidding, almost out of control, all the way to the bottom.

2:30 P.M. There must be five thousand people here now, all peasants from the mountains or cane-cutters from the flatlands beyond the Sierra Maestra. They all seem sure that Fidel is coming, although there still has been no announcement. They are shy, quiet people, extremely good-looking. When they catch me photographing them, they laugh embarrassedly and half turn away.

The roar of an airplane motor overhead turns all eyes expectantly toward the sky. But it is not Fidel; it is an old red biplane used for crop dusting. As it flies in low over the crowd, a man standing at an open door in the fuselage casts a basketful of fresh flowers into the slipstream. Everyone races to catch them, children, peasants, soldiers, yapping dogs. With each new pass another cheer goes up as the flowers come drifting down. The *campesino* men, with their rough clothes and leathery faces, look sheepishly at the flowers in their hands. Now that they have them they don't quite know what to do with them. Some sniff them self-consciously. Others just hold the blossoms and stare at them. One soldier has stuffed a pink flower into the muzzle of his rifle. The plane disappears behind a mountain, then is seen again making one final pass toward us low over the water. This time the man in the doorway shakes out a large basketful of miniature Cuban flags for the children. They flutter down gaily, and the little boys and girls dance and squeal under them, snatching excitedly to catch one before it hits the ground. The little red biplane dips its wings and flies away eastward. The man, still standing in the open doorway, waves good-by.

4:15 P.M. The official program has now been under way for an hour: speeches, gymnastics, a pageant—in which the schoolchildren, brandishing giant pencils, attacked a cardboard model of the Uvero garrison, the walls falling down to reveal a new school inside—and now a band concert. Beneath the sour brass another, guttural sound is heard, a distant racket growing sharper and louder. A shout goes up. Out across the plateau, one, two, three big olive-green Russian helicopters are descending to earth as slowly as dragonflies. Fidel for sure! The program stops abruptly. A large part of the audience breaks away and races toward the whirling, coughing machinery. Soldiers quickly form a restraining line around the helicopters, but there is great pushing and shoving.

The door of the first 'copter opens, to great cheering. But it is a false alarm: Castro's bodyguards pile out. Stern-faced, tommy guns strapped across their backs, they take up positions around the second aircraft, facing the crowd. Then, after what seems a long pause, a pair of boots is seen, and a shout goes up in earnest, for there is no doubt this time. They cheer him all the while he is stooping and squeezing his bulk through the low hatch, descending backward to the ground. At last, sturdily erect, he turns around and waves to them. The crowd waves back and the din of their shouting grows louder. Then suddenly, surprisingly, the polyphonic confusion blends into a single, clear rhythmic chant: *"Fi-del! Fi-del! Fi-del! Fi-del!"* Grinning, he waves his cap to them. At this, the chanting grows faster and hoarser; the lines of spectators surge forward toward him, threatening to break through the human barricade. The soldiers shout threats, curses, pushing the crowd back. Castro's bodyguards grip their weapons and plant their feet, their faces menacing. Fidel quickly puts his cap back on, turns away, and begins shaking hands with the officials around him. The spell is broken. The chanting ceases. Reluctantly, the mob dissolves, and the people straggle back to their places in front of the reviewing stand.

During the excitement Raúl Castro has stepped out of the third helicopter, almost unnoticed among a group of other officials. He is the minister of Cuba's armed forces and second-in-command of the government, the man who would succeed Fidel if he were killed. Raúl is not at all like his brother, either in looks or personality, and he suffers a good deal from invidious comparisons with him. This is partly because there is nobody, anywhere, like Fidel Castro, and partly because of a certain meanness in Raúl's aspect and an unfortunate snarling quality in his voice. In reality, although he is as tough as he looks, he is a serious, quiet, remarkably courteous young man with an affable sense of humor.

Raúl, standing near me, does not watch his brother dealing with the crowd. He is gazing at the flags flying atop the high hill over the plateau, scratching his smooth chin uncertainly. I say hello, and he greets me with surprise. "What—again in Cuba?" He shakes my hand warmly. I ask what is bothering him about the flags.

"I'm just trying to remember how everything happened," he answers. "I haven't been back here since the battle. Eight years! It's hard to remember where everything was."

I repeat the story that the *miliciano* told me, including how Raúl had begun the battle by killing the sentry with his knife.

He snorts and kicks the ground, smudging the toe of his polished jump boot. "Crap! I didn't do any such thing. I just fought like any other soldier, and I was damn lucky I didn't get killed!"

He looks toward the hill again. "Now I see what's wrong. The flags are in the wrong place. Fidel's command post was down there, on the lower hill, and we went down its slopes and attacked from there, and there, and there." He laughs. "Ay, these *campesinos!* Isn't the truth itself heroic enough for them?"

6:00 P.M. Away to seaward the sky is still a clear, pale blue. But from the north a flotilla of gray clouds had gradually pushed its way across the mountaintops, and now it has begun to rain softly.

Castro has been speaking for more than an hour, extemporaneously, as is his custom. He is in expansive form. This is the kind of audience he most enjoys: the patient, unsophisticated people of the mountains who live out their lives next to nature and expect nothing more from a man than that he talk to them straight. The Revolution has done more for them than for any other population group in Cuba, partly because they were formerly the most underprivileged people in the country, and partly because of Castro's own special fondness for them. He had passed his childhood among them, and it was here that he had later returned to open his rebellion against Batista. When he needed their help, fleeing from Batista's pursuing troops, the *guajiros* had hidden him and his men, fed them, and cared for their wounded, risking torture or execution if found out. In return, he had paid in full for whatever he took, kept his promises, and what astonished them most, treated them always with personal dignity, as equals.

When victory came, they had been its first beneficiaries. Out of gratitude, Fidel had showered them with hospitals, schools, roads, farmlands, clothes, and higher wages. For the first 26th of July celebration almost the entire peasant population of Oriente had been carried by truck and bus into Havana. In starched new white *guayaberas* and yellow straw sombreros, their machetes at their belts, they had shuffled in silence through the nightclubs and casinos and tracked up and down the vaulted staircase of the Havana Hilton Hotel, gaping in wonder at so much opulence of glass and steel, the wealth and power of a true palace. Afterward, in the Plaza de la Revolución, Fidel had thanked them and said that all of this belonged to them now; that they had won it for themselves and their children; and for the first time they had had a glimmering vision of the magnitude of the enemy they had put to rout.

In the seven years since 1959, Fidel has spent nearly as much time among them in the mountains as in Havana, coming back whenever there was an excuse. The city, he has said, is his office, but the mountains are his home. And he keeps returning, because, like every politician who must endure the distempers and abrasions of high public office, it soothes him to go home from time to time to his own constituency.

For the *campesinos*, for generations inured to the circumscribed lives of feudal serfs, their transformed status is still too revolutionary for them to have fully absorbed it. Incomprehensible to them, for example, is that they should have been deemed so important that a law was passed indefinitely banning any new housing construction in the city of Havana because the cement was needed for building homes and schools and hospitals in the countryside; or that the government should have gone to the expense and bother of sending thousands of high school students into the mountains with kerosene lamps and textbooks to stay there many months just to teach the peasants how to read and write. And now Fidel is here, standing up in the rain and telling them that their transformation has only begun, that now they are going to reforest the mountains, start cocoa and coffee and mango industries, plant some kind of crop in every acre of soil, much of which has never been tilled; that they are going to have the paved highway brought from Santiago through Uvero all the way around the peninsula to Manzanillo, that there are plans to build beaches and tourist hotels all along the coast, not only for tourists, but for the peasants themselves to enjoy; and more, still more.

It is wonders heaped upon wonders, a vision of bounty too rich to be imagined. As Castro speaks, the peasants are as attentive as children listening to a magician announcing the tricks he is going to do. As each project is announced, they applaud. They cheer the loudest when he describes how Cuban scientists are now conducting experiments in seeding the clouds in order to make rain artificially in times of drought; of course, this would be the greatest miracle of all.

6:30 P.M. Castro is talking about plans to increase the use of machines to cut the sugar cane in future harvests. A combine can cut thirty times as much cane as a *machetero* can. But they should not be afraid of losing their jobs. The combines, he says, will make more wealth and more jobs for all.

There is a commotion in the front row. A Negro *machetero* with a black cigar is shouting, trying to get Castro's attention. Fidel pauses, unruffled. It is quite common for him to be interrupted in the middle of a speech, and he enjoys an opportunity to banter with the crowd.

13

FIDEL: Right, *viejo?* You are from here in the Sierra, no?

MAN: Yes.

FIDEL: And when did you come here, in what year?

MAN: In 1925, Fidel. I was a cane cutter. I used to cut cane on the plantation of your *papá.*

FIDEL: Really? Well, things are different there now, you know. Now it's a people's farm. (*The crowd laughs.*) Anyway, if you worked for my father, then you helped to pay for my college education! (*More laughter, followed by loud applause.*)

7:00 P.M. The clouds have suddenly closed in, the rain is driving down off the mountains in diagonal sheets. Castro is still talking. Though the downpour has plastered his uniform to his skin and filled his dark beard with raindrops, he has another fifteen minutes in his head and he is not going to omit one sentence. About half the crowd has fled to shelter—they can hear the rest on the radio. The remainder, some of them huddled under sheets of plastic, stay on to the end, applauding with undampened enthusiasm.

He is explaining the significance of the battle of Uvero. It was important for two reasons, he says: first, because it was the time when the rebels began to learn not to be afraid; and second, because it taught them that they did not need help from outside the country, for "the weapons for our victory were in the hands of the enemy." This, says Fidel, is a fundamental principle of guerrilla warfare, and their having learned it and understood it marked the beginning of victory for the Revolution.

"*¡Patria o Muerte—Venceremos!*" The speech is over. Dripping, Castro turns from the microphones and almost instantly is swarmed upon by members of the audience who are scrambling over the barricade. Some are old friends; most of them have a grievance to air or a favor to ask; many wish only to touch him. The bodyguards are hard-pressed to keep them back, and finally give up the attempt, standing by with sullen faces, their eyes sharp against any untoward movement.

Like an actor who has just come off the stage after a virtuoso performance, Castro is still stimulated, still a little high. With expansive good humor he greets all the *campesinos* in turn, submits to their embraces, and listens to their pleas, bending down his glistening beard so that the mountaineers, short people, can shout into his ear in their staccato dialect. One aged peasant woman, her head swathed in a terry-cloth mantilla, comes up and without a word grips his beard tightly in her gnarled hand, to Castro's pained surprise. When he finally manages to loosen her fingers, she throws her arms around him, sobbing, and cries, "Ay, Fidel—how fat you have gotten!"

Now a very old *campesino* is helped through the crowd into the circle around Fidel. He wears a peasant straw hat and a starched white *guayabera*. His face is wrinkled with age, his mouth a toothless pit. But his back is youthfully straight and his eyes clear and lively.

"Fidel, you don't remember me because I am an old man. But I remember you."

"Now just a minute, I do seem to remember a very old man, not such a bad man. He lived in a shack by the river. But you couldn't be that one—he would be dead by now."

"No, Fidel, it's me, it's me! You remember everything, even my house."

"Really, you are the same? Well I am glad to see you alive and so energetic, *viejo*. Tell me, what can I do for you?"

"Fidel, I want a pension."

"What, at your age you don't have a pension?"

"No, Fidel. They wouldn't give it to me."

"Don't tell me! Well," Castro says, taking out pencil and notebook, "I am going to look into this personally. Give me your name and all the details." The old man gives the information. He does not know how to spell his last name.

"All right, *viejo*. But tell me, since I see that you have your health and are living well enough, what do you need a pension for?"

"Ah, Fidel. I want it so I can start a little business with cocoa trees. They grow very well in this soil—"

"What? At your age you want to go into business with cocoa trees? What madness! Listen, how old are you, *viejo?*"

"Only eighty-seven, *Comandante.*"

"Eighty-seven! What sheer madness! *Viejo*, don't you know that at eighty-seven you should be spending your remaining years in peace instead of going into business for yourself? That's what a pension is for."

"But I will live many more years yet, Fidel. I feel very strong. I am all alone. I must have something to do. I don't think I will live with any more women."

"Help! No more, no more! You will have your pension, *viejo*. Ay, these *campesinos*, going into business when they are nearly ninety. They are never going to understand what socialism is all about, that's for sure." (*Much laughter.*)

Suddenly, impulsively, Castro is leaving, shouldering his way down from the platform and through the crowd toward a waiting jeep, surrounded by his guards and the peasants orbiting around them, racing to keep up with his long-legged gait. An orderly helps him into a quilted green nylon field jacket. Without a word he hops into the front seat of the jeep, which abruptly takes off at high speed with two bodyguards clinging to the running boards, scattering bewildered peasants right and left in its trajectory.

Not knowing what else to do, I jump onto the back fender, my cameras clattering. Gonzales, a chief of Fidel's bodyguard, reaches out and shoves me in the chest, sending me sprawling. "Some other time, *caballero!*" he snarls as they pull away.

I pick myself up, surrounded by excited, confused peasants running in all directions to get out of the way of other jeeps whose drivers, taken by surprise, are gunning their engines through the semidarkness to catch up to Fidel. I see Korda hanging from one of them. I run alongside, and he hauls me up just as the driver shifts into high gear, his other hand clamped over the horn.

9:00 P.M. We are in an army encampment, deep in the woods, about a mile from where the celebration took place. It is dinnertime, and Fidel, other *comandantes,* and guests are filing into the large mess tent. I stumble in the darkness and literally bump into Raúl Castro, who motions to me ambiguously. "Shall I come in?" I ask in English. "*Da, da!*" he replies, gesticulating. Then, embarrassed, he corrects himself: "I mean, yes, yes. Come, please." He offers me a chair next to him at the table, opposite Fidel. In Spanish now, he explains that he has been traveling around with a group of Russians for several days. Since he knows only a few words in either Russian or English, he gets the two mixed up. He points toward the far end of the table, where three young foreign-looking men are sitting, somewhat in isolation from the rest of the group, talking quietly among themselves. Two are blond, and the third, dark and skinny, with a craggy face and large Adam's apple, looks familiar. He is Sergo Mikoyan, Raúl tells me, the son of Anastas Mikoyan, the former President of the Soviet Union.

The dinner, served by an energetic detail of Cuban GIs in fatigues, is sumptuous. The main course is *lechón asado,* roast young pig, a specialty of the region, with crisp skin and sweet, delicate flesh. There is Cuban beer and Spanish white wine in abundance. The conversation is ebullient, rollicking, full of repartee. As usual, Fidel dominates it. Enthusiastically, he talks about today's "act," and how the peasants responded to his speech. They are all learning a great deal, he says. Someone down the table asks whether he remembers the Negro in the crowd who shouted that he once worked for Fidel's father. Fidel says yes, he does. Then, in a curiously detached voice, he begins to speak about his father. He had owned a large sugar plantation on the other side of the mountains. He had been a *latifundista,* a wealthy landowner who exploited the peasants. He had paid no taxes on his land or income. He had "played politics for money."

Someone else inquires how many *caballerías* of land his father had owned. Fidel names a figure. Raúl Castro breaks in. "No, Fidel, it was less," and he names a lower amount. Fidel disagrees. The two brothers dispute heatedly for a moment, but without conclusion. Raúl finally desists. Fidel continues talking.

More platters of food are brought in and passed from hand to hand. Everyone serves himself copious portions and devours them ravenously. The sound of popping corks seems bizarre inside a tent. Glasses are refilled and filled again. Fidel's appetite matches his energy: enormous. Beginning with a jar of yogurt (which, he says, he learned to like in Russia because "it prepares the stomach"), he devours a full meal of roast pig, fried chicken, rice, *fou-fou* (a starchy fruit of the banana family, indigenous to the region, which is rolled into heavy, sticky balls, the size of matzoh balls, then boiled), *malanga* (a starchy vegetable something like boiled, mashed white turnips), ham-and-cracker sandwiches, tomato slices and lettuce salad. Then, just when we are all gasping and looking forward to coffee and cigars, José María, Fidel's personal army cook, ducks under the tent flap with a gigantic filet mignon spitted on a stick, still sizzling from the fire. He places it on the *Jefe*'s plate. Fidel stares at it for a moment, grimacing. It would make a meal in itself. He pokes it with his fork. At last, heaving a sigh, he cuts into the juicy meat and manages to consume about half of it before satiety forces him to push the dish away and signal for the table to be cleared.*

Saturday 6:00 A.M. A tattoo on the canvas over my head wakes me up: it is storming again. I am in a large tent with about forty others, mainly soldiers and guards, sleeping on double-decker army cots.

"Good morning!"

It is young Sergo Mikoyan. He and the other two Russians are already up, straightening their beds in the far corner of the tent. We have passed the night together under one roof, in unwitting peaceful coexistence.

"How did you sleep?" Sergo asks. His English is flawless, nearly without accent, but he has a slight stutter. He walks toward me, hugging himself tightly. He is wearing only the short-sleeved sports shirt and thin blue slacks that he wore yesterday. They are still damp from the rain, and his bony frame is vibrating pitiably from the cold.

His face has the same dark features as his father's but is sharper and bonier, with keen, deep-set eyes. He also has his father's characteristic gloomy scowl, which made me think, when I first saw him,

* *Castro can also go to the other extreme. Sometimes he will go an entire day without eating anything, and occasionally he will fast two or even three days running for no special reason.*

that he was somewhat aloof and taciturn. Instead, I find that he is friendly and eager to talk. He has a quick intelligence and an eager curiosity.

Sergo has come to Cuba as scriptwriter with a Russian film team making a documentary film on Cuba. They had been with Raúl Castro for several days. On the spur of the moment Raúl had invited them to accompany him to Uvero. "Only for one day—we'll be coming back to Santiago the same night, so you won't need any clothes," he had promised them. Though his teeth are actually chattering, Sergo is able to tell the story with an admirable sense of humor.

His real profession is economics. He has a desk job in Moscow's Institute of World Economics and International Affairs, but every so often he becomes bored and looks around for something more interesting to do, like this trip to Cuba. He has been here twice before, with his father. He wishes he could find excuses to come more often, Sergo says. He finds the Cubans warm and sympathetic, and Fidel Castro an exciting man.

We chat briefly about international relations, Cuba, the Cold War. With conviction, he says, "What is most important is that your country and the U.S.S.R. must remain flexible in these days." He is concerned that Secretary of State Dean Rusk may not be imaginative enough to handle such a policy. However, he has "a great respect" for President Johnson, who is "less narrow-minded than Harry Truman," a remark that I find astonishing, since within the last four weeks the United States has intervened to put down the revolution in Santo Domingo and begun bombing raids on North Vietnam, and the Soviet press has been comparing Lyndon Johnson with Adolf Hitler.

6:30 A.M. The flap to Fidel's tent is open, so I go in. Castro has been up since five, too restless to sleep. As usual, he is in motion, and his high, hoarse voice easily dominates those of the people around him. Clad in boots, fatigue pants, and a quilted green nylon parka over his bare chest, he is regaling his guests by reading them the latest AP and UPI wire service reports on the bitter civil war in Santo Domingo. (The cables, together with the newspapers, intelligence reports, and communications of state, are delivered to him by helicopter twice a day, wherever he is.) The men around him listen silently, shaking their heads and clucking their tongues. After each passage, Castro pauses to offer a sardonic commentary, slapping the sheaf of cables with the backs of his long fingers like a sly rabbi. "What madness!" he chuckles. "What a book of fiction could be written about this poor little island! What a cast of characters! Caamaño! Imbert! Tapley Bennett! Thomas Mann! The O.A.S.! The U.N.! The United States!—It could make a trilogy!"

We go to breakfast in the mess tent. The menu is exactly the same as last night's: roast pig, ham sandwiches, etc., even beer. This time Fidel, after some yogurt, limits himself to a plate of *fou-fou* and mashed *malanga,* which he downs rapidly and with gusto. Helping himself to seconds, he notices that neither Sergo nor I have tried it, and he ladles a couple of *fou-fou* balls onto our plates.

"You must eat *fou-fou*," he says in English. "It is a great delicacy. Very healthy, too, very full of vitamins. We practically lived on it in the Sierra. For us, it was our beefsteak. Now that I live in Havana I miss *fou-fou* very much."

I try it, but it is extremely bland, and its consistency, like that of raw dough, nauseates me slightly. It is obvious that Sergo also does not share the *Jefe*'s enthusiasm for the dish. I can understand its value as a staple to the guerrillas when food was scarce, though: it is very, very filling.

9:00 A.M. Raúl has left, taking the Russians and most of the others who stayed overnight in the camp with him. Still sitting in the mess tent, we hear the ack-ack of helicopters rising through the thick mountain mist en route to Santiago.

Fidel, chewing on a long, tan cigar, complains about the weather. It is good for the crops, he says, but bad for his plans. He wants to make a trip in a small motor launch westward along the shore of the peninsula, around Cabo Cruz, and then northward to Manzanillo, a distance of about 130 miles. Cabo Cruz, at the western tip, is where Castro and his seasick revolutionaries landed in December, 1956, after a miserable six-day trip in the rickety yacht *Granma* from Mexico's Yucatán Peninsula, and started the Revolutionary War.

Puffing contentedly, his chair tilted back against the tent post, Castro reminisces about that historic voyage. He recalls how, in spite of his hunger and physical wretchedness after the long crossing and his tremendous excitement at being about to land again on Cuban soil, he had been moved by the raw beauty of the coastline, with the craggy green mountains of the Sierra Maestra rising straight out of the water, and he resolved once he came to power to turn this area into a center of tourism. "Now," he says, "even though it is still a few years before Cuba will be able to support a tourist industry, and the Blockade poses great limitations, I want to have a close look at the area and start making plans."

So we are going to stay here and wait for a turn in the weather.

4:00 P.M. It has been a long, lazy day, humid and dark, orchestrated with intermittent heavy rains. The mountains, yesterday the color of pistachio, have turned a more deeply saturated shade of green. The dirt paths around the tents have become slick mud. Everything and everybody that is not soaking wet is damp. Even when it is not raining, the sky continues to drip heavily, like a plaster ceiling covering a network of leaky pipes. The atmosphere is oppressive. I feel as if I were living in an underwater landscape, that it would be easier breathing if I had gills.

I have brought my tape recorder, hoping to make at least a beginning on the long interview which Fidel has promised me. Being here in the mountains, isolated by the weather, seems an ideal opportunity for it, since Castro presumably has nothing better to do. But when I had Korda approach him about getting started, he didn't seem to be interested.

Korda and I have been hard-pressed for something to do. I have been taking pictures but in a rather inhibited fashion, not being quite sure what my status in the camp is. Although everyone is aware that I am an American, I seem to be welcomed wherever I go. Yet Korda cautioned me to go slowly and not to take photographs of Castro relaxing unless he is there too. So I have spent most of the afternoon in our tent, talking to Korda, reading, or dozing on my bunk.

9:00 P.M. What does the Prime Minister of Cuba do to pass the time when he is holed up all day in a tent in the rain in the mountains?

He plays dominoes.

At least that's what he's been doing since ten o'clock this morning, nonstop except for a short nap in the afternoon and without pausing for lunch or dinner. All this time I have been waiting for a chance to talk with him. Not that he is physically inaccessible. On the contrary, in Fidel's tent lack of protocol is the order of the day. I and, it seems, just about everybody else in camp are free to come and go as we please. There is always a soldier on duty outside the tent-flap, seated on a card chair, his poncho draped over all but the muzzle of his tommy gun, but the only time he has stopped me so far was once when Castro was taking a nap.

Inside, Fidel's tent looks like an all-male hunting camp anywhere: informal and rather disorderly. There are cigar and cigarette butts all over the dirt floor. The rows of army cots, unmade, are littered with jackets, newspapers, orange peels, pistol belts, and state papers. To the left of the tent-flap is a small table with two bottles of Armenian brandy, half-a-dozen exquisite cut-glass brandy glasses, and some demitasse coffee cups. There is a bit of brandy left in one of the bottles, but most of the glasses are stuffed with cigar butts and cigarette stubs. Night has fallen, and the tent's interior is illuminated by three bare bulbs hung high overhead, no more than forty watts each, powered by electricity from the Russian-built portable generator which provides light for the whole camp.

The weather having grown uncomfortably warm and clammy, the tent's interior is like the inside of a hothouse, and the card table upon which Fidel and his friends are playing dominoes has been moved into the doorway to catch what little air strays in from the oppressive night without. Everybody is either in his undershirt or stripped to the waist. Fidel sits in the most comfortable spot, his back to the open tent-flap. Under the dim incandescence of the light bulb, his beard casts a dark, bib-shaped shadow upon the smooth skin of his chest and belly, stretching and contracting as he leans forward to play, backward to observe, or turns and twists on his narrow seat with eternal restlessness.

They play partners, two against two. The players are all old revolutionary comrades, men with whom Fidel can let himself go. It is a boisterous game, accompanied by shouts, joking, and loud laughter. The wit of the group is Pepín Naranjo, the stocky, cherub-faced mayor of Havana. An irrepressible clown, he is one of Castro's close associates and travels with him often. Pepín cracks jokes constantly and cheats outrageously wherever he can. He is caught about half the time. It is part of the fun.

Armando Acosta is a short, broad, paunchy man of about forty. His round, swarthy face and thick black mustache make him look more Sicilian than Cuban. Armando is one of the regime's work horses. He holds the chief military, political, and administrative posts for Oriente Province and wears the bronze star of a *comandante,* Cuba's highest military rank. His serenity of temper makes him a natural butt for the others' jibes. He answers each one with only a slowly broadening smile.

Comandante Guillermo García is built like Armando, but harder and thicker. His heavy chest and his massive head, with its wide, impassive face and close-cropped sandy hair, remind me of a great stud bull.

These three are the regulars. From time to time one of them rises from the table, stiff and bleary-eyed, to be spelled by one of the four or five lesser intimates watching the game from nearby cots or chairs. Fidel, however, never leaves his seat. He plays every game with utter absorption. The hours go by, and the others grow bored or tired, or both, but Castro's enthusiasm never flags, and he never fails to evince genuine unhappiness at losing a hand.

Midnight. It is apparent that everyone else is exhausted. Yet, still they go on playing and joking because Fidel wants to, because it seems to relax him, although now even the humor begins to seem a

21

little forced. For Castro, "relaxation" appears to be a relative term. Even while he is laughing loudest at a joke, he is studying the dominoes and planning his next move. His intensity of concentration and his unremitting desire to win are impressive. In a simple game of dominoes, as in everything else, Fidel Castro is a zealot.

Sunday. 10:00 A.M. The weather seems to be turning better. The sky has lightened considerably. Now and then a hazy shaft of sunlight, vagrant, lights up the raindrops clinging to leaves or grass like beads of quicksilver. Some of the soldiers who have had to stand guard duty in the continual rain are draping parts of their uniforms on the roofs of the tents to dry.

All quiet. Fidel is sleeping late. He was playing dominoes until 3 A.M.

I go for a stroll around the camp—and stumble across the answer to a question that had been bothering me: how does Castro maintain communications with his government and the outside world while stuck away here in the woods? The answer is a radio-telephone, complete with portable generator, manned by two poncho-clad soldiers under a large tree near the edge of the camp. Like practically all the matériel I've seen, it is Russian. Its aerial is strung up in the tree like the tangled string of a fallen kite. As I walk by I overhear one of the young soldiers speaking, or rather shouting, an official message to some nearby point for relay to Havana.

"—Go to the house of Raúl and get a box of mangoes! *Sí, mangos!* Also a uniform that the *Jefe* left there and a bathing suit. *Bath*ing suit. *Correcto.* Send it in a plane to Santiago, then by helicopter to Chivirico—"

After breakfast, I have a chat with Guillermo García. He is a hero of the Revolution, the first peasant to join Fidel's forces in the Sierra Maestra. Today he is commander in chief of the armies of the three western provinces and a charter member of Cuba's eleven-man politburo. Spinning a butane lighter on the table top with his ponderous hand, the trace of a thin smile occasionally illuminating his otherwise expressionless face, Guillermo reminisces about the Revolution.

He had been a simple *campesino* who traveled through the mountains buying cattle from other peasants for one of the rich landowners.

"I met Fidel for the first time on the twelfth of December, ten days after he landed in the *Granma*. I remember the moment very well. We were walking through a field of *plátanos* [bananas]. Fidel said, 'Are we already in the Sierra Maestra?' I said, 'Yes.' And Fidel said, 'Then the Revolution has triumphed!'

"At that moment we were four men, with two rifles and one hundred and twenty-seven bullets." Guillermo's barely visible smile indicates that he is tremendously amused.

"And did you believe him?" I ask.

"Did I believe him?" Guillermo gives the lighter a heavy spin. "If I didn't believe him I wouldn't be here now, *chico*," he says softly. He picks up the lighter and begins clicking the top up and down rhythmically, working carefully on another thought.

"You know, Fidel spoke with so much emotion—you had to believe him. Even in that *plátano* field, though it seemed crazy, I believed him. And now, look where we are.

"And something else. There we were in the mountains, far away from civilization. We had no troops, no arms, no clothes, no food. Yet even then Fidel was always studying. We hadn't even started to fight the enemy and Fidel was already analyzing international affairs. I remember we would be worrying about where we could find something to eat, and Fidel would be talking about America and Eisenhower and making plans for the future. He always had that way. He always analyzed the enemy's reaction in advance and prepared for it.

"Another thing. Fidel had never been in these mountains before. But in six months he knew the whole Sierra better than any *guajiro* who was born here. He never forgot a place that he went. He remembered everything—the soil, the trees, who lived in each house. In those days I was a cattle buyer. I used to go all over the mountains. But in six months Fidel knew the Sierra better than I did, and I was born and raised here."

I ask Guillermo if there ever were discussions about political ideology while they were in the mountains. He gives a short, nasty laugh.

"*Chico*, who had time for that? For all of us, there was only one thing on our minds. To beat Batista. We spent all our time worrying about that. How to get more guns, more men. In my first battle, at La Plata, I had only twenty bullets for my rifle. We let Fidel do our thinking for us."

When Castro came to power, many guerrillas went to Havana to fill important government posts. Guillermo was one of them. He did not like the city.

"When I came to Havana I was ignorant, like any *guajiro*. If they had given me an examination, I would only pass the second-grade level. I didn't even know how to make an official telephone call. But it was necessary to do the work of the Revolution. I worked in my job all day, from eight to six, every day. Then I had to study from seven o'clock to eleven o'clock every night, in order to get up to the sixth-grade level. Even today I am still studying."

"What are you studying now?"

"Marxism-Leninism." He pauses. Then he gives the lighter a spin. "The task of the party is very difficult," he adds, gazing at his hands as they keep the lighter revolving.

A long silence.

"But I will tell you one thing: Fidel has not changed. He is exactly the same as he was in the Sierra."

Another silence.

"*La Sierra Maestra*," Guillermo García muses softly, his eyes still fixed vacantly on the lighter. "*Una cosa interesante. Nuestra maestra.*" *

1:00 P.M. The sun has disappeared again. The air is filled with a misty drizzle being blown off the mountain tops, the sky a backdrop of smoky whiteness across which dark clouds are scudding like dirty sponges. Periodically one of them, as if wrung out violently, unleashes a sudden splatter of fat, gray drops.

Castro is up, lounging on his bed in only trousers and boots, puffing on a big cigar. He is reading aloud from the Cuban newspapers, which have just arrived. The others are sprawled in chairs or lying on cots, listening attentively and puffing on "Fidel Specials." The tent is filled with their pungent fumes. In a bed in a far corner of the tent, Pepín Naranjo is still sleeping.

Later, Fidel suddenly invites me to sit down, and we have a short conversation in which he does most of the talking. He seems on edge; perhaps the inactivity is beginning to get to him. Casually, at top speed, he glides over a wide stretch of subject matter, first in Spanish, later shifting into somewhat broken English.

"People are beginning to appreciate the value of work. Material incentives, though important as a stimulus, are not the most important factor. More important is the moral incentive being felt by the people. These are the first fruits of socialism here. People used to think, before the Revolution, that work such as cutting cane was dirty—let others do it. But now they are beginning to understand and feel the true value of work itself. They are making their own future, and they see the results. With this has also come perhaps our most important accomplishment—the instillation in the people of a revolutionary consciousness."

We talk briefly about the Soviet Union, which buys half of Cuba's sugar and supports her economy. Then, somehow the conversation wanders onto the subject of Stalin.

"Stalin was a very strong man, but very strange," Fidel says. "I think that he made very many mistakes, especially in the last years of

*"*The Sierra Maestra. An interesting thing. Our teacher.*"

his life. He was very jealous, very much afraid. That is why he made the pact with Hitler: he was afraid that Germany and England would ally against him.

"Stalin—he had no contact with the people. Living alone for so many years, inside the Kremlin, never going out. . . . I think perhaps he was a little senile in his last days. He executed so many men, all the heads of the army, the party. And for what?

"Khrushchev was a man who did many good things, and also some bad things. He was much better than Stalin. I don't think Stalin would have made so many compromises for the sake of Cuba as Khrushchev did. He was too strong-minded and too nationalistic. Nikita came to our aid at a moment when we needed much help. That was a good thing that he did." Castro pauses and examines his cigar. "But he also did some things to Cuba which were very distasteful," he adds significantly.

"Meaning the Missile Crisis?"

Fidel exhales a cloud of smoke that all but obliterates his face. He puffs and exhales again.

"Yes."

In silence, he watches the smoke ascending and swirling in hazy layers around the light bulb overhead. At length, he continues:

"I think that there can never be another Stalin or another Nikita. The fact that Khrushchev was substituted for by a vote of the entire Central Committee, after full discussions—this means more democracy in the Soviet Union, more collective leadership, and it will be more difficult in the future for a strong man to rise to the top. Because there will be too many persons. . . ." His voice trails away, leaving the thought incomplete.

The conversation shifts. Castro begins to speak about the United States, developing his thoughts with mounting excitement until he is off the bed, on his feet, haranguing me, punctuating his accusations with jabs of his smoldering cigar in my direction.

"Johnson! He is very smart! He conducted a very good campaign against Goldwater, and now he is doing everything that Goldwater talked about! Everything!

"I think that now international tensions are going to become worse. Because of Santo Domingo, especially. And Vietnam. In Santo Domingo, Johnson has made a Declaration of No Independence for all of Latin America! How can he do such a thing? What right has he? And the crisis in Santo Domingo has set back the United States' good will in Latin America forty years. It has killed the Alliance for Progress. It has killed the O.A.S.! Every time the United States makes a mistake, it embarrasses its allies!

"And now the same thing in Vietnam. Does your country think it has the unilateral right to intervene wherever and whenever it wishes? Eventually the United States will be fighting all alone on three continents, against the future. I think that the Soviet Union will not allow the United States to follow this 'Johnson Doctrine.' It would be impossible to suppose that 'peaceful coexistence' means that the United States can do anything it wishes!"

As suddenly as he had begun, he stops and hurls himself back upon the bed, crossing his boots on the sheet and pulling hard at his cigar, which has gone out. After a moment's silence, he apologizes for his outburst. It was not, he wishes me to know, directed at me personally, but at my government. He picks up a Cuban paper. On the front page there is a venomous story about McGeorge Bundy, the special envoy of President Johnson who has gone to Santo Domingo to try to settle the crisis.

"But tell me," Castro asks, sitting up again, "Who is this McGeorge Bundy? I do not understand. Didn't he come from Harvard? I have always heard that Harvard is a very liberal university. How is it possible for such a man to be the agent who carries out the reactionary policies of Johnson?"

He stares at me, a challenging gleam in his eyes, eager for a reply. I am at a loss to answer a question put in such a way. It reminds me of the accusing question of the peasant militiaman on the mountaintop at Uvero. It shocks me to realize that Fidel Castro, with all his analytical brilliance, is really out of touch with the day-to-day realities of American political and social life. In his way, he is as biased about America as Americans are about him.

4:00 P.M. Raining heavily again, without cease. The ground is so thoroughly inundated that it can hold no more water. The footpaths have turned to pudding. The guards, soaked to the skin in spite of their ponchos, have given up trying to find shelter beneath the trees and now are standing exposed to the full tropical downpour. In their misery, they no longer even attempt to keep their gun barrels dry.

The domino marathon has been under way again since early this afternoon. I watch until I feel myself growing drowsy with boredom. As I am leaving the tent, I hear Fidel bang down a domino, exclaiming: "History always favors the intrepid!"

9:00 P.M. With Korda, I am again in Castro's tent, the only place in camp where anything interesting is going on.

The night packet of messages, cables, and newspapers arrives. Fidel has been waiting impatiently for them. He jumps up from the domino table and goes to his bed, followed at a respectful distance by the entire assembly. After a brief, intensive scrutiny of the official mail, he hands the day's sheaf of wire service cables to Pepín to read aloud. Fidel lights a cigar, clamps it in his mouth, and settles back comfortably on the pillow, his arms folded beneath his head.

The first batch of cables is from Prensa Latina, Cuba's own wire service and propaganda arm. Pepín runs through them at top speed, a series of short, dull, one-dimensional reports from various world capitals, most of them in socialist countries.

Then, more slowly, he reads the dispatches of the UPI. The first dozen or so, filed from different date lines, are all about Santo Domingo. One is a sardonic report on the material inconveniences the civil war is causing in the capital city of Santo Domingo: hotels are short of chambermaids, and there is no food to serve the guests; various embassies are without phone service; the erratic water supply is causing many Dominican families to do without baths. This last elicits a faint chuckle from the *Jefe*. Now Pepín turns to an AP cable.

"Tokyo. May 30th. For the third day in a row the People's Republic of China has attacked the Soviet Union for taking a soft line on the U.S. intervention in Santo Domingo. The Chinese government said, in an official broadcast of Radio Peking monitored here this morning, that. . . ."

Pepín stops and cocks an ear. Fidel's eyes are closed. From under the cigar comes the faint, rhythmic sound of snoring. Armando smiles. As we tiptoe out of the tent, Pepín is drawing a blanket up to cover him, while Armando gently extracts from Castro's mouth the still smoldering cigar.

Monday. NOON. After another morning of eternal dominoes (now even Fidel is playing without enthusiasm), we go to lunch. Castro apologizes for not having spent more time talking to me. He has not been feeling well. An infection has swollen his right forearm and caused spots on the rest of his body, and he hasn't been able to sleep well, he says. He thinks it comes from having eaten a certain kind of fish which at this time of year carries infectious bacteria.

"Anyway, I hope you haven't been bored," he says, smiling. "What would your State Department say if they knew you had been kept incommunicado in the Sierra Maestra with Fidel Castro for three days?"

I answer, "Probably they would say, 'Tell us, what's he *really* like?' "

1:00 P.M. Much excitement in front of the *Jefe*'s tent. Fidel has just decided that, bad roads or no, we are going to leave this place. We will try to get as far as Chivirico, a distance of perhaps twelve miles, where the launches for our sea trip are waiting for us. A squad of Castro's bodyguards are applying their lungs to the nozzles of two bright orange rubber life rafts, testing for leaks.

2:00 P.M. Fidel bursts from his tent, climbs into the lead jeep, and we are away at last, in slipping, sliding, jouncing four-wheel drive. We barely navigate through the ruts out of the camp and turn onto what is left of the main road. After about two hundred yards we come to the first stream, now quite a respectable river. Fording it, two jeeps get stuck, one of them our own. It takes us fifteen minutes to come loose. Halfway across the next stream we suffer the same fate and sit there until a passing band of *campesinos* delivers us with a hearty push to the far shore. Another quarter of a mile, and we juggernaut to the top of a rise to view a formidable sight below: the Rio Grande River. Only three days ago it had contained hardly enough water to wet our tires; now it is a racing, swollen torrent. And right in the middle, half-submerged, is one of the jeeps. Fidel? No, he is still on our side, getting out of his own jeep and striding angrily to the bank. As we join him, out onto the running board of the stranded vehicle steps Pepín Naranjo. He waves a handkerchief and shouts jokes, but they are inaudible in the roar of the river, which is coursing right through the floor of the jeep and over his boots in a small but powerful waterfall.

Fidel sits on a rock, chin in hand, stony-faced, watching Pepín and two of the guards wade toward us through the hip-deep water holding their guns high over their heads. Clearly we cannot go farther in the jeeps. However, help is nearby. In a few minutes a helicopter sputters out of the clouds and makes a gentle landing in the roadway, practically at our feet. In three separate loads, we are airlifted to Chivirico, a trip of only eight minutes.

I am in the second flight. By the time I reach Chivirico, a large crowd has already gathered around Fidel and more or less thrust him into the local *tienda del pueblo* (state-run general store). I find him in the very rear of the store, standing with his back against the counter, completely hemmed in by *campesinos* and looking very morose. Word has spread quickly through the small town; more peasants are continually arriving and jostling their way into the narrow, rapidly filling store. All the peasants in the front rank are trying to talk to him at once, while those in the rear strain and press forward or hold up their children to get a better look. The few guards with him do their best to keep order, but it is impossible. Fidel endures the bedlam stoically. Normally a crowd like this would make Castro expansive, but today it only irritates him. He is impatient to be going.

3:30 P.M. At last we have reached the boats, and Castro is dividing up the party. There are two twin launches, each with a capacity for three of us plus a pilot. The rest will travel on two large gray Russian-built Coast Guard gunboats which always convoy Fidel at sea—one forward, the other aft, both always to seaward of him. We are going to Santiago, about sixty miles down the coast. I have been accorded a place in the launch Fidel is not in, so that I may photograph him.

The launches are small, no more than eighteen feet long and seven across the beam, but extremely swift, powered by two new-looking Chrysler engines. Castro is piloting his own launch. As we clear the docks, he opens up the throttle and does a couple of rings around our launch, waving, then pulls away to eastward down the coast.

Moments later one of his engines conks out. A crewman works on it for a while, then gives up. We shall have to travel all the way to Santiago at half speed.

4:30 P.M. Again the weather closes in. The coastline, its jagged mountains wreathed in veils of swirling mist, grows steadily fainter. To seaward the two escort gunboats have disappeared completely into the haze. All we can see now is Fidel's launch, a couple of hundred yards ahead, bobbing like a pea in the rough water.

A squall line marches up from the southwest and smacks our stern with winds and shingles of rain. Our pilot throttles down the engine and leaves the wheel to haul out the canvas side curtains. While I stand forward and clutch my cameras, trying to keep them dry, the other two passengers lend the pilot a hand. They have a difficult time fastening the curtains into place, for the canvas has shrunk.

Castro's launch, apparently having lost its heading in the storm, has now made a 180-degree turn. As I watch, it suddenly speeds up and comes toward us on a course that will take it straight across our bow. With curtains up on all sides, Castro can't see us. At the last moment, I grab the wheel and spin it to starboard, gunning the engine. Fidel's boat races by, narrowly missing ours. Our pilot is still fussing with the canvas. Feeling the boat swerve, he bounds to the controls. For at least a minute he just stands there silently, his hands on his hips and a rueful grin on his face, staring after the other little boat, which, now back on course, is once again receding into the mist.

9:00 P.M. Well after dark, after more than four hours on the water, we find the Santiago lighthouse and inch into the long, narrow harbor. Our shared ordeal has given all of us in our boat a new feeling of camaraderie. As we glide at low throttle through the calm, iridescent waters of the harbor, one of my fellow passengers, Isidoro Malmierca, an old-time, prerevolutionary Cuban Communist who has not said so much as a word to me in any language during the four days we have been together, suddenly puts his hand on my shoulder and whispers conspiratorially, in halting English, "You know, we made a mistake. This is not Santiago—we are in Santo Domingo!"

"Good," I reply, "please take me to the Embajador Hotel." * At this dubious riposte Malmierca laughs uproariously.

At the bottom of the harbor we tie up at the dock of one of the party's guest houses, some rich merchant's former villa. Fidel is already in the living room with his feet up and an army greatcoat over his shoulders, sipping brandy. He offers me a glass.

"I have to return to Havana tonight," he says. "A delegation of Italian Communists is waiting to see me. I am sorry you haven't had a more interesting excursion. But, anyhow, I will see you again soon, and then we will talk."

He gulps down the brandy, springs to his feet, shakes hands, and is off, flanked by his bodyguards and Pepín. They leave a trail of wet bootprints on the polished sandalwood floor.

Monday. 10:00 A.M. After a shower and a good night's rest, Korda and I take the first available flight for Havana. Before going back to sleep, Korda tells another story about his surprise trip with Castro to the Soviet Union in 1964.

After twelve days in the U.S.S.R. they flew home to Cuba in the same Russian plane which had brought them. It was early Sunday morning when they landed at Havana's Rancho Boyeros airport. Due to a mix-up in communications, there was nobody waiting to meet them: no officials, no press, not even a government car. The airport was empty.

Castro strode across the deserted apron and into the terminal. He seized the nearest telephone and dialed the private home number of Osvaldo Dorticós, Cuba's President.

"Hello, Dorticós?" Castro shouted, holding the phone away from his mouth. "This is Fidel. What's doing?"

"Fidel? Hello, where are you?"

"I'm in Moscow," Fidel yelled, winking broadly at the appreciative audience now clustered around him.

"Oh, fine. How are things going? When are you coming home?"

"I'm flying back tomorrow. But listen, do me a favor. When I arrive, I don't want any welcoming committee. No ceremonies, no newsmen, not even any officials. I just want to come in quietly."

* *Where the U.S. Marines landed and set up their headquarters during the civil war.*

"But Fidel, we've got everything planned for your arrival. Don't you think it's important for the press to be there?"

"No. I don't want anybody."

"But Fidel. You are the chief of state. At least for the sake of protocol I should be there—"

"Hey, Dorticós!" Fidel interrupted. "You know what? I'm at Rancho Boyeros right now!"

He slammed down the receiver on what must have been a startled President, walked through the terminal doors, calmly got into a taxi-cab with one of his aides, and rode home.

Korda laughs, enjoying the scene all over again.

"Of course when he got to his house Fidel didn't have any money to pay for the cab," he says. "But the funniest thing of all is that the driver was a *gusano*.* He kept giving Fidel hell all the way home!"

* Gusano, *literally "worm," is the term Castro coined to describe "disgruntled bourgeois elements with counterrevolutionary tendencies."*

Left: *Korda, the photographer*
Above: *Cane trucks bringing* macheteros *to the celebration at Uvero*

Cane cutters and militiawomen of the Sierra Maestra arriving at Uvero
Legend on truck reads: "Let not a single cane stalk remain in the soil"

Militiamen on the hilltop from which Castro was supposed to have directed the battle of Uvero

Left and Above: *The two soldiers who talked to the author*
Below: *A bemused peasant with a flower dropped from a plane*

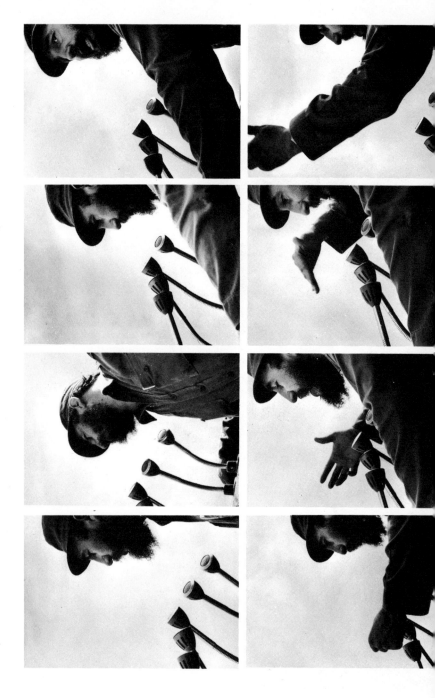

*Fidel speaks. Cuba's peasants, once the most underprivileged class,
have been the Revolution's greatest beneficiaries*

OLD MAN: *"Fidel, you don't remember me, because I am an old man. But I remember you!"*

FIDEL: *"Now just a minute, I do seem to remember a very old man, not such a bad man, who lived in a shack by the river. But you couldn't be him —he would be dead by now."*

OLD MAN: *"No, Fidel, it's me, it's me! You remember everything, even my house!"*

FIDEL: *"Really, you are the same? Well, I am glad to see you alive and so energetic, viejo. Tell me, what can I do for you?"*

OLD MAN: *"Fidel, I want a pension."*

FIDEL: *"What, at your age you don't have a pension?"*

OLD MAN: *"No, Comandante, they wouldn't give it to me."*

FIDEL: *"Don't tell me! Well, I am going to look into this personally. Give me your name and all the details." (The old man gives Castro name and address. He does not know how to spell his last name.)*

"All right, viejo. But tell me, since I see that you have your health and are living well enough, what do you need this pension for?"

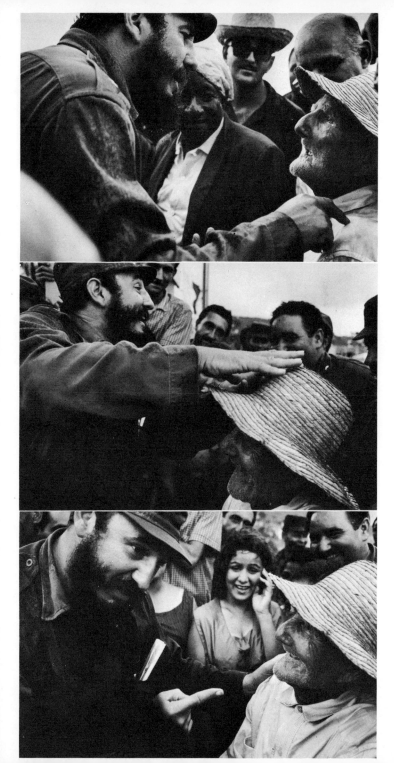

OLD MAN: *"Ah, Fidel! I want it so I can start a little business with cocoa trees. They grow very well in this soil—"*

FIDEL: *"What! At your age you want to go into business with cocoa trees? What madness! Listen, how old are you, viejo?"*

OLD MAN: *"Only eighty-seven, Comandante."*

FIDEL: *"Eighty-seven! What sheer madness! Viejo, don't you know that at eighty-seven you should be spending your remaining years in peace and quiet, instead of opening up a* new business for yourself? That's what a pension is for."

OLD MAN: *"But I will live many more years yet, Fidel. I feel very strong. But I am all alone. I must have something to do, because I don't think I will live with any more women."*

FIDEL: *"Help! No more, no more! You will have your pension, viejo. Ay, these campesinos, going into business when they are nearly ninety. They are never going to understand what socialism is all about, that's for sure!"*

"Ay, Fidel— how fat you've gotten!"

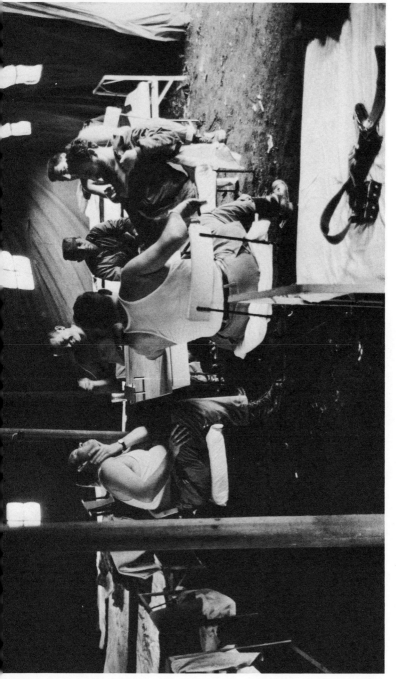

In Castro's tent, a three-day marathon game of dominoes

Pepín Naranjo, mayor of Havana

*Castro's launch, with Fidel at the wheel, loses its bearings
in a rough storm off the coast of Oriente*

two:

with Castro on the Isle of Pines

"I will see you again very soon, and we will have our talk," Fidel Castro had promised in May. Now it was August, and I was still waiting. I had come to Cuba intending to stay only about two months, and I was beginning to run out of time and money and, most of all, patience. My most vexing problem was that I had lost all contact with the top. I had no way of finding out when my interview would be, or whether it was even going to take place at all.

It is a general characteristic of countries where one man rules that there are no "normal" channels through which one may gain access to him. This is especially true in Cuba, where the process of institutionalization has been lagging, and where the leaders carry on their affairs with studied informality, as though they were still guerrillas in the mountains. Moreover, because the regime has been troubled throughout its seven years in power by defections and betrayals of people in key positions, and because he himself is so busy, Castro has come to guard his channels of approach more and more jealously.

The only sure way of reaching Castro while I was in Cuba was through one of two people: René Vallejo, his aide-de-camp, or Celia Sánchez, his secretary. They are both old, infinitely trusted comrades from the guerrilla days, Fidel's right and left arms and his closest personal friends. Vallejo, a gifted surgeon, doubles as Castro's physician, while Celia includes among her multiform duties that of keeping house for Fidel. (In Havana she lives in the same house, in the apartment below his.) So time-consuming are the demands imposed by the excessive congestion of authority that both of them are in motion all day long, attending personally to an enormous range of details on Castro's behalf, many of which, in an atmosphere permissive of greater trust, might easily be delegated to others. Castro, who himself works an average twenty-hour day, expects his associates to do likewise.

The problem of direct access to Castro would not be so crucial if ministers, heads of departments, and other officials were able to make important decisions on their own authority or at least to transmit requests to the top and report back the decisions. But such is the chaos and the insecurity in Cuba's ever-shifting administration that most officials, like the general public, must reach Castro through either Celia or Vallejo, sometimes for even the most minor requests. Thus, the information chief of the Ministry of Foreign Relations, Ramiro del Río, a capable and intelligent man who should have been my normal channel to Castro, was totally unable to find out anything about the status of my interview. (Most of the time he couldn't even get Vallejo on the telephone.)

While I was feeling frustrated, the thought occurred to me that there might be thousands of Cubans in a similar predicament, unable to get satisfaction from lower authorities and equally impotent in their efforts to communicate with the Maximum Leader. Take, for example, the case of Celia Sánchez' telephone.

Celia is a hard-working, warmhearted woman with a sympathetic ear for everybody's problems. As a result, she has long been *the* person in Cuba to go to when direct intervention without red tape is imperative. The problem is, how to reach her? Because so many people call her all day long (and much of the night too), she has an unlisted telephone number. It is given out to individuals only with her personal permission and only after a solemn pledge of secrecy is extracted. But Cubans are notoriously unable to keep secrets. So, every few months, when the volume of calls rises to an uncontrollable level, Celia is forced to change her number without notice.

Moreover, once you have obtained her number and dialed it, you are given a final chance to reconsider the urgency of your call. A professional radio announcer's voice recites the following tape-recorded admonition:

"If you are calling to discuss a personal matter—about a home, an intervened farm, a house at the beach, furniture, refrigerators, automobiles, accessories for the same, scholarships, exit from the country, or prisoners—direct yourself to the appropriate organization. I do not work in any of those departments. After seven o'clock at night, do not call me. If it is not urgent, *do not call me.*"

My own contact was not with Celia Sánchez (I had not yet met her) but with Comandante Vallejo, whom I knew from prior visits to Cuba. With him I had worked out the arrangements for my trip by phone and letter from New York. Before I left, he had assured me that

I would have an interview with Fidel Castro—not a "press" interview, but a longer, informal conversation extending at least two or three days, as I had specifically requested. Soon after I arrived, over a convivial luncheon at his own home, Vallejo had reconfirmed Castro's enthusiasm for the idea. "In a very few days," he promised, "you will be sitting down with Fidel, and you will have as much time as you want."

That was early in May. Since then I had made two trips with Fidel and spoken with him briefly on half a dozen other occasions. Each time there had been some reason for not starting the interview at that moment, and each time he had promised, "I will see you very soon," after which weeks would go by during which nothing happened. I called Vallejo frequently; he always assured me, in the same enthusiastically cheerful tone, "It's going to be very soon now. Be ready." And after that, each time, silence.

By mid-July, Vallejo wasn't even coming to the telephone anymore when I called (out of embarrassment at not being able to give me a definite answer, I later learned). Korda, usually an alternate source of information because he saw Vallejo and Fidel often, had gone to Paris as a photographer with a junketing Cuban cultural ensemble. The Foreign Ministry people often took me to lunch or dinner and urged me to be patient, but could do nothing and knew nothing.

It was not difficult to find reasons for Castro's seeming unwillingness to talk to me. There were extenuating circumstances. A week before my arrival, the United States had sent troops into the Dominican Republic, only 100 miles away from Cuba's southern shore. This "Yankee aggression" reawakened memories of the Bay of Pigs and ma¹e Cubans bitter and uneasy. The island was in a state of official alert when I arrived.

Two weeks later, the U.S. suddenly began bombing North Vietnam, Cuba's sister socialist republic, with whom Castro and most Cubans feel a militant solidarity that is remarkably personal in tone—given the distance between the two countries. At this moment the vilification of the United States by Cuba's leaders and press, already at a shrill pitch, grew even louder and more vituperative.

Finally, when Castro, on a steaming hot afternoon at the 26th of July celebration in Santa Clara, devoted part of his speech to a tirade against the "false and cynical reporting" of the resident AP and UPI correspondents, denouncing them as "paid lackeys of the Yankee press," I gave up hope. In such an atmosphere, I decided, Castro would hardly be in the mood to sit down for a long interview with an American journalist. So as soon as I returned to Havana, I set about winding up my affairs and booked a seat for the following Monday on the weekly flight from Cuba to Bermuda.

The Friday night before I was to leave, I went to a movie (a horrible East German wide-screen color musical called *Love Has Its Harvest in Summertime*). Afterward, I joined some friends at El Carmelo, a swank outdoor restaurant famed in prerevolutionary times for its ice cream and which, surprisingly, still has it.(You pay for the luxury, however: a sundae, for example, costs $1.50.*) It is a gathering place for Havana's intellectuals and artists. Around midnight, I began walking back to the Hotel Nacional, about a mile away.

The summer night was warm and sultry. Walking down Twenty-first Street, I stopped for a moment to wipe the perspiration from my face and was suddenly aware of a pair of large white eyes peering carefully at me out of the darkness. It was a Negro soldier, very black, whom I recognized as one of Castro's bodyguards. He was posted on the street corner, a tommy gun slung over his back. Across the street was the Hotel Capri, which in other times had housed one of Havana's gayest casinos, operated by George Raft and Las Vegas money. In the hotel's angled driveway I saw Fidel's fleet of Oldsmobiles gleaming under the light of the neon signs. Other bodyguards were lounging against the cars and in the hotel doorway, smoking and laughing and eying the passing girls. Their presence was a sure sign that Castro was somewhere inside the hotel, and their relaxed state indicated that he was not expected to emerge very soon.

My own hotel was only two blocks away. I decided to make one last try to arrange the interview. I went back to my room and quickly wrote a letter to Castro. I reminded him of his many promises to talk with me and of the long time I had been waiting. I opined that he was about to forego an unusual opportunity to communicate directly with the American public, the long-range advantages of which, I thought, ought to outweigh any rancor that he might be feeling at the moment over present U.S. foreign policy. I said that he had a reputation of being a man of his word and voiced the hope that he would keep his word to me.

Back at the Hotel Capri, the bodyguards were still deployed. I struck up a conversation with one of them, who informed me that Fidel was meeting with a trade delegation from Spain who were quartered in the hotel. More than an hour passed. Finally, shortly after 2 A.M., there was a flurry of activity, the guards quashed their cigarettes

---

* In 1967, under Castro's direction, the Government went into ice cream production itself. The "Coppélia"—an enormous ice cream parlor for the masses, white, modern and of adventurous design—was opened in Havana. It offers ice cream of excellent quality in more flavors than Howard Johnson's, and there are usually long lines outside it on evenings and weekends. Smaller Coppélias have been built in each provincial capital.

and manned their posts, and Castro then pushed energetically through the glass doors leading from the hotel lobby, preceded and followed by other green-clad guards moving in particle-like trajectories toward the automobiles. Two strides behind him came Vallejo. I called to him and gave him the letter.

"Fine," he said, "I'll read it to him in the car right now!" and he ran to catch up with Castro's automobile, which was already moving out of the driveway, one rear door still open, and jumped in.

The next morning at eight o'clock, Vallejo woke me with a phone call, his voice excited. "Fidel liked your letter very much! Don't go anywhere! Be ready for a car to pick you up anytime after noon!"

Two weeks and six postponements later, at precisely one o'clock of a Sunday afternoon, I stood under the porticoed entrance of the Hotel Nacional with my gear as a guard-laden Oldsmobile eased across the slowdown bump at the mouth of the driveway, roared down the long approach, and shrieked to a stiff halt in front of me. Without a word of greeting, Gonzales, the crusty second-in-command of the bodyguard, motioned me into the back seat. I got in, juggling cameras, tape recorder, and knapsack, between two tough-faced soldiers who paid no attention to my efforts to squeeze into the narrow space. On one side, a submachine-gun bolt was digging into my ribs; on the other, a bulky pistol prodded my kidney. My knees were drawn up tightly, cramped by the heavy leather sling across the back of the front seat, which bulged with tommy guns, pistols, bullet clips, grenades, and a large quantity of ammunition.

We raced down onto the Malecón, the picturesque drive that girdles Havana's splendid harbor, and headed with urgent speed toward Vallejo's home in Nuevo Vedado. The silence in the car was broken only by instructional grunts from Gonzales to the driver: *"Doble aqui. . . . A la izquierda. . . . No, por allí por allí!"*

After about fifteen minutes we turned into a secluded side street and halted in the driveway beneath Vallejo's modern, split-level home. The driveway was already filled with other Oldsmobiles, parked at different angles for fast exit to the street. The guards shoved open the doors, leaped out like paratroopers, and headed for the house. "Shall I come with you?" I called to Gonzales. "Stay there—don't move!" he shouted over his shoulder.

Shortly, the door of the house next to Vallejo's was opened, and Castro strolled out onto the porch alone, a long tan cigar in one hand and a gold snaptop lighter in the other. He sniffed the air and peered contemplatively at the uncertain sky. As he was about to light his cigar, a large charcoal-gray dog streaked out of the house behind him and hurtled against his calves with such force that Castro jackknifed backward, dropping the lighter, and almost fell flat. The dog, a young German shepherd, bounded around the lawn in high spirits, then ran back to Castro's side, panting and frisking its tail. Fidel, recovering from his surprise, laughed and patted its flank, talking to it affectionately.

I got out of the car. Castro saw me, picked up his lighter, and came down the steps. As we shook hands, we were knocked apart by the dog, which then leapt onto its hind legs and put its forepaws on the *Jefe*'s shoulders, moaning with excitement. The dog minuetted with Castro, who staggered backward, laughing and fighting it off as it exuberantly tried to lick his beard.

"His name is Guardián," Fidel shouted proudly, ducking as the dog leapt again. "He is not very well trained yet! I got him as a puppy and raised him myself. I think he will make a good watchdog, no? Heel, Guardián!" he ordered sharply. The dog paid no attention. "Heel! Heel!" But Guardián only redoubled his efforts to kiss him. "Come," Castro said finally to me, giving up. "I must not stand outside here. It is too exposed. Let's get into the car."

We got into the back seat of Fidel's automobile—the three of us. The dog occupied half the seat, hulking and shifting nervously, leaving the Premier and me jammed together. Our thighs and shoulders were locked so tightly that as we talked we were forced to look straight ahead, unable to turn.

"I want to apologize," Castro said seriously. "I am very sorry about all the delays we have had in getting together. There have been many problems. Lately there were so many delegations arrived for the 26th of July whom I had to see. . . . And then there was the international situation. . . . Your letter was very good, very good. It reminded me about you, what kind of a person you are, and so I decided to do the interview, not for myself, but for you, because you are trying to do an honest piece of work. . . . So now we are going to the Isle of Pines, where I am hoping to get a little rest. We will have all of tonight to talk, as late as you wish, and then perhaps a little time tomorrow morning if there are still some questions. We have a plane ready to take you back to Havana tomorrow so that you can make your flight."

I thanked him. "But," I said, "I really feel that one night will never be enough. I think we are going to need two or three days. So if you are going to stay on the Isle of Pines a while, and you wouldn't mind my being there, I could postpone my departure one more week, now that we've finally gotten together, and we could talk whenever you have the time."

Castro pursed his lips and frowned.

"Very well. But you must understand that I am going principally because I need to relax. I want to do some hunting and fishing. Also, I have a great pile of books to read. But I have no objection if, perhaps when I have an hour before breakfast, or sometimes in the evening. . . . Only you must make a pact with me. You can stay at my house, but you must be there as simply one more guest and live like everybody else. You can go fishing or hunting with us, take pictures if you want to. But I don't want to feel any pressure. . . . I must not feel pressure when I look at you and think, 'Well, he is waiting for his interview.' Do you agree?"

"Of course," I said. "In fact, I would prefer it."

The doors were flung open. Vallejo and the driver piled hastily into the front seat, and we set off again with characteristic abruptness. We sped through the narrow Havana streets, flanked front and rear by Oldsmobiles filled with guards and guns. The drivers handled their cars like motorcycles, shimmying back and forth across the road and feinting dangerously close to the oncoming traffic, maintaining a clear path for Castro's racing sedan. They rode four to a car with the windows down. The two in the rear sat back to back, sideways, facing the windows, clutching their tommy guns tightly, nervously alert. They shifted their heads and eyes constantly, searching for danger. The drivers used no sirens or blinking lights to clear the corridor. Instead, whenever a civilian car accidentally got too close, one of the escort vehicles would veer at him sharply, almost brushing his fender; simultaneously, the two guards on his side thumped ominously on their door with open palms and swore savagely at the by now thoroughly frightened driver.

Once out of the city traffic and onto the highway, all the cars faded into a single line as we accelerated to Fidel's customary cruising speed of over seventy. Vallejo turned around, smiling with remarkably white teeth through his long, gray, Smith-Brothers-cough-drops beard.

"How do you like that dog? Some dog, huh? After you get through with Fidel, I'm gonna get you an interview with Guardián. He knows all of Fidel's secrets!"

Guardián, after some nervous experimentation, had found a position that suited him. He had stretched himself out with his rear legs planted on the back seat and his forepaws resting on the top of the front seat. His large head hung directly over Fidel's rotund little chauffeur, upon whom he was drooling copiously. "He-he-he-he," laughed Fidel, as the dog, in a paroxysm of puppyish affection, suddenly began to lick the driver's face with his long, lavishly moist tongue. Castro watched with glee and made no move to restrain the dog, while the poor driver struggled to keep the speeding auto on the narrow, two-lane highway.

"I want to show you something," Major Castro said, as we turned and drove up a dirt road and came to a stop before a large stand of sugar cane. Everyone got out of the cars and traipsed through the mud to the edge of the field. The cane was taller than any I had seen in Cuba, easily nine feet high. The field was guarded by two armed soldiers who saluted laconically as we walked up.

"This is my own private experiment." Castro's voice rang with pride. "One *caballería* of land.* Look—the cane is only five months old, and already it is very high. I think it is going to be the tallest in the world! You see, by using the proper fertilizer, phosphates, and using them correctly, that is, not mixing them directly into the soil, which contains much iron, but dropping them into holes and covering them, holes correctly spaced apart in relation to the cane, and by supplementing the rainfall with controlled irrigation, and by planting the cane in a line parallel to the line the sun makes across the sky, so that the leaves receive the maximum sunlight, I have proven that we can get twenty-five percent greater yield per acre than they get in Hawaii, which has the highest production yield in the world. I believe we will set a world's record in sugar cane with this method! The only thing that I fear is the strong wind, which blows the cane down and stunts its growth. Well, what do you think of it?" he asked enthusiastically.

"It's wonderful!" I said, feeling very stupid, since I know absolutely nothing about agriculture. I had a vision of other Cuban political officials, equally untutored in the subject, desperately taking cram courses in sugar-cane production in order to be able to talk about it intelligently with their Maximum Leader.

At a boat slip near the coastal town of Batabano, we boarded the same two motor launches in which we had traveled through the storm in May in Oriente Province, eight hundred miles away, at the other end of the island. The two escort gunboats were there too. Observing military form, Castro made a quick inspection of the ship's crews, accompanied by Guardián, who strained and tugged mightily on the leash and at one point almost yanked his master overboard into the sea.

The moment he stepped onto the deck of his launch, Fidel's manner grew buoyant and relaxed. As he took the wheel and ignited the pow-

* Thirty-three and one-third acres.

erful engines, his eyes lit up with excitement. He uncovered the compass and, consulting a sea chart which a crewman had spread out beside him, set it for the proper bearings. He reached into a cupboard and took out a white commodore's cap, looked at it, thought better of it, and put it back. Vallejo handed him a long, blonde "Fidel Special" cigar. He bit off the end, stuck it into his mouth, lit it, shifted into gear, and gunned the motors.

It was a bright, warm afternoon with a light rain falling from a heavy cumulus cloud off to starboard. As we raced into the open sea, flanked by the gunboats and trailed by the second launch, Fidel shouted into my ear, above the growl of the engines, a catalogue of the boat's vital statistics.

It was a new boat, built that year in a Cuban shipyard at Playa Girón (the Bay of Pigs) and fitted with Chrysler engines imported from Canada. It had great speed and range. "In this boat we could be in Key West in three hours! We could even make it all the way to New York!" he cried gleefully, nudging me with his elbow. "If we started right now, we could be there—let me see—inside of twenty-four hours. We could go right up the East River to the U.N.!"

In the same shipyard, he said, they were now building another launch which will be fifty percent faster. At this, Comandante Vallejo emitted a loud groan. "You almost drowned in that rough sea off Oriente that last trip in this boat! Now you are getting a faster one? ¡Ay, mi madre!" he cried ruefully, slapping his bald pate.

We covered the distance from Batabano to the Isle of Pines, about 120 miles, in less than two and a half hours. Fortunately the sea was flat calm all the way.

The Isle of Pines is a small, cauliflower-shaped island that lies due south of Havana. It has a colorful history, dating from the days of the Spanish Main, of piracy, rum-running, slave-trading, and smuggling, and it may have been the setting for Robert Louis Stevenson's *Treasure Island*. It remained a center for all kinds of illicit trade right up until the Revolution in 1959. In modern times the island has also served as the traditional internment center for political prisoners under Batista and Castro alike.* Prisoners make up about one-half of the resident population of 17,000.

Prior to the Revolution the entire island was owned by only four men. Much of the land is still wilderness, with almost untapped opportunities for hunting and fishing. For Castro, the total sports enthusi-

---

* For his attack on the Moncada Barracks, Castro was imprisoned in a solitary cell on the Isle of Pines in November, 1953. On May 15, 1955, he and his surviving co-conspirators were pardoned by Batista, after Castro had served less than 19 months of a 15-year sentence.

ast, this is the island's chief attraction. It is just as isolated as the mountains of the Sierra Maestra, his first love, yet it has the advantage of being considerably closer to the seat of government at Havana.

The sun was close to the sea as we eased into a narrow river overgrown with the tangled roots and branches of mangrove trees. We put in at a small military dock, where we transferred to another waiting fleet of automobiles. A delegation of local officials took us on a rapid but arduously thorough tour of the island's agricultural high spots. It was nearly dark when we finally arrived at Castro's country retreat, a modern ranch house situated in a tropical setting at the top of a hill, well off the main road and protected on all sides by tall trees.

The second unit of Fidel's guard had arrived earlier and were already deployed in positions in the tree thickets around the house and down the slopes of the hill. At the bottom, at the turnoff from the main road, there was a guard shack with two soldiers on duty. Behind it was a cleared field, the landing strip for a courier helicopter which brought the newspapers and the affairs of state from Havana twice daily and stood ready to airlift Castro back to the capital in the event of an emergency, or to the other side of the island to go fishing.

"This," said Fidel with a proprietary flourish of his hand as we stepped onto the veranda, "was once the manor of one of the four feudal barons of the Isle of Pines. If I am not mistaken, he is at this moment enjoying his retirement in Miami."

It was a single-story, white wooden ranch house in an architectural style common to the American Southwest. Built in the shape of a long L, its entire length was fronted by a porticoed veranda, lined with rocking chairs and other pieces of outdoor furniture, which faced a green, well-tended lawn and a garden of flowering tropical shrubs. There were several bedrooms, each having a separate door leading directly onto the veranda, much like a motel. Castro's room, at the bottom of the L, was the largest. It contained a king-sized bed. Next door slept Vallejo, also alone in a large room with a double bed. Next to him was a twin roomful of double-decker army cots, the barracks for the bodyguard. The rest of us slept two to a room, each pair of rooms having a common bath. I was assigned the room adjacent to the guards' barracks. I shared it with Dr. Cambó, a quiet and rather humorless old army doctor who travels with Castro as backup physician for Vallejo. At the top of the L was the dining room and behind it, the kitchen. There was another door inside the dining room through which I was never invited; I assume it to have been a kind of command post. Beyond the kitchen, two steps led down to a microwave communications room with a small dormitory next to it for the radio operators, on duty 24 hours a day. All the rooms were equipped with American air conditioners, kept running all day long because of the heat.

Dinner was ready when we arrived and was served in the dining room immediately. Without protocol, we took chairs around a single large table and served ourselves, boardinghouse style. Fidel, according to his custom, was at the center of both table and conversation. Since Castro had proposed to begin the interview directly after the meal, I was laying plans to leave the table early to get my tape recorder ready, but before the dessert had been served Fidel stood up, stretched, yawned, bit into the end of a cigar, and spat the tip onto the floor.

"Well," he announced, "I'm going to bed." With that, he strode from the room. I looked questioningly at Vallejo. He smiled. "Tomorrow, I guess," he said. "Here, have a cigar."

Even before all the dishes had been cleared, a domino game was under way: Pepín and Vallejo against "Chomi," * a studious young vice minister of public health, and Dr. Cambó. I watched for a while, puffing an H. Upmann Number 1 cigar. Then I went for a walk. Forty feet down the road I was challenged silently by a guard who materialized out of the darkness with his gun at port arms. I turned back and sat in a chair on the veranda, where I rocked for a while, listening to the strange, raucous calls of the wild birds until my cigar went out. Then I went to bed.

The next morning Fidel did not come to breakfast. He sent word to me that he would be tied up all morning with visitors from Havana. I was to be given a tour of the island. So, with Vallejo and the two *responsables* of the Isle of Pines, I spent the morning in a jeep traveling the back roads, visiting orange and grapefruit groves, pasture fields, cattle farms, and prison camps. I was encouraged to photograph and talk with some of the political prisoners. But, being understandably intimidated by the array of officials who accompanied me, they did not have very much to say.†

We returned to the house for lunch. Castro again did not attend. Later, I was in my room preparing the tape recorder when Vallejo entered.

"Fidel's still talking to those people from Havana," he said. "He says you should see some more of the island." Frowning, he went on:

"Look, I'm a little worried. I know Fidel. The way things are going you could be here a week and never get to talk to him. He always has a

* Since 1967, rector of the University of Havana.

† See Chapter 6, Political Prisoners.

million things to do and people coming to see him. Besides, he could get a call any minute to rush back to Havana, and once he's there you can forget about the whole thing. I mean it! So I'm going to ask him to give you a full day, maybe tomorrow, just devote one whole day to you, starting early in the morning and going right into the night as late as you want. I know that's not what you want, but believe me, at least that way it's sure that he talks to you, so I advise you to take it. Okay?"

I said I would take it. I spent the afternoon back in the jeep, now minus Vallejo, seeing more trees, more cows, and more prisoners. When I finally persuaded my guides to take me home, around six o'clock, I found the camp empty. Castro and all the others except for a few guards had gone off in the helicopter to do some hunting.

I prowled about the empty house, feeling tired and exasperated and also very much out of place. I wandered into the dining room looking for a cigar. As I opened the door I heard what was for me, after three months in Cuba, strange music. One of the kitchen crew was playing a phonograph (it must have been left behind by the "feudal baron" when he fled). It was a record of Harry James playing "Smoke Gets in Your Eyes." The soldier was sprawled in an easy chair with his cap and shirt off, his boots crossed upon the inlaid wooden dining table, waving his arms dreamily in time to the music. The incongruity of this scene, on top of my already distracted mood, gave me a distinct sensation of hallucination. This was heightened a moment later as I sank upon the couch and noticed, hanging on the wall, another relic of a former era and culture curiously left in place: a framed, printed excerpt from Coleridge's poem "Kubla Khan":

A damsel with a dulcimer
In a vision once I saw:
It was an Abyssinian maid,
And on her dulcimer she play'd,
Singing of Mount Abora.
Could I revive within me
Her symphony and song,
To such a deep delight 'twould win me,
That with music loud and long,
I would build that dome in air,
That sunny dome! those caves of ice!
And all who heard should see them there,
And all should cry, Beware! Beware!
His flashing eyes, his floating hair!
Weave a circle round him thrice,
And close your eyes with holy dread,

For he on honey-dew hath fed,
And drunk the milk of Paradise.

"Where were you?" Castro said, stamping mud from his boots and shucking his field jacket at the same time. "I wanted you to go with me and photograph me shooting! I shot five birds! Well, maybe we can go again before you leave. Anyway, tomorrow we work, eh? The whole day, starting very early, eight o'clock, perhaps? Until we finish! I hope we finish tomorrow, because I want to relax!"

At eight o'clock the next morning, under the watchful eye of a guard, I set up my tape recorder and microphone on the card table outside Castro's door. He appeared at nine and went to have breakfast. It was nearly ten when we finally sat down, I in the middle, facing the lawn; Castro on my left; Vallejo across from him. We all lit cigars, and I started the tape recorder.

"Ah what a fine machine!" Fidel exclaimed, leaning forward to get a closer look. "So small! Show me how it works."

I gave him a demonstration, which deepened his curiosity. For fifteen minutes he asked question after question, curious to learn every little detail—how many speeds it had, how long it played on its battery, how the controls worked, where it was made, how much it cost—and he pushed the buttons himself experimentally with great delight. Finally, he approved: "This seems a most efficient way of working. I think we shall do good work with this wonderful machine."

I started the tape again.

"Wait—" he said, holding his hand over the microphone until I stopped the recorder. "First I want to know if you have a plan. What is your plan as to how we shall work?"

As I gave a brief outline of the subjects that I hoped to cover he listened with absolute attention, his dark eyes fastened on mine. I had the feeling that he was already composing answers to questions that I might ask. "But," I said at the end, "this is only a general list of things we might talk about. I hope you won't expect them all in exactly the same order. I would like to keep this conversation informal and ask you questions about anything that comes up while we're talking, even if it takes us afield temporarily."

Fidel rubbed his bearded right cheek thoughtfully with his knuckle.

"Very well," he said finally. "A good plan. A conversation—that is much better than an interview, I agree. Only we must hurry, so that we can finish today. You have mentioned many things. . . ." He sighed. "Okay." He pulled his chair up behind him and leaned forward intently. "What is your first question?"

And so at last, almost to my disbelief, I started the tape and the interview began.

It was a far-from-auspicious beginning, however. For one thing, I had had little experience at conducting interviews before, and the job of having to think of the questions, listen to Castro's answers, and simultaneously man the controls of the tape recorder (it was a new machine to me too) was taxing at first. Moreover, Castro's earlier reluctance to give the interview and his expressed longing to be done as hastily as possible were an added pressure that made it difficult to establish the intimate, easy atmosphere that I wanted.

Added to this was the complication that it was necessary, for the sake of absolute clarity, that Vallejo translate both my questions into Spanish and Castro's answers into English a sentence at a time. This cumbersome machinery at first irked Castro, who has the declamatory habit of many years of public speaking and tends to unfold his thoughts in long, repetitious, convoluted sentences of baroque syntax whose meaning is carried forward almost as much by the cadence of the phrases as by the connotations of the words. However, after a somewhat stilted beginning, Vallejo's translations gradually integrated themselves, Castro's impatience diminished, and the conversation began to develop its own rhythm.

Then came a moment of crisis. In the middle of one of Fidel's involved answers I noticed that the tape recorder was not recording. What was more, I had no way of knowing how long the tape had been running blank.

"What is wrong?" Fidel asked, interrupting himself as he noticed my consternation.

"The contact in the microphone cord seems to be loose," I said as casually as I could. "Maybe it's the humidity."

He watched with surprising patience as I searched for the trouble. As I had hoped, it was only a loose connection. I repaired it in makeshift fashion by taping the cord firmly to the table.

"But how did you know that it wasn't recording properly?"

I showed him a meter on the side of the machine and explained how, when the machine is recording, the little needle jumps and falls with each impulse of sound. He nodded, fascinated. We started again. I asked him whether he could give his last answer over again from the beginning. Although at least fifteen minutes had passed, he still had the train of thought fully in his mind and was able to repeat his answer word for word and sentence for sentence.

While he talked, I turned occasionally and checked the meter to make sure that the connection hadn't come loose again. Each time I did this, Castro shook his head. Finally, he covered the microphone with his hand and said, "Don't worry—I am watching it. I will tell you if it isn't working."

The passing of this moment of tension somehow served to relax all of us and from then on the conversation flowed easily forward. We passed smoothly from the subject of farm production to the counter-revolution, political prisoners, the Bay of Pigs, and back to agriculture again. Castro's answers grew increasingly involved as he became more and more engrossed. I noticed that he seemed to savor the pointedness of some of the questions.

Suddenly, he looked at his watch, unbelieving.

"Two-fifteen!" he exclaimed. "We must have lunch!" He rose and stretched. Vallejo, smiling, pointed toward the end of the veranda. The other guests were grouped around the dining room door, watching us and waiting patiently for the *Jefe* to come to the table.

Fidel put a hand on my shoulder and walked me across the lawn, his head lowered.

"I can see now that we are going to need a lot more time. There are many things we will need to talk about," he said, steering me away from the porch toward the trees. He went on, thinking out loud. "Today is Tuesday . . . I think we will need all of today . . . and tomorrow . . . Thursday . . . maybe part of Friday. . . . Then I have something I must do, a little adventure for the weekend . . . then some meetings next week. . . ." He stopped, facing me. "I think you should plan to stay another week, make another trip to the interior if you want, and then next Friday you can come to my house in Havana. We will have lunch, spend the day. Surely we can finish by the end of next weekend. What do you think?"

"That sounds excellent," I said, "but I absolutely must leave on next Monday's plane. I have already been here six weeks longer than I intended, I've postponed my departure several times, and now—"

"Yes, yes, I know, you have postponed your departure. You have waited all this time to see me, because I didn't know how important this conversation was going to be, you see," he insisted. "But now that we have begun, surely one more week is not too much, if I promise you the time?"

"I know," I said, "but I promised my wife on the telephone that I was coming home on Monday. I told her this was the last time I would say that. If I don't keep my word I may have no more wife when I get home."

"Oh, if it's your wife, then there's no problem! She can come here for a week. As my guest!"

"But that's impossible."

"Ah yes," he mused. "The State Department." He bent down and tore off a fistful of grass. He kneaded it for a moment, then opened his hand and let it drop, fluttering down. "Well, then, why not have her fly to Mexico City? You can go on the plane to Mexico City on Monday, say hello to your wife for a few days, and then come back here on Friday. If it's a problem of money, I will loan it to you personally. I know this problem of a wife can be very important—"

"Thank you, but it's not a question of money," I said. "Perhaps the best thing would be if we just wait and see how things go this week. Then, Friday or Saturday, I can decide what I have to do."

"Very well," Castro replied unhappily. "But I know what is going to happen." We were now walking rapidly toward the dining room. "*Ay,*" he sighed, "and I was really hoping to relax just a *little!*"

After lunch, we sat down to work again and talked until dark. With time out for a short dinner, we went back at it again until well after midnight. Now that he was interested, Castro's enthusiasm for the conversation became indefatigable. Whenever we would take a break —and that happened rarely—his mind would go on working, and he would return to the table charged with excitement, impatient for me to get the machine going so that he could record a whole new set of ideas on whatever it was we had last been discussing.

At 1 A.M., Castro finally called a halt, and we went to bed, promising an early start the next morning. Limp with exhaustion, I lay on my back and heard the sound of Fidel's voice echoing in my mind as insistently as if he were still sitting next to me. It was going to be a hard week, and I was already tired out after only one day. As I drifted quickly off to sleep, my last conscious thought was the rueful reflection that I was like a moth who had set out looking for a little light and had flown straight into a laser beam.

The next morning there was a new face alongside our little table: Tamargo, Castro's paunchy and bespectacled chief stenographer. He had been summoned from Havana at 5 A.M. because Fidel had now decided that he wanted a running transcript of the interview to check over each night. But after a second full day of conversation, it had become obvious that Tamargo alone was going to be insufficient to cope with the flow of words. That evening we stopped early so that he could be shuttled back to Havana in the helicopter. Besides his own notes, he took with him my tapes from the previous day. He and his crew labored all night at the Presidential Palace transcribing them in order to produce a typescript for Castro the following morning.

By 9 A.M. Tamargo was back, grubby and unshaven, with the transcript and two young assistants with portable typewriters. They set up a little office in my room and worked in shifts, one of them always on the veranda recording the conversation in shorthand while the other two were typing up their notes in the room.

The interview continued for five more days. Several hours each day we sat with the microphone between us, Fidel, Vallejo, and I, around the little table on the porch outside Castro's bedroom, talking softly, like three men at a seance. Vallejo, on my right, chain-smoked cigars (which kept going out because he had to do so much talking) and perspired heartily from the effort of concentration. To my left sat Fidel, sometimes in fatigues, sometimes, in the mornings, with a white cotton pajama top hanging over his trousers and black leather slippers over blue socks. He too smoked constantly, alternating between strong Cuban cigarettes and his own brand of mild, extra-long cigars.

While we worked we were left completely alone by the rest of the company, who kept to the other end of the veranda in deference to Fidel. His by now total immersion in the interview may have had a disrupting effect on the regular governmental routine, for every morning, and sometimes in the afternoons, new people arrived, officials from Havana or even farther away, to see the *Jefe* on some matter. They would have to wait for hours to catch a few quick words with him during a break. Sometimes, when I looked up past Fidel's shoulder diagonally across the lawn, I would see them congregated in rocking chairs, all in a row, rocking back and forth, hour after hour, in silence, their eyes fixed unwaveringly—and, I imagined, resentfully—in our direction.

At night we often talked long after everyone else had gone to bed, our muted conversation scarcely louder than the silken chatter of the crickets. Once in a while we would be startled by some wild bird shrieking like a lunatic in the dark.

A conversation with Castro is an extraordinary experience and, until you get used to it, a most unnerving one.

In the first place, unless you are very firm, it is not properly a conversation at all, but something more like an extended lecture, with occasional questions from the audience. This is not to say that Castro is rude, for he is not; in fact, socially he can be as courtly as a Castilian nobleman. Nor does it imply that he is not interested in what you have to say. It is simply that he is one of the most enthusiastic talkers of all time. A ten-word question can program him for an answer lasting fifteen or twenty minutes. His mind is as precise and organized as a watch and ticks out its ideas just as inexorably. He is seldom irrelevant or banal, and he never loses sight of the original point he started to make, no matter how many embellishments, circumlocutions, or interruptions may occur along the way. His memory is prodigious. If you change the subject before he has finished with it, he will reply to your new question first, in as much detail as it needs, then return to his previous thought and complete it. In developing an argument, he is as careful, as patient, and as logical as a spider spinning a web; its conclusion leaves you gasping and entangled, yet marveling in spite of yourself at the inevitability of its symmetry, and at pains to remember where it all began.

For Castro, trained as a lawyer, and an orator and a politician since his university days, the primary use of speech is demagogic: that is, its purpose is not so much to exchange ideas with someone as to convince another of his own. This is true whether he is addressing half a million people in public or conversing privately with one man. It is not enough that you understand; you must, if at all possible, be convinced. To this end, he bends his considerable energy and intellect with enormous concentration. As the carefully formed sentences flow out in cadence, every word has the ring of absolute conviction, the product of a mind never in doubt.

But what is even more compelling than Castro's mind is his manner, the way he uses his voice and his body, especially his eyes, to reduce a listener to surrender. If he is effective in a public speech, where the listener is at a relatively safe "aesthetic distance," in a private conversation, focusing the full force of his personality upon you at close quarters for hours at a time, he is formidable.

Replying to a question, Fidel would usually begin in a deceptively detached, conversational tone of voice, his eyes fixed on the table, while his hands fidgeted compulsively with a lighter, a ball point pen, or anything else at hand (I had to tape down the microphone stand so that he wouldn't move it inadvertently).

As he gradually warmed to his subject, Castro would start to squirm and swivel in his chair. The rhythm of his discourse would slowly quicken, and at the same time he would begin drawing closer to me, little by little, pulling his chair with him each time, until at last, having started out at right angles to my chair, he now would be seated almost alongside me. His booted foot, swinging spasmodically beneath the table, would touch my foot, then withdraw. Then his knee would wedge against mine as he leaned still closer, his voice becoming steadily more insistent. As he bent forward, his hands, surprisingly delicate and fine-boned, moved gracefully out and back in emphatic cadence with his words; then they would begin reaching toward me, tapping my knee, touching my chest, plucking softly at my shoulder, still in the same hypnotizing rhythm. As he continued speaking, I would become aware of his rich, dark, brown eyes, glittering in the frame of his tangled beard, peering fervently into my own eyes from only inches away. He would remain thus sometimes for as long as a quarter of an hour, touching me rhythmically as he spoke, then looking away, then swinging back and fixing me in his mantic gaze, as if we were the only two people in the world, and he had an urgent message to give me which words alone could not carry.

By the third day of the interview, Castro's insatiable energy had begun to wear me down (and Vallejo as well, who had to work the hardest of all of us). One morning, after we had worked until 2 A.M., the door of my room banged open at 7:30 and Fidel was at the end of my bed, pulling at my feet and shouting "Get up, Lee, get up! We've got to go to work!" He paced about impatiently while I put on my pants and hunted groggily for the tape recorder and microphone. I staggered down the veranda, rubbing my eyes sorrily in the brilliant sunlight and trying hard to wake up, propelled insistently by Castro, wide awake and bursting with vitality, who exclaimed,

"I haven't been able to sleep! I went to bed with so many ideas in my head that I kept waking up all night long. Are you ready? I've been up since very early, waiting for you to wake up. Finally I couldn't let you sleep any longer!"

Another day, Fidel decided to go on a skin-diving expedition. He left by helicopter right after lunch, taking most of the camp with him, for the other side of the island where there were coral reefs abounding with large fish. Vallejo and I stayed behind. "Fine," Vallejo said delightedly. "Once he gets into the water he won't come back until late tonight," and he promptly went to bed.

Around six o'clock, I heard the unmistakable clatter of the helicopter. It was followed in a few moments by the tire screeches of the arriving jeeps, and Fidel burst into the dining room with great, stomping strides. His eyes glowed exultantly, and his mouth kept breaking into wide grins.

"I broke a world's record!" he cried. His beard was still damp, and he was panting slightly. "Four hundred and six pounds of fish," he announced, tapping my chest with his forefinger. He swiveled and strode toward Vallejo, who had sleepily entered the room. "Four hundred and six pounds, Vallejo! In only three hours and forty-five minutes!" Vallejo looked pleased. "Wonderful," he said admiringly.

"Yes, wonderful!" the *Jefe* repeated, pacing energetically around the room, then back again in the other direction. Then he veered toward me again, expansively breaking into English. "I think I maybe swam . . . five or six miles under the water. I wish very much that you were there, to photograph." He laughed. Then his face became serious. "But you know," he said, "all the time I am beneath the water today, I am thinking about the book, worrying about the questions. . . . It is not so good . . . I catch much . . . many fishes, but all this time I cannot free myself mentally from the questions. So finally I said, 'Let's go home, I have to get back to work.' " He walked slowly away, vacantly perusing the floor, then turned and came back and stood in front of me, very close. "I want to know that we have finished," he said. "I imagine that until we have finished I will worry a lot. It is important that I relax. But I cannot relax until my mind is free from the subject. Don't you think that we will finish soon?" He was smiling, making a joke, but his eyes were solemn.

Life at Castro's island retreat was informal. Most of the guests were comrades-in-arms from the guerrilla days, people whom Castro trusts and feels at ease with. They are the closest thing he has to a family.

Comandante (Dr.) René Vallejo is tall and lean despite his middle age, with a long salt-and-pepper beard but little hair on his head. An easygoing man with a ready laugh, he is a surgeon-turned-politician who still performs operations occasionally to keep sharp his skill, which is reputed to be considerable.

Like many Cuban doctors, Vallejo served his internship and residency in the United States, in Boston. During the Second World War he was a doctor with the U.S. Seventh Army in Germany, and his fluent English is still laced with GI slang. After the war, he worked for UNESCO in Europe. By the time Castro went into the mountains, Vallejo was back in Cuba, operating a successful clinic and private practise in Manzanillo. One day he simply left it to join the Revolution. He was nearly forty years old. Today, he holds the rank of *comandante*—major—Cuba's highest military rank. He is Castro's aide-de-camp but holds no official function, a position which allows him to operate behind the scenes most effectively. His devotion to his leader is unabashedly worshipful. Except for Fidel's brother, Raúl, he is probably the man closest to Castro in all of Cuba, as well as the individual upon whom Fidel relies most. Earlier in the year, Vallejo had undergone two operations for circulatory disorders during which he narrowly missed losing his life. He had spent a month in the hospital recuperating. I asked him how Castro had managed to get along without him. "Well," he said, "Fidel came to the hospital every night."

Celia Sánchez, one of the legendary figures of the Revolution, arrived on the third day and stayed the rest of the week. Black-haired, olive-skinned, petite and sinewy, gracious, soft-spoken, and often smiling, Celia (as everyone calls her) embodies that combination of sweetness and toughness typical of the women of northern Spain, where her family originated. As was her custom in the mountains and as she does today in Havana, Celia took immediate but unobtrusive charge of Castro's personal housekeeping as soon as she arrived on the Isle of Pines. Moving into the room behind his, she polished his boots, supervised the soldier detail which daily cleaned his room, and made sure that the kitchen detail took special pains in preparing the food. Now, one night for dinner there were fancy hors d'oeuvres; another night, a layer cake. Days, when she was not away on some commission for Fidel, she would sit on the veranda, her feet tucked under her, making careful architectural drawings in an artist's sketchbook for a new restaurant and recreation area which she was designing, to be built near Varadero. In one sketch the restaurant had a giant tree trunk growing right through it, its branches above the roof like a green parasol.

Celia always dressed in army fatigues, but her blouse was tailored and she wore heelless shoes, like ballet slippers. She smoked nervously and often, extracting the cigarettes one at a time from a pack of Winstons that she kept concealed inside her trouser pocket (so that I would not notice that they were American, I suspect). At night there was usually a group around her on the veranda. They took turns reminiscing about the Revolutionary War, reliving old exploits, some of them tragic, but most of them humorous, and fascinating to listen to. Occasionally, when one of them began a story he was suddenly interrupted by the surprised exclamation of another who had participated in the same action; it would turn out that neither had known until now that the other had also taken part. They spoke in voices full of excitement and laughter, yet charged with a piquant nostalgia for the adventurous and relatively irresponsible days in the Sierra Maestra, when all they had to do was fight, and there was no paper work. One night, after a round of tales had extracted its last chuckle, there was a lull, and then I heard Celia say, her low, husky voice throbbing in the darkness as though in reverie: "Oh, but those were the best times, weren't they? We were all so very happy then. *Really*. We will never be so happy again, will we? *Never. . . .*"

One evening, while Fidel was occupied with reading and revising the transcript, I had a long bantering talk in English with Comandante Manuel Piñeiro, the gruff head of Cuba's G-2, whom Cubans call *Barba Roja* because of his bright red beard. I had noticed that both he and Pepín Naranjo smoked Chesterfield cigarettes and seemed to have an unending supply. "Where do you get them?" I asked. "Mexico? New York? Spain?"

"Oh, no," said *Barba Roja*, "nothing so complicated. They come to us free of charge, courtesy of the CIA. You don't believe me? But it is true. The CIA's agents bring them in, in large quantities, hoping to use them to win over new people. We capture them, and we smoke them. Very generous, the CIA, no? My favorite brand!"

The Cuban G-2 chief was also the victim of one of Fidel's practical jokes. He slept in the room adjoining mine with Pepín Naranjo. One morning at two o'clock, after an all-night work session, the *Jefe* tiptoed into their room with Guardián cradled in his arms and carefully placed him into bed with the sleeping *Barba Roja*. When the dog began to lick his face, Piñeiro awoke with a startled roar that roused everyone in the house and brought the guards running. The next morning Castro was still chuckling about it.

True to Fidel's world, I was accepted from the beginning by everyone in the house as simply one of the guests. Considering the ever-present fear of those close to Castro that a U.S. agent might someday infiltrate Castro's inner circle and attempt to assassinate him, I had remarkable freedom of movement. No one seemed to pay much attention to where I went or what I did, except for the guards, who said nothing, but were, I felt, a little on edge at having an American photographer around with unrestricted access to the area and to Castro himself. It's probably just as well that they never found out that Dr. Cambó, the army doctor who shared my room, went away for an entire afternoon and left behind his loaded pistol in the recess of our common night table.

By the end of the week, Castro and I had discontinued evening taping sessions so that he could busy himself with the transcripts. He was now working far into the night, correcting, revising, making additions, and reading excerpts aloud to Pepín and *Barba Roja* in their room as they lay in bed. Saturday night he was up working until dawn. Around eleven on Sunday, he emerged, still in pajamas, and beckoned me into his room. Vallejo was already there, working. Pages of transcript were spread out everywhere, on tables, covering the bed, on the floor.

"It's much more work than I thought it would be," Fidel said, throwing up his hands in a gesture of resignation. "I'm not going to be finished before you leave. I will need about one more week. We will have to send the finished transcripts to you in New York." He was anxious to show me what he had been doing, to reassure me that he wasn't rewriting the interview—only "improving" it. "Don't worry, I'm not going to change anything. I'm just making it clearer, more exact, I promise you. You will like it much better." He picked up a sheaf of transcript, spotted something that needed fixing, and a moment later he was back at work again, totally absorbed. I said good-by and went to pack.

I flew to Havana that afternoon and left the following morning for home. It was another two weeks before the finished version of the interview transcript was delivered to my apartment in New York by an official of the Cuban U.N. mission: five bound volumes, more than four hundred and twenty pages of neat Spanish typescript. With it came a note from Vallejo, saying that Castro had been working on it continually, seven or eight hours a day, ever since I had left, and had only just now finished. "I hope you will be satisfied," he added.

Although most of the revisions Fidel Castro made were minor ones (clarifications, corrections of fact, etc.), there were in his transcript one or two deviations from the tape recordings in which I felt the sense had been significantly altered. On my own responsibility, I have restored these few statements to their original state.

I am solely responsible for editing and reorganizing the interview into the form in which it appears here. The original conversation, which comprised nearly twenty-five hours of tape recordings, has been reduced to less than half. Secondly, since most important topics were touched upon more than once, often several times in the course of the week-long interview, it was necessary, for the sake of clarity and readability, to do some cutting and pasting in order to present the interview subject by subject and theme by theme. Moreover, I have arbitrarily correlated these various sections under three main chapter headings: "Castro's Cuba," "Fidel's Fidel," and "Castro Looks at the World."

Although I was under no obligation to do so, as a matter of courtesy, since I had done such a drastic editing of our original conversation, I returned to Cuba in May, 1966, and showed the new version to Castro. I was especially anxious to assure him that none of his answers had changed its meaning in being transposed from its original context. I spent three days with Castro in a retreat in the mountains of Oriente Province, during which he and Vallejo read every word of the manuscript carefully. He made a number of changes, most of them either slight adjustments of wording for greater clarity or minor corrections of fact. At the end, he pronounced himself satisfied with the result. He said that no statement of importance on any subject had been omitted, that the only element missing was a good deal of polemic against the United States which on second thought might seem gratuitous and was therefore expendable anyway. Before we parted, he signed and dated the final page of the manuscript.

I should also say that this edited version of the interview was the only portion of the manuscript seen by Castro or by any other Cuban prior to the publication of this book.

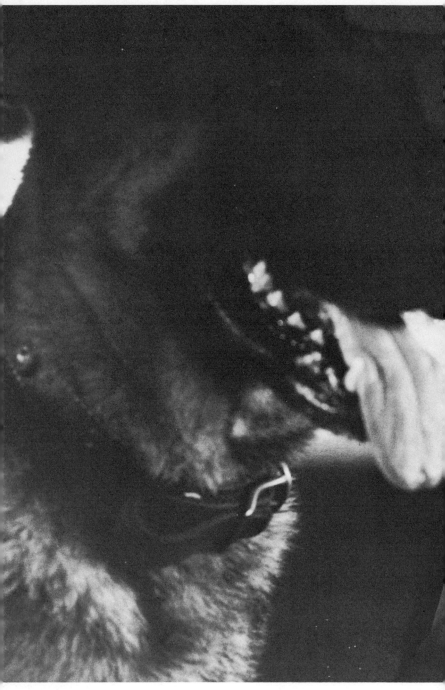

With "Guardián"

Above: *Castro, a restless sleeper, is already up at 6:00 a.m. reading diplomatic cables in his Isle of Pines dining room*

Below: *Comandante (Doctor) René Vallejo and Celia Sánchez—Castro's right and left arms*

three

Castro's Cuba (interview— part one)

AGRICULTURE

LOCKWOOD: What is occupying most of your time these days?

CASTRO: I am spending most of my time on agriculture, specifically problems of agricultural technology. I think the application of technology is essential in agriculture, and if we who direct the country didn't have any technical knowledge, we would have to depend on the technicians. But technicians often have conflicting ideas and do not analyze production problems from a political point of view. So we must know at least enough to be able to evaluate their opinions.

Our need for technology in general is so important that we are conducting a training program for agricultural technicians such that within ten years we will graduate fifty thousand technicians of the middle level and above, most of them chosen from among the farm laborers. This is in addition to all the student workers who are graduating from institutes of industrial technology and farm engineering, college level and above. We hope to have one of the most modern agricultures in the world.

LOCKWOOD: The other day you showed me an experimental sugarcane farm that you are running personally. Are you becoming an agricultural technician too?

CASTRO: Naturally there are many technicians carrying out experiments here. I personally am doing a small experiment on one *caballería*—thirty-three acres—cultivating it with all the resources of technology, taking many factors into account. For example: the choice of seeds, their prior fertilization, planting them during the month that I believe ideal for sowing so that the maximum vegetative growth of the plant coincides with the days of most sunshine. In addition, I am experimenting with the direction in which the furrows are situated in relation to the rays of the sun; the distance that I believe optimum between the seeds and between the rows; and, what is most important, the preparation of the soil, the formula of the fertilizer, the mode of applying it, the quantities and the dates in which it should be applied.

I expect to obtain the equivalent of eight tons of sugar per acre in one year. The maximum reached on the plantations of Hawaii is some eleven-and-a-half tons in two years. This means producing approximately twenty-five percent more than the maximum reached on the best plantations of Hawaii. And from the way this experimental planting is going, I am certain that I will obtain those quantities.

LOCKWOOD: How do you find time for this sort of thing when you have so many other things to do?

CASTRO: Look, when each day there are more people on whom it is possible to depend because of their ability, when the work is well divided, and when things are not very much centralized, then one can take time to study. I often study in the morning, also at night, but every day I try to spend at least three or four hours. Sometimes I take the whole day. I feel that this is one of the most useful things I can do. In fact I have tried to get all the party leaders in the provinces and regions of the country to study. I have distributed many technical books, and they have organized their own study circles.

My problem is that I didn't take a technological course in school. I studied law. And now I find myself required to make an extra effort, because in order to understand some of these technical problems an education in basic sciences is required: chemistry, physics, mathematics, biology, botany. So I have had to spend part of my time studying just to acquire a little of this basic knowledge, and I regret not having understood the importance of technology when I was younger.

LOCKWOOD: But is agriculture really so important that you yourself must spend all this time on it?

CASTRO: What does agricultural development mean to our country? It means the quickest satisfaction of the fundamental needs of the people: food, clothing, and shelter. It means the immediate utilization of the major natural resources which our country possesses. What are they? The resources of our soil and of our climate. Our being situated in a semitropical zone offers us exceptional conditions for cultivating certain crops. For example, there is no other country in the world, in my opinion, that has the natural conditions for the production of sugar cane that Cuba has.

We also possess exceptional conditions for livestock production. We are able to make use of pastures all year round, and I think our per-acre productivity of meat and milk can be double that of any industrialized country of Europe; likewise tropical fruits, which are becoming more and more in demand in the world. Here on the Isle of Pines alone we are going to have an area planted with citrus trees as extensive as all of that which Israel has, and we expect to achieve a yield as high as theirs per acre. It is possible that Cuba's overall national production of citrus fruits will come to triple theirs between 1970 and 1975, when the groves will come into full production. That will make us the leading exporters in the world. We also have good conditions for growing winter vegetables, fibers, and precious woods, including some types that are found only on our soil.*

With these natural resources and with a relatively small investment in farm machinery, seeds, fertilizers, and insecticides, and with the labor of the people, we will be able in a very short time to recover our investments and at the same time to obtain a considerable surplus for exportation.

Of course, the possibilities of which I am speaking also existed before the Revolution. That is, the natural conditions were the same. What was lacking? Markets. We lacked both internal and external markets. The internal market was limited by the quantity of men and women working in the country and by the salaries which they earned. The external market was limited by a policy of compromise, which prevented Cuba from taking advantage of all the existing possibilities for world trade.

Almost all our trade was with the United States. In a sense, this originally had a natural basis—that is, it was an exchange of products which Cuba easily produced and which the United States needed for products which the United States produced and Cuba needed. But it had been deformed by a series of tariff privileges for American goods that the United States had imposed upon Cuba. In this way, North American industrial products had acquired a notorious advantage over those of other countries. Naturally we opened up a little trade with the rest of the world, but under the circumstances it was far below the true potential. Sometimes it happened that Cuba had a chance to develop some crop or some product which we were buying from the United States. Then the sugar interests exerted every type of internal pressure against this production, alleging that this would affect North American interests and would occasion reprisals in the purchases of sugar (the sugar quota).

This caused the complete stagnation of our economic development. In the last thirty years before the triumph of the Revolution the population of Cuba had doubled. Yet in 1959 seven million people were living on the income from practically the same amount of sugar ex-

* In addition to these programs, all of which have been carried out, Castro has expanded the diversification of Cuban agriculture considerably since this conversation took place. Among the new crops now under intensive cultivation: rice, gandul (a type of bean useable for both food and cattle fodder), and coffee. In the spring of 1968, more than one hundred ten million coffee seedlings were planted in Havana Province alone.

ports as when we were only three-and-a-half million inhabitants. An enormous unemployment developed, and—as if this were somehow related to the imbalance of trade—the North American business interests here were sending back to the United States, during the last ten years before 1959, one hundred million dollars a year more in profits than we were receiving. The little underdeveloped country was aiding the big industrialized country.

If you came to Havana in those days, you saw a city with many businesses, many neon signs, lots of advertisements, many automobiles. Naturally this could have given the impression of a certain prosperity; but what it really signified was that we were spending what small resources were left to us to support an elegant life for a tiny minority of the population. Such an image of prosperity was not true of the interior of Cuba, where the people needed running water, sewers, roads, hospitals, schools, and transportation, and where hundreds of thousands of sugar workers worked only three or four months a year and lived in the most horrible social conditions imaginable. You had the paradoxical situation that those who produced the wealth were precisely the ones who least benefited from it. And the ones who spent the wealth did not live in the countryside, produced nothing, and lived a life that was soft, leisurely, easy, and proper to the wealthy. We had a wealthy class, but we didn't have a wealthy country.

That false image of prosperity, which was really the prosperity of one small class, is the image which the United States still tries to present of Cuba before the Revolution. They try to hide the true image of that epoch, the image of terrible economic and social conditions in which the vast majority of the country lived. Naturally we have not made this majority rich, but we have extraordinarily improved the conditions of their lives. We have guaranteed them medical assistance at all times, we have blotted out illiteracy, and we have offered facilities and opportunities for study to everybody, children as well as adults. Tens of thousands of housing units have been built, as well as numerous highways, roads, streets, parks, aqueducts, sewerage systems—in short, we have done everything that is within our means to improve the living conditions of this vast majority, although all this has happened to the detriment of the luxurious life which the minority led here.

For some years now we have not imported automobiles, but we have imported tens of thousands of tractors, trucks, pieces of construction equipment, etc. We are certainly not opposed to there being automobiles when the nation reaches a high level of development. But having food, shoes, clothing, medical attention, education, full employment, and sufficient housing for all the people and developing economically are far more important right now. A country cannot permit luxury to take possession while many things essential to the material and spiritual life of man have not been fulfilled.

And so by what way, along what roads, shall we set out toward the solution of our problems, the satisfaction of our needs, the growth of our economy? By investing hundreds of millions of pesos in costly industrial installations, which take years to build and to begin production, and which moreover require thousands of qualified engineers and workers, simply in order to produce some articles of which there is an excess in the world? Or else, by taking advantage of our natural resources and utilizing the hundreds of thousands of men and women capable of doing simple tasks, to begin creating wealth rapidly with a minimum of investments, producing articles of which there is a great shortage in the world?

Fruit is scarce, for example; vegetables are scarce, at least during certain times of the year; meat and milk are scarce; sugar is scarce. In short, *food* is scarce in the world, and the population of the world is growing at a rate much greater than that at which the production of foodstuffs increases. Consequently, a country that develops the production of foodstuffs along scientific lines, as our country is able to do, will be producing something for which there is an unlimited need. To the degree that numerous areas of the world become more and more industrialized, the position of the food-producing countries improves, because it is easier for an industrialized country to produce an automobile than to produce a bull.

What is happening in Europe? Industry is well developed, the workers earn relatively high wages, many of them have refrigerators, television sets, record players, washing machines, tape recorders, even automobiles. Nevertheless, they want to eat more meat, which is very expensive and often beyond the reach of their wages; they want to eat more fruit, more vegetables; they want to improve their diet. Moreover, the Socialist countries are now achieving an extraordinary industrial development. But at the same time their full employment and social development have brought about an enormous need for food. If we add to these all of the underdeveloped countries, such as Egypt, Morocco, and others, which are trying to develop their economies, it can be clearly seen that everything we are able to produce in agriculture has a market.

So we have come to the conclusion that our main source of immediate returns lies in agriculture, in which we must invest our present resources while we are preparing the people and developing our general and technical education. This means that until the year 1970 we will devote ourselves fundamentally to the development of agriculture. Then, from 1970 to 1980, we will proceed to the development of other lines of industry which require a higher level of technique and investment.

Naturally, there are some industries that are indispensable during this period for agricultural and social development: for example, the construction industry, the thermoelectrical industry, the fertilizer industry, the sugar industry. There must also be investments in ports, in sea and land transportation, just as we also need to develop the industry for the manufacture of agricultural implements.

By 1970, we must reach the level of approximately one billion, three hundred million dollars in exports. That is to say, between now and 1970, within five years, we will actually double our dollar exports. I believe that no other country in Latin America has that immediate prospect. Our commerce is growing, confidence in our economy is being strengthened, and you see that at this moment, when prices for sugar on the world market are lower than ever before, in Cuba there are no layoffs of laborers nor centers of sugar production shut down nor lowering of wages, such as in Peru, in Brazil, in the Dominican Republic—which in great measure caused the discontent which gave rise to the revolution there. On the contrary, we have produced *more* sugar, we have *raised* wages, and instead of closing sugar centers, we are increasing the planting of sugar cane and the number of sugar mills.

What allows us to do this? The vast market that we have for sugar —in the Soviet Union, in the People's Republic of China,* in the other Socialist countries of Europe and Asia, which need sugar and which at the same time produce numerous articles that we need.

LOCKWOOD: But they pay you a premium price† for sugar. Moreover, isn't it true that the Soviet Union doesn't really need all the Cuban sugar they are buying, that actually they can produce most of what they need themselves, and they merely buy from Cuba as a form of economic aid?

CASTRO: Of course in buying our sugar they help us, and that has been one of the factors determining the accords they have made with us. But, at the same time, they are not sacrificing their economy. On the contrary, it is economically advantageous to them. Why? Because the needs of their country are great, their level of sugar consumption

* *But in February, 1966, the Chinese, who had been accepting Cuban sugar mainly in barter for rice and manufactured products, cut back their trade drastically over a political dispute with Castro, who retaliated with a speech accusing China of economic imperialism. The future of China as a market for Cuban sugar remains doubtful as of this writing.*

† *6.11 cents a pound, as opposed to the 1965 world market price of less than 2 cents a pound.*

can increase considerably over what it is now, and sugar would cost them much more to produce than it costs us.

LOCKWOOD: Even when you add on the costs of transporting it in ships almost halfway around the world?

CASTRO: That is a very small cost if you consider the total value of the sugar. Even if Cuba were to sell them all the sugar she produced, the Soviet Union's potential consumption would still be greater. Even with five million tons of sugar from Cuba, they still have to produce close to ten million tons, since the Soviet population—more than two hundred and thirty million people, living in a frigid zone where the need for calories is greater and with a level of consumption similar to that of the population of the United States—requires approximately fifteen million tons each year.

In 1965 we produced six million tons of sugar. In 1966 we expect to produce between 6.4 and 6.5 million tons. It depends more or less on how the rains behave, but very probably we will reach that figure.* In the year 1967, we plan to reach 7.5 million tons. We have obtained a great quantity of agricultural equipment, and we have very much increased our capacity for plowing and sowing the soil. We expect to plant for the 1967 season six hundred and twenty-five thousand acres, of which part is completely new and part is the re-employment of areas already planted.

This year, also, some four hundred thousand acres of cattle pasture will be planted. We have at present close to seven million head of livestock. Moreover, we are using artificial insemination on an increasingly large scale in order to improve our livestock with purebred stock especially acquired for that purpose. By the end of the year we should have about one thousand inseminators. When the Revolution came to power, there weren't even half a dozen in the country. By the end of the year we will have approximately seven hundred thousand cows in the program of artificial insemination. That is fourteen times the number there was at the beginning of this year.

We also have a plan for reforestation, in which we are planning to plant approximately a million acres in timber trees in the next five years, if possible.

---

* However, the rains behaved very badly. During the calendar year 1965, Cuba suffered the worst drought in its recorded history, severely curtailing the maturing of the cane for the 1966 harvest. Then in the spring of 1966, at the height of the harvest, the country was inundated by torrential rains, rendering the cane difficult to cut and further reducing the harvest. As a result, instead of the 6.5 million tons predicted by Castro, the 1966 sugar yield fell to a poor 4.45 million tons, indicating a tight financial situation for Cuba in 1967.

For future discussion of predictions versus actualities, see the Afterword to this book.

LOCKWOOD: Does that include citrus trees?

CASTRO: No, in the next five years we will also plant no less than one hundred and fifty thousand acres in citrus trees.

LOCKWOOD: All this could not be accomplished without a great deal of organization and planning.

CASTRO: Well, there is much better organization, and above all there is more knowledge, more seriousness and responsibility in everybody, and there is also the party, which is well organized, and there is a great eagerness among the people for work. A proof of that was the last *zafra* (sugar cane harvest). Whereas six million tons could formerly be produced only with difficulty when there were hundreds of thousands of unemployed, now, when there is no unemployment in the countryside, the cane necessary to produce six million tons of sugar was cut easily. Of course, some gathering machines and combines contributed, but it would not have been possible without the eagerness for work that exists. Tens of thousands of workers from the city were mobilized.

LOCKWOOD: When you mobilize thousands of workers from the cities to cut sugar cane, doesn't it interfere with the work in the factories, industries, and offices?

CASTRO: Actually not very much, because traditionally, and also since the Revolution, you might say that we have had an overabundance of office workers. At present, measures are being taken to reorganize the work in some administrative and industrial centers where there is an excess of personnel. But how do we solve the problem? We don't lay off anybody; instead we choose the youngest in those centers and put them to studying even while we go on paying their wages. Why? Because we realize that it is preferable that those persons, instead of doing work of little importance, should be studying, and the same money that would be spent on them without producing anything is used to train them.

Throughout the country where there had been a lot of unemployment, this tendency to work in public offices developed. In Havana, for example, which is a very large city, too large for our country, it used to be that almost all the girls would study shorthand and typing and train to work in offices. At present that is not so. Tens of thousands of girls are studying to be teachers or nurses or in the technical schools or the technological institutes. The Cuban woman is now being trained for productive work. This is a completely new situation. Right now we have enough trained office personnel so that we won't have to send a young boy or girl to work in an office for the next ten years. Of course, you understand, only a revolutionary government can do such things.

INDUSTRIALIZATION

LOCKWOOD: From not long after you came to power until quite recently you were following a policy of crash industrialization and deemphasizing agriculture. Why did you change your mind about industrializing and decide to push agricultural development again?

CASTRO: The problem of industrialization, as a generic concept, has been used as a slogan by nearly all underdeveloped countries. It would be clearer and more exact to speak of *economic* development, because it is a more complete term that includes both agricultural and industrial development. The possibilities I have just been explaining are the result of analyzing the experiences of that period. We didn't know them, and really we couldn't know them then; the conditions which existed in 1959 for our trade, our conditions for markets, were radically different from those of today. At that time, the greater part of our trade was still with the United States, and our economy was tightly interwoven with the North American economy. In those days we were, practically speaking, wholly ignorant of the enormous market possibilities that we had in the Socialist camp, even though there was tied to the slogan of industrialization another slogan, also vague and generic, which other countries are still using today: "extensive trade with all the nations of the world."

Naturally, "extensive trade with all the nations of the world" was something that would have clashed directly with the interests of the United States. Also, in those days everybody talked about revolution, about structural changes, and naturally those changes in social structure were also going to clash with the interests of the United States. At that time the United States didn't talk about agrarian reform; at that time the United States didn't talk about structural changes. That is, they didn't speak about land reform, tax reform, or about social development. That is a language the United States began to use some years later, out of the fear that new revolutions like the one in Cuba might break out in Latin America.

We were speaking in vague and generic terms about "industrialization," "wide trade," "revolution." Today, these ideas have been made more clear, concrete and real: structural change that is full and profound; economic development along the road of our agriculture; priority in this period to those branches of industry which serve as a basis for a modern agriculture; an educational plan of enormous breadth for the preparation of technicians for agriculture and industry, without which economic and social development are impossible.

LOCKWOOD: Would you say that the leaders of the Revolution made many mistakes during those first years?

CASTRO: We made many mistakes, many small mistakes, but no serious errors whose consequences might endure for a long time. That is, whenever we have taken a false step, we have been able to correct it immediately.

Could we have avoided making mistakes? I think not. Not to make mistakes would have meant anticipating each situation perfectly before it came up. That was absolutely impossible.

LAND REFORM

Now then, I am going to give you an example of what could have been a grave mistake in agriculture.

At the beginning of the Revolution, if we had followed the classic path which other countries have followed, we would have divided up the land. This would have been a mistake of such transcendence that its consequences would have been felt for a long time. You will remember that even in my Moncada speech, "History Will Absolve Me," and also when I was in the Sierra Maestra, I spoke not about dividing up the land but rather of organizing cooperatives—large enterprises of production in a cooperative form.

I found upon the victory of the Revolution that the idea of land division still had a lot of currency. But I already understood by then that if you take, for example, a sugar plantation of twenty-five hundred acres where the land is good for sugar cane, in the vicinity of a sugar mill, and you divide it into two hundred portions of twelve-and-a-half acres each, what will inevitably happen is that right away the new owners will cut the production of sugar cane in half in each plot, and they will begin to raise for their own consumption a whole series of crops for which in many cases the soil will not be adequate. Accordingly, if we had undertaken that kind of agrarian reform, dividing up the land, we would have mortgaged the agricultural future of our country, and none of the agricultural projects could have been carried out, as we are now doing, using the land in the most practical way, utilizing machinery, irrigation, fertilization, and technology on a large scale. The small landowner produces primarily for his own sustenance. And that is why small landowning is not the answer for providing food for the dietary needs of a population with a decently high standard of living. The only way to meet those needs is by the use of machinery to the greatest possible degree, and by employing fertilization, irrigation, and all the techniques which permit intensive production. This can be achieved only through the kind of management where the machine, the labor force, and technology are employed in an optimum, rational way. That is the concept of the *granja,** or "people's farm."

* *Pronounced* grán'ha.

LOCKWOOD: How did the *granja* idea originate?

CASTRO: Many factors contributed to the development of this idea.

For example, there was an experience we had while we were in the mountains of the Sierra Maestra. On one occasion we had confiscated some herds which belonged to some Batista collaborators, and we distributed them among the *campesinos*. We gave them one cow for each family—these were families which had many children and needed milk. What happened? Within a few months practically all the cows had been slaughtered and eaten. Of course, different reasons could have contributed to this: a certain fear of losing the cow, or a certain insecurity stemming from the fact that a war was going on. Yet there were some who kept the cow and didn't kill it. So I came to the conclusion that the majority of the *campesinos* had killed their cow because they preferred the immediate benefit of being able to eat it to the longer-range value of having the milk.

So then we made new distributions and set down certain legal requirements prohibiting the killing of the cows. And still, many of them—although a smaller number—slaughtered their cows. They would come and tell us that the cow had fallen down the hill or that it had had an accident! This naturally fortified my conviction that the land of the *latifundistas** should not be divided but should be organized into cooperatives.

When the Revolution came to power a new problem arose. On the sugar-cane and rice plantations it was easy to organize a cooperative, since these crops needed many workers. But when we came to the case of the great cattle ranches, vast extensions of land where a few men managed thousands of head of cattle, the question arose, what should be done? Organize a cooperative? It would have been a cooperative with very few people, and, as owners of the herds, they would have been made rich. What then? Send hundreds of people there whose work wasn't needed? That would have made a better distribution but it would have added nothing to the nation's wealth. Moreover, that labor force would have been underemployed, because it takes only a few men to manage a herd.

It was in thinking about these problems that I reached the conclusion that it was necessary to search for a superior form of social ownership of those lands. Thus the people's farm arose, which immediately presented itself as the ideal kind of organization for all the lands that had not been divided.

Even the concept of the cooperative, though a form superior to that of small-scale landholding, is inferior to the system of socialist ownership of people's farms which we have now established, because with

* *Owners of large landholdings.*

this system you can utilize the land in an optimum way, absolutely rational, determining at each moment that whatever crop benefits the nation shall be produced. And you guarantee to the workers a satisfactory income, housing, schools, roads—all those social benefits that are needed as much by the man who is planting sugar cane as by the man who is planting tobacco or tomatoes or sisal grass. The benefits reach all the agricultural workers, whatever the crop, and they are paid according to the quality and the quantity of their work.

LOCKWOOD: What exactly is a people's farm?

CASTRO: It's an agricultural production center whose lands are the property of the nation and which is operated as an enterprise of the nation.

I will give you a more concrete example. The United Fruit Company owned some three hundred and twenty-five thousand acres of land. Its stockholders lived in the United States and received a profit there, an income, without ever having visited those lands. The company assigned an administrator—naturally they tried to assign a good one—who ran things like a huge agricultural enterprise. Today, the substantial difference is that there are no foreign stockholders who own the business and receive the profits. Today, the enterprise belongs to the nation, which uses its profits for economic and social development for all—for schools, hospitals, roads, housing for workers, the acquisition of machinery, etc.

Thus, our success consists in having a good organization, designating good administrative groups, with a further advantage that the North American company could not have. The North American company was in constant social conflict with the workers, while the *granja* acts in permanent cooperation with the workers, who have their party organizations, their union organizations, their youth organizations, their women's organizations, who work there, who study, who receive the greater part of the profits and many benefits they did not receive before, who have the possibility of progressing in accordance with their level of experience and preparation, since from their own ranks come the men who occupy the posts of management and of responsibility.

And this also allows us to introduce mechanization. The U.S. company could not introduce mechanization. Why? Because there was a lot of unemployment in the country. If they had gone ahead and put in a machine to cut the sugar cane, the workers would not have permitted it, because that would have meant a shortening of the three or four months of the year in which they worked, a reduction of their incomes. Today, since there is work for all, no laborer fears the machine or looks upon it as an enemy; on the contrary he sees the machine as a friend, because he is changed from a manual worker to a mechanical worker who is going to have better living conditions, more income and easier work.

Finally, the company had to limit production because the country had limited markets. It had no reason for introducing fertilizers, irrigation, or methods of extensive production. Today, we are able to apply all these methods and increase production as much as we want, because we have the markets. We maintain full employment, and at the same time we considerably improve the living conditions of the workers and their families.

Alongside the system of people's farms there still exists the system of small landowners who own their own farms. The small farmers can hold up to one hundred and sixty acres of land. Of course in a country like Japan one hundred and sixty acres would be considered a vast estate, but in Cuba they are considered small farms. Also, there are some exceptions made for very efficient farmers who have always completely fulfilled their obligations to the State. Under the policy adopted by the Second Agrarian Reform Law toward the most competent, dependable, and hard-working farmers, there are some unusual cases of holdings up to nine hundred acres.

The Revolutionary Government sustains these individual landowners, it gives them credit and resources and buys their surplus produce, whatever they do not need for their own consumption. They can even sell individually, provided it is not in wholesale quantities. A neighbor who wants to buy from them, individual people, thus can go and buy.

Obviously, there are some exceptions. A product like sugar cane, which requires an industrial process, can only be bought by the sugar mill. But many other things, like eggs, chickens and milk, can be traded freely on a small scale. Sales in large amounts are made only by the State.

LOCKWOOD: There is a limit on how much they may sell?

CASTRO: They cannot sell over a certain quantity in each case. They can sell to any family as much as they wish to buy for their own consumption.

What happened, for example, with regard to eggs? Before, when production was limited, the small farmers sold eggs at an exorbitant price, at thirty cents an egg. When the Government's program of egg production was developed, the price was reduced to six, seven, and eight cents. They can now consume the eggs they produce or sell them at that price, which is a fair one. The best way to fight speculation, in our experience, is not by taking measures of a legal nature, but by increasing production.

Although some small farmers have organized their own cooperatives, we do not exert pressure on them to do so. In fact, we are not even interested in organizing them into cooperatives. Why? First of all, out of respect for their traditions, for their habits as small individual property owners. Any effort to organize cooperatives could have clashed in part with those feelings. Second, because we believe that with the passage of time every one of these small farms will progressively become a part of the National Common Lands Fund. How? Through expropriation? No. Through new agrarian reforms? No; we have promised them that the era of agrarian reform laws is already ended. How, then? By buying the land whenever there is a farmer who wishes to sell out.*

There are cases of farmers whose children go into the army or who are away studying in schools or in technological institutes. They have been left completely alone, and some of them are old. So they want to sell out. There are other cases of farmers who grow too old for farm work and want to retire. When such cases have come to our attention, we have bought the land and given them a pension. The possibility of selling his farm and receiving a pension besides is one of the incentives that allows us to go on acquiring new lands. But in no case is any pressure ever applied. His right to his piece of land will be respected absolutely.

LOCKWOOD: How many small farmers are there in Cuba now?

CASTRO: There must be, I believe, some one hundred and fifty thousand, counting the smallest. But actually, considering only those with any kind of economic productivity, I figure that there must be around one hundred thousand.

At present, 70 percent of the land is nationalized, 30 percent is

* *Another important reason for protecting the small farmer which Castro does not mention is that his production is often higher and of better quality than that of state-run enterprises raising the same crop in the same area.*

During recent years, as diversification of Cuban agriculture has been accelerated on a massive scale, the involvement of the small farmers in central planning has also increased. In areas where the state has decided to raise a single crop such as coffee or gandul beans, Castro, in order to obtain the small farmers' co-operation without disturbing their autonomy, has devised a kind of "semi-collective," wherein they are offered seed, fertilizer, the use of tractors, technical assistance and other inducements free of charge, in return for which each agrees to raise only that crop (or in some cases to meet a state-set quota).

Elsewhere (notably in San Andrés, Pinar del Río), full-scale collectives have been formed. The government provides not only farming supplies but new, furnished homes, utilities, roads, schools, stores and everything necessary for setting up a self-contained social unit. Members of the collective elect their own party and administrative officials.

Though the small farmer is often under considerable social and political pressure to join one of these plans, the economic advantages offered by the state are considerable and are seldom refused. His legal ownership of his land is still guaranteed, as are the profits from his production (though the latter, of course, are severely regulated by the state, which sets both quota and price).

privately owned. It does not matter to us if within twenty years 20 percent of the land is privately owned, if within forty years 90 percent is nationalized and 10 percent is privately owned. It doesn't matter how long it takes. It will be a completely evolutionary process.

LOCKWOOD: Do small farmers have the same privileges as those who work for the state—medical care, scholarships for their children, and so forth?

CASTRO: Yes, and they have that right without any kind of discrimination. Indisputably, the owner of one hundred or one hundred and fifty acres of land has a larger income than a farm laborer, but nothing would be gained by establishing a different system with regard for social services—for example, to charge for education, to charge for medical care—because the nation socially benefits from having the children of small farmers study and become technicians. Furthermore, the Revolution has established free education and medical care for all citizens. Politically and socially, it wouldn't be right to exclude them, and it wouldn't be conducive to educating the new generations of those farmers in socialism.

Formerly, you must realize, those small farmers were exploited. They paid rent, they received very low prices for their produce, they were charged high interest rates on loans, they had no roads or schools or hospitals. The Revolution has freed them from paying any rent, it has offered them many benefits, and it has given them peace of mind by promising that there will be no new measures of an agrarian nature for them. This creates the conditions for the union of the *campesinos* with the Revolutionary Government. It is very important to follow a correct policy toward the farmers, because the power of the Revolution is based on the intimate union of the workers and peasants.

Our belief that we have resolved this problem correctly is borne out by the fact that the counterrevolution has not been able to penetrate the mass of farmers. Of course there are always exceptions of individual peasants or workers who are won over by the counterrevolution, just as many people of the middle class have been won over by the Revolution. But essentially the support of the Revolution among the farming and working sections is very great, and I believe that as the years pass it will become greater and greater, better organized and more efficient.

LOCKWOOD: Weren't many of those who supported the counterrevolution in the Escambray Mountains small farmers who were afraid they were going to lose their land, even though the Agrarian Reform promised they wouldn't?

CASTRO: Well, although its main social base was among the middle-class and wealthy farmers, it's true that some of the small farmers of

Escambray supported the counterrevolution. Revolutionary *esprit* is not the same in all regions of the country. There are places where, for historical reasons, it is much stronger, as for example in the Sierra Maestra, in the mountains of Oriente Province.

During the Revolution, an organization was active in the Escambray called the Second Front of the Escambray. It was composed of elements who played an insignificant role in the war, who behaved very despotically toward the farmers and lived off them parasitically. Thus, the same sympathy for the Revolution did not develop there that developed in other farming regions of the country. There, they had an unfavorable image of the Revolution right from the beginning, unlike what happened in Oriente Province, where we paid for everything we bought, where we respected the farmers and were very careful in our relations with them.

After the victory of the Revolution, this group began to conspire and to organize the counterrevolution in the Escambray. Unquestionably, the fear of Communism was an influence too, because they (the counterrevolutionaries) arrived and told the farmer that the government was going to nationalize his land. That could have been one influence. Another could have been a certain circumstance that is peculiar to the peasant when he has a low political level. For example, there were some young men who had not joined the Revolution and later saw that others who did join had acquired positions and had ascended socially; these now thought that the counterrevolution offered them an opportunity which they should take advantage of.

And one factor that undoubtedly contributed a lot in their favor then, but that later counted against them, was terror. The counterrevolutionary bandits committed a whole series of murders so that the peasants would not give information to the revolutionary troops, so that they would help them and keep their mouths shut. The result was that some peasants were frightened and collaborated out of fear, even though everybody saw and detested the things the counterrevolutionaries were doing.

Because of this, when we organized our systematic campaign against them, we were able to mobilize the farmers and the workers of Escambray, and the vast majority of them demonstrated that they stood with the Revolution. When the Revolution mobilized its forces, it could count on more than ten thousand workers and farmers of the Escambray. It is with that force, fundamentally, that the bandit gangs were eradicated.

LOCKWOOD: This was the mountain militia?

CASTRO: Yes, the Farmers' and Workers' Militia of the Escambray.

Thus the vast majority of the population fought against the counterrevolutionaries there, and the gangs never developed a fighting spirit. They stayed on the defensive, because they weren't thinking in terms of starting a victorious war, but rather of winning a certain merit for themselves for the time when an invasion might come and they would be counted among those who had risen against the Revolution.

They never hoped to win by their own effort, even though they received arms from the United States, many modern arms, and a lot of food. They fought only when they were surrounded, in order to try to escape; they stayed always on the defensive; and they never developed the offensive spirit that we had in the Sierra Maestra. Because we didn't hope for somebody else to resolve our problems, we had to solve them ourselves. Do you understand? In that way, then, they were subjected to incessant and tenacious pursuit, until they were totally defeated.

This proved that it is impossible to organize guerrillas against a revolution made up of peasants and workers, just as there is no way of crushing a guerrilla war organized by peasants and workers.

LOCKWOOD: Is that also why the Bay of Pigs failed?

CASTRO: Well, that was not a guerrilla war, but a frontal attack, with planes, tanks, etc.; it was a conventional war. But it failed for the same reason, because the invaders—supported from the outside—fell beneath the crushing force of the people.

LOCKWOOD: When did the campaign against the counterrevolutionaries take place?

CASTRO: More or less from 1960 to 1964. The CIA organized groups in Pinar del Río too, in the province of Havana, in Matanzas, in Camagüey. The only place they were never able to penetrate was Oriente Province. They were eliminated slowly. The most important fighting was that of the Escambray Mountains—it was a systematic struggle.

LOCKWOOD: Why do you call them "bandits"?

CASTRO: We have to call them bandits because we cannot call them revolutionaries.

LOCKWOOD: Or counterrevolutionaries either?

CASTRO: All right, but remember that they did many things that were real acts of banditry: the murder of teachers, the murder of members of the literacy brigades, the murder of managers, of farmers, of workers. In reality, "bandit" is a political term, but the things they did were things that won them the name of bandits. They committed many absolutely unjustifiable excesses in order to sow terror there, things we never did while we were struggling against Batista—never!

We never employed terror. In our struggle the one who employed terror was Batista. He came with airplanes, he dropped bombs, he murdered farmers! We never used aviation in the Escambray, we never dropped a bomb, we never took measures that would affect the population, we never sowed terror. We may have used means to keep them from helping the bandits, but not inhuman means, not burning houses, not torturing, not murdering.

HAVANA

LOCKWOOD: Havana, you have said, is much too expensive for revolutionary Cuba. I suppose that now one of your biggest problems must be how to maintain it. It's growing old, it's crumbling, it lacks facilities. . . .

CASTRO: That is true. Havana, in the first place, is too large a city for a country of our size and geographic configuration. Our country is long and narrow. It has this city, its capital, at one end, and in precisely the smallest province. The problem of water supply is extremely serious on account of the uncontrolled way in which the city grew. It gets its supply from underground water, since there is no river, and in a warm country, with a tropical climate requiring a great consumption of water, this is a serious problem. Furthermore, very fertile lands in the vicinity of Havana are deprived of water on this account. Perhaps in the long run we will have to use desalinized sea water in the city. But this procedure is still very expensive. At present we are studying techniques to increase the rainfall, and it seems that the prospects of this are good.

Another problem is that the population of Havana receives approximately one-half of the wages that are paid out in the whole country, and almost one-half of the resources of the nation are invested there. Before the Revolution, practically nothing was ever built in the countryside, neither roads nor hospitals nor schools. Most of the public works were undertaken only in the capital of the republic. We inherited an overdeveloped capital in a completely underdeveloped country. A modern city has many expenses; to maintain Havana at the same level as before would be detrimental to what has to be done in the interior of the country. For that reason, for some time Havana must necessarily suffer a little this process of disuse, of deterioration, until enough resources can be provided.

Of course, everything that's essential will be taken care of in Havana, the public services: transportation, water, sewerage, streets, parks, hospitals, schools, etc. But construction of new modern buildings—like those lavish skyscrapers that were built before the Revolution, to the detriment of the interior of the country—has been discontinued for the time being.

Moreover, under the Urban Reform Law of 1960 all rents were reduced and many people are now paying no rent at all.

LOCKWOOD: How does the law work?

CASTRO: First, rents on all dwellings were reduced by an average of 40 percent immediately. Second, people living in houses that had been built twenty years or more before 1960 were required to pay rent for only five more years. In the more modern buildings they would have to pay longer, up to a maximum of twenty years for the most recent ones. Third, in all new housing being constructed, the occupants pay a flat rent of ten percent of the family income.

At the end of 1965, the first five years of the Urban Reform were concluded, and around 80 percent—I don't know the exact figure—of the urban population then owned their own homes and ceased paying rent. One result of this is that urban family incomes have increased by tens of millions of pesos.

LOCKWOOD: Still, there obviously is a housing shortage in Havana, isn't there? I don't know how many stories I've heard about young men and women who want to get married but can't, because they have no place to live. I've met couples who have been engaged for two or three years and are still living with their families, waiting for an apartment to open up so that they can get married.

CASTRO: If the resources were invested in the construction of the housing required to satisfy the needs of Havana, all the rest of the island would have to be sacrificed. Moreover, the number of young persons who have jobs today and are leading their own lives has considerably increased. Before, it was very rare for a boy seventeen or eighteen years old to be thinking of getting married. Many young people had to wait till they finished their studies at the university, and many others had to wait until they could find a job. Today, the boy works and the girl works. So the number of marriages, as well as the number of births, has increased considerably.

LOCKWOOD: Is the scarcity of living quarters in the cities one of the reasons why you have permitted the continuation of that old Cuban institution, the *posada?* *

* Posada (*literally "boarding house" or "inn"*) *is slang for a motel-like place where couples go to make love, no questions asked. There are at least three dozen in Havana alone, former private enterprises which are now run by the Revolutionary Government. Generally located in secluded streets at the edge of town, the* posadas *are refreshingly accommodating, avoid any possible embarrassment to the lady, who can, if she wishes, enter and leave without ever having been seen. Rooms are cheap (about $2.65 for the first three hours, 50 cents an hour thereafter) and comfortable, equipped with a large double bed, private bath and shower, radio, telephone, bar room service, etc., even two sets of slippers. Furnishings vary from sparse and dingy in the older ones to near-*

CASTRO: Well, that is a much more complex problem. I don't know whether you want to go into an analysis of that problem too.

Actually, a great effort is being made to eradicate prostitution. But the problem of the *posadas* also poses a series of questions of a human kind that will have to be analyzed in the future.

Traditions and customs can clash somewhat with new social realities, and the problem of sexual relations in youth will require more scientific attention. But the discussion of that problem has not yet been made the order of the day. Neither customs nor traditions can be changed easily, nor can they be dealt with superficially. I believe that new realities, social, economic and cultural, will determine new conditions and new concepts of human relations.

LOCKWOOD: You mean, concepts shorn of the religious traditions that still form the basis of popular attitudes toward sexual relations?

CASTRO: I think it's not only a matter of religious traditions, which naturally have an influence, but also of certain traditions derived from Spanish customs, which are stricter in this aspect than, for example, Anglo-Saxon traditions.

Naturally, those centers to which you refer have been in operation because they satisfy a social need. Closing them makes no sense. There have not, of course, been resources to augment them. But what has definitely been fought is prostitution. That is a vicious, corrupt, cruel thing, a dead weight that generally affects women of humble origin who, for an infinite number of economic and social reasons, wind up in that life. The Revolution has been eliminating it, not in an abrupt, drastic, radical way, but progressively, trying to give employment and educational opportunities to the women so that they might learn other skills that would permit them to work and earn their living in a different manner. This has advanced slowly but effectively.

All this raises the future necessity, too, of approaching the problems of sexual relations in a different way. But we believe that these are problems of the future that cannot be determined by decree—not at all. I believe that people are developing new concepts as a result of a more scientific training, of a superior culture, of the abolition of certain prejudices; and all this is taking place gradually, as has happened in other countries.

LOCKWOOD: There has apparently been an organized effort by men in your government to deal firmly with homosexuals, some of whom

---

sumptuous in those built just prior to the Revolution (an entire modern cottage, including air conditioning and TV); all are kept immaculately clean. Couples generally arrive by car or taxi for the sake of privacy. However, on Friday and Saturday nights there is often a long line waiting for rooms in front of some posadas, *sometimes extending a block or two down the street.*

were in positions of responsibility. It seemed that a general, naïvely conceived effort was under way to stamp out homosexuality.

CASTRO: That problem has not been sufficiently studied nor sufficiently analyzed. Nor do I believe that definitive norms exist yet anywhere in relation to this very delicate problem.

We have considered it our duty to take at least minimum measures to the effect that those positions in which one might have a direct influence upon children and young people should not be in the hands of homosexuals, above all in educational centers.

LOCKWOOD: Is it your position that if one is a homosexual he cannot be a Revolutionary?

CASTRO: Nothing prevents a homosexual from professing revolutionary ideology and, consequently, exhibiting a correct political position. In this case he should not be considered politically negative. And yet we would never come to believe that a homosexual could embody the conditions and requirements of conduct that would enable us to consider him a true Revolutionary, a true Communist militant. A deviation of that nature clashes with the concept we have of what a militant Communist must be

But above all, I do not believe that anybody has a definitive answer as to what causes homosexuality. I think the problem must be studied very carefully. But I will be frank and say that homosexuals should not be allowed in positions where they are able to exert influence upon young people. In the conditions under which we live, because of the problems which our country is facing, we must inculcate our youth with the spirit of discipline, of struggle, of work. In my opinion, everything that tends to promote in our youth the strongest possible spirit, activities related in some way with the defense of the country, such as sports, must be promoted. This attitude may or may not be correct, but it is our honest feeling.

It may be in some cases a person is homosexual for pathological reasons. It would indeed be arbitrary if such a person were maltreated for something over which he has no control. You can only ask yourself, when assigning a person to a position of responsibility, what are the factors which might help that person do his job well, and what are those that might hinder him?

EDUCATION

LOCKWOOD: You seem to have awakened a great interest in education. It seems that there is hardly anyone in Cuba these days under the age of seventy who is not studying something.

CASTRO: That is true, an extraordinary interest has been awakened.

If you remember that our population is some seven-and-a-half million inhabitants, about 30 percent of the population is studying, that is, some two-and-one-half million people. That includes one million adults.

LOCKWOOD: One of the first big programs that you created was the system for training student-teachers in Minas del Frío* and elsewhere. How has that worked out—are you satisfied with the results?

CASTRO: Yes, it has been a great success. Before, it was very difficult to get teachers who would go to teach in the mountains. Now, students from every province and from all the towns of the country go into that school, and when they graduate they begin to teach in the mountains. At present we have some fifteen thousand young people† studying to be teachers. In 1965, the first thousand graduated; beginning in 1968, four thousand per year will graduate; and between 1970 and 1980, we will graduate a total of fifty thousand teachers. And we have this well organized. During their last two years of school the students study and teach. By 1968, practically all the primary schools in Havana will be staffed by students from the Teachers' Institute, and the present teachers, through advanced training courses, will go on to teach in the secondary schools. This program is progressing very well.

LOCKWOOD: I've seen some of the young teachers in action—they have a great deal of enthusiasm.

CASTRO: Terrific spirit! Really, great teachers have developed. We also have about ten thousand ‡ workers studying in the agricultural technology institutes, workers from the countryside who have been outstanding in their work. We send them first to elementary school courses until they reach the level of the eighth grade, and afterward they study for two years in agricultural technology centers. When they finish and go back to work, they will have a level of preparation that will allow them to matriculate in the university through correspondence courses.

Really, it would be worth the trouble if all these things that are being done today in Cuba, which in our judgment are the only way in the long run to resolve the problems of the country, could be compared with what is being done elsewhere. Is anything similar being carried out in other Latin American countries?

We stand ready to show these things to everybody who might come

---

* *Minas del Frío* (*"The Mines of the Cold"*) *is a school camp for student-teachers located in Oriente Province high in the Sierra Maestra Mountains. It is the first stage in Cuba's unique crash program to acquire a corps of trained teachers for the rural area schools.*

† *By 1968, the figure had risen to twenty-nine thousand.*

‡ *Fifty thousand in 1968.*

to Cuba in good faith, to make an objective appraisal. We would show them everything, in order that they should see both good and bad, what would please them and what would displease them, things that are going well and things that are not. We are sure that the balance is very positive. The years we are now going through are the most difficult, and they are already being left behind. Within four or five years the position of Cuba will be incomparable; it will be superior to that of any other country in Latin America.

LOCKWOOD: Is it true that a young man cannot enter the university unless he is a revolutionary?

CASTRO: Well, there is no regulation, but there is a policy that is applied through the students' organizations, by means of agreements that are discussed and adopted in public general assemblies, in which the mass of all the students of a department participate. It is required at least that one not be *counter*revolutionary.

To train a university-educated technician costs thousands upon thousands of pesos. Who pays for that? The people. Should we then train technicians who later on are going to leave to work in the United States? I don't believe that is right. The country, in making this expenditure, has the right to the guarantee that it is training technicians who are going to serve the country. The future intellectuals of the country are being educated in the university, and without any hesitation we must try to see that those intellectuals are revolutionaries.

LOCKWOOD: How can you expect a young man of sixteen or seventeen to have made up his mind politically? Even you yourself, in fact, were not a revolutionary when you entered the university.

CASTRO: True, I was not a revolutionary; hardly anybody was. I was one of the privileged when I went to the university.

LOCKWOOD: But isn't that a rather early age at which to expect a young man to have formed himself politically?

CASTRO: No, at seventeen a boy can be politically developed. However, that wasn't the real problem. The problem was that, on account of compulsory military service, some persons from bourgeois families who had already left school and who were not seventeen, but twenty-five, twenty-seven, or thirty, tried to enroll in the university to avoid fulfilling this obligation, since university students are exempted.

LOCKWOOD: But that was before. I am asking about now—why is it not possible now to allow young men to enter the university even if they have a questioning attitude about political and social matters?

CASTRO: We have to insist on certain intellectual requirements; that is, a good record in studies, high motivation, and good conduct. Even a questioning attitude about political and social matters could not be a good reason to prevent young people from going into the university.

If that young person has "human sensibility," science and truth will convert him into a revolutionary.

LOCKWOOD: What does it mean that a student must have a record of "good conduct"?

CASTRO: Good conduct means his behavior as a student and as a citizen.

LOCKWOOD: In his private life too?

CASTRO: Academic and civil. But a boy doesn't have to be necessarily a Marxist-Leninist in order to study at the university. For example, a Catholic boy can enroll, a Protestant boy can enroll.

LOCKWOOD: Can he be neutral to the Revolution and still be accepted?

CASTRO: It is enough if he is an honorable individual who is willing to study in order to live and work in the country and who embodies the necessary requirements of capability and motivation. You must not forget that in a revolution there are hardly any neutrals.*

POLITICAL INDOCTRINATION

LOCKWOOD: To what extent does the curriculum in Cuban schools include political indoctrination?

CASTRO: What you call political indoctrination would perhaps be more correctly called social education. After all, do not forget that those children are being educated to live in a Communist society. From an early age they must be discouraged from every egotistical feeling in the enjoyment of material things, such as the sense of individual property, and be encouraged toward the greatest possible common effort and a spirit of cooperation. Therefore, they must receive not only instruction of a scientific kind but also education for social life and a broad general culture.

LOCKWOOD: Is this "culture" to which they are exposed selected from a political point of view?

CASTRO: Of course some knowledge is of a universal kind, while other subjects that are taught may be influenced by a definite conception. For instance, history cannot be taught as a simple repetition of events that have occurred without any interrelationship, in an accidental way. We have a scientific conception of history and of the development of human society, and of course in some subjects there is and will be influences from our philosophy.

LOCKWOOD: A Marxist influence?

* This last sentence was added later by Castro. At the same time, he deleted the first sentence of his original reply; "It doesn't matter whether he is neutral toward the Revolution."

CASTRO: Yes.

LOCKWOOD: What about in the arts? Is there an attempt to teach the history of art and literature and their criticism from the Marxist point of view?

CASTRO: We have very few qualified people as yet who could even try to give a Marxist interpretation of the problems of art.

Concerning art criticism . . . I think that that too is a complex problem. I have the intention of calling together a group of outstanding students in the humanities faculty of the university who are totally lacking in prejudice and put them to thoroughly studying the problems of culture and art, so that we might one day have a team capable of correctly approaching these problems. We don't suppose that all the political leaders should have an encyclopedic knowledge and be in a position to speak the last word on matters of culture and of art. I would not consider myself sufficiently skilled to make decisions in that realm without professional advice from really qualified people in whose sound and revolutionary judgment I could trust.

As a revolutionary, it is my understanding that one of our fundamental concerns must be that all the manifestations of culture be placed at the service of man, developing in him all the most positive feelings. For me, art is not an end in itself. Man is its end; making man happier, making man better. I do not conceive of any manifestations of culture, of science, of art, as purposes in themselves. I think that the purpose of science and culture is man.

LOCKWOOD: Those words "happier," "better," can be interpreted very broadly—

CASTRO: They *should* be interpreted in a broad sense. I don't think there has ever existed a society in which all the manifestations of culture have not been at the service of some cause or concept. Our duty is to see that the whole is at the service of the kind of man we wish to create.

But doesn't this mean that perhaps every work must have a political content in itself? No, that is not necessary. I believe that the content of any artistic work of any kind—its very quality for its own sake, without its necessarily having to carry a message—can give rise to a beneficial and noble feeling in the human being.

CENSORSHIP

LOCKWOOD: Is there any attempt to exert control over the production of art in Cuba? For example, of literature?

CASTRO: All manifestations of art have different characteristics. For example, movies are different from painting; movies are a modern industry requiring a lot of resources. It is not the same thing to make a film as it is to paint a picture or write a book. But if you ask whether there is control—no.

LOCKWOOD: One thing that is surprising is the amount of creative freedom given to your artists, the painters and sculptors, as compared with other Socialist countries. However, this liberalism seems to apply to a lesser extent to literature.

CASTRO: Because literature involves the publication of books. It is principally an economic problem. The resources that are available are not sufficient for all the needs for the printing of textbooks, for example, schoolbooks, reference works, books of a general nature. That is, we cannot waste paper. That is one of the limiting factors. This doesn't mean that the political factor doesn't have its influence too. A book that we did not believe to be of some value wouldn't have a chance of being published.

LOCKWOOD: In other words, an author who wrote a novel that contained counterrevolutionary sentiments couldn't possibly get it published?

CASTRO: At present, no. The day will come when all the resources will be available, that is, when such a book would not be published to the detriment of a textbook or of a book having universal value in world literature. Then there will be resources to publish books on the basis of a broader criterion, and one will be able to argue whatever one wishes about any theme. I, especially, am a partisan of the widest possible discussion in the intellectual realm.

Why? Because I believe in the free man, I believe in the well-educated man, I believe in the man able to think, in the man who acts always out of conviction, without fear of any kind. And I believe that ideas must be able to defend themselves. I am opposed to the blacklists of books, prohibited films and all such things. What is my personal ideal of the kind of people that we wish to have in the future? People sufficiently cultivated and educated to be capable of making a correct judgment about anything without fear of coming into contact with ideas that could confound or deflect them. For example, how do we think of ourselves? We think that we could read any book or see any film, about any theme, without changing our fundamental beliefs; and if there is in a book a solid argument about something that could be useful, that could be positive, that we are capable of analyzing and evaluating it.

May all the men and women of our country be like this in the future! That is the kind of man we wish to shape. If we did not think like that, we would be men with no faith in our own convictions, in our own philosophy.

LOCKWOOD: But such an atmosphere is not possible at the present time?

CASTRO: It would be an illusion to think so. First on account of the economic problems involved, and second because of the struggle in which we are engaged.

LOCKWOOD: Is it also in the name of that "struggle" that the Cuban press writes so one-sidedly about the United States?

CASTRO: I am not going to tell you that we don't do that. It's true, everything that we say about the United States refers essentially to the worst aspects, and it is very rare that things in any way favorable to the United States will be published here. We simply have a similar attitude to the attitude of your country. I mean that we always try to create the worst opinion of everything there is in the United States, as a response to what they have always done with us. The only difference is that we do not write falsehoods about the United States. I told you that we emphasize the worst things, that we omit things that could be viewed as positive, but we do not invent any lies.

LOCKWOOD: But it amounts to the same thing. By emphasizing only our bad qualities, you create a distortion that is the equivalent of a lie.

CASTRO: That depends on what you mean by "lie." I agree that it is a distortion. A lie is simply the willful invention of facts that do not exist. There is a difference between a distortion and a lie, although unquestionably they have some effects of a similar kind.

This is not ideal. But it is the result of realities that have not been imposed by us. In a world of peace, in which genuine trust and respect among peoples existed, this wouldn't happen. And we are not responsible for this situation.

LOCKWOOD: But if you persist in promoting these distortions, which encourage only hostile feelings in your citizens, how can you ever expect to have peace?

CASTRO: Again, we are not the ones responsible. It is the United States who cut all relations with Cuba.

LOCKWOOD: I don't think that has anything to do with the question.

CASTRO: I am simply fulfilling my duty of speaking to you with complete frankness when I tell you how things are from our side. I have the honesty to speak like this—how many leaders of the United States would speak in the same terms?

LOCKWOOD: You are most frank. But I would like to insist on this point a bit longer. In my personal opinion, you have more to gain by keeping your society open to knowledge of all kinds about the United States than by persisting in painting a distorted image of us. For example, in recent years there has been an increasing effort on the part of our government to support the Negroes' fight for civil rights, and strong legislation has been passed. This is something which could also be covered by the Cuban press, besides the fact that there are

Negroes rioting in California, or that the Ku Klux Klan is marching in Georgia and Alabama, which is the only kind of thing you ever publish here.

CASTRO: It is my understanding that news of that legislation was published here, although naturally we have a substantially different point of view about it than you do. We believe that the problem of discrimination has an economic content and basis appropriate to a class society in which man is exploited by man.

This is clearly a difficult, complex problem. We ourselves went through the experience of discrimination. Discrimination disappeared when class privileges disappeared, and it has not cost the Revolution much effort to resolve that problem. I don't believe it could have been done in the United States. It would be a little absurd to speak at this moment of a revolution there. Perhaps there will never even be a revolution in the United States, in the classic sense of the word, but rather evolutionary changes. I am sure, for example, that within five hundred years North American society will bear no similarity to the present one. Probably by that time they won't have problems of discrimination.

LOCKWOOD: But why not speak of the evolutionary changes in the United States too? Why not tell the Cuban people the whole story?

CASTRO: Because altogether there have not been any evolutionary changes in a positive sense in the United States. But rather, politically speaking, a true regression. From our general point of view the policy of the United States, above all her foreign policy, has advanced more and more toward an ultrareactionary position.

LOCKWOOD: We were not talking about United States foreign policy.

CASTRO: In reality that is what affects us most.

LOCKWOOD: Since we're on the subject, it also seems to me that anybody who has a point of view substantially different from the governmental line about almost anything has very little opportunity to express himself in the press here. In fact, there is extremely little criticism of any kind in the Cuban press. It seems to be an arm of the government.

CASTRO: Well, what you say is true. There is very little criticism. An enemy of Socialism cannot write in our newspapers—but we don't deny it, and we don't go around proclaiming a hypothetical freedom of the press where it actually doesn't exist, the way you people do. Furthermore, I admit that our press is deficient in this respect. I don't believe that this lack of criticism is a healthy thing. Rather, criticism is a very useful and positive instrument, and I think that all of us must learn to make use of it.

LOCKWOOD: Don't you think that there are Cuban writers who

would make use of that instrument if there existed an atmosphere in which their statements would be taken as constructive criticism?

CASTRO: Criticism, yes—but not work in the service of the enemy or of the counterrevolution.

LOCKWOOD: But who is to decide at any given point which criticism is constructive and which is counterrevolutionary?

CASTRO: Well, we are in the midst of a struggle, a more or less open war, and when, for example, the United States has been faced with such situations, what they have done is to repress without consideration all those who opposed the interests of the country while it was at war. When you were at war against the Nazis, you had such a policy.

LOCKWOOD: But you haven't answered the question. Who is to decide?

CASTRO: Under such circumstances, the party decides, the political power, the revolutionary power. Naturally, when we no longer live under these circumstances, the causes that require severe measures will actually disappear.

LOCKWOOD: But in the meantime there is almost no criticism of any kind in your society, either in the press or in the literature, radio and television, or in any of the other organs of communication in Cuba.

CASTRO: Certainly there is a minimum of criticism. And there is something more: we have to pay attention to the training of the journalistic cadres, because millions of people read what they say and write. If we are going to have a people of wide culture, then the men who have daily contact with them must have a wide culture too, to be really qualified for the social function which they perform. We believe that journalism in its different forms has an extraordinary importance in modern life.

Not that I would tell you we delude ourselves that under the present circumstances journalism can have any other function more important than that of contributing to the political and revolutionary goals of our country. We have a goal, a program, an objective to fulfill, and that objective essentially controls the activity of the journalists. I would say that it essentially controls the labor of all the intellectual workers. I am not going to deny it.

LOCKWOOD: But isn't there a certain danger inherent in suppressing all forms of criticism—?

CASTRO: I agree! I do not say at all that the absence of criticism can be useful. On the contrary, it could even be harmful.

LOCKWOOD: What do you think has been responsible for the growth of this atmosphere?

CASTRO: I believe various circumstances, but fundamentally the situation of emergency and strain under which the country has been living, required to survive by the skin of its teeth. Almost all activities have had to be subordinated to the need for survival.

LOCKWOOD: One thing which may have influenced this atmosphere of inhibition is your own strong personal position against "counterrevolutionary" attitudes. Isn't it possible, once this climate has been established, that an intellectual may come to fear that any critical idea may be interpreted by the government as counterrevolutionary? That is, perhaps the strong position you have always taken has shut off a line of communication between you and people of intelligence who are in a position to see that something is wrong or who may have a better idea. By stifling critical comment, don't you make it unlikely that you will hear any ideas but your own?

CASTRO: I confess that those are themes which we have to pay attention to in the near future. Because other things have been occupying our attention, we have not been able to concern ourselves with such obvious deficiencies as these.

LOCKWOOD: This lack of a critical perspective seems to apply in education as well. In my visits to schools in various parts of the country I found generally that the children are being taught to accept concepts at face value rather than to question them. Don't you feel that this is potentially dangerous to the intellectual future of your country?

CASTRO: I think that the education of students depends very much upon the level of training and capability of the teacher. That is, it is not a question of policy. The child must be taught to think; to develop his intelligence must be the essential objective of teaching.

Anyway, I am going to concern myself with the observations you have made. One of our fundamental concerns has been the training of a corps of teachers on the highest pedagogical level. It must never be forgotten that the conditions under which we have lived are not normal ones; they are conditions of violent class struggle, clashes of ideas, of judgments, of feelings. All this can contribute to the creation of a certain environment, a certain atmosphere of inhibition. . . . However, this was not what we were most concerned about in these first days. What concerned us much more was to open a school in a place where there was no teacher, to teach the ABC's, to teach reading and writing. In that first stage we were concerned with the elemental things in education, and many things had to be improvised because we lacked skilled personnel.

I think it is logical that we should make sure that the children now in elementary school and who are going to be the future intellectuals, the future citizens of our country, should not be educated in a dogmatic way, but should develop their capacity to think and to judge for themselves.

LOCKWOOD: I've also noticed in the classrooms a tendency to approach facts dogmatically. For example, we were talking before about how the Cuban press purposely does not paint a well-rounded picture of the United States. Well, the interpretations and the "facts" about the United States which are presented to the students in their classes are precisely those printed in the newspapers, repeated without clarification. What is going to happen when all of these young boys and girls who have been receiving this one-sided picture all through school, perhaps ever since the first grade, become adults?

CASTRO: Without doubt they will have a very bad opinion of the United States and about everything it represents, in the same way that in the United States children are educated with a very bad opinion of Communism. It is lamentable, but it is a reality.

LOCKWOOD: Someday the United States and Cuba are going to have friendly relations again. When that happens, won't you have to deal with the legacy of this bad feeling with which you are indoctrinating your youth?

CASTRO: That is not an easy question to reply to. Besides, nobody has ever before posed this question. Actually this is the first time that I have heard it posed by a North American. Nor have we posed it to ourselves; it can be said that we have never been consciously concerned about that problem.

Perhaps that is due partly to our great pessimism about whether the American people really have much opportunity to express their own opinions, or to change a situation. It is possible that even we ourselves have not fully understood how deeply the feeling of solidarity with the Negroes has penetrated the hearts of the North American people. That is, we have no faith at all in the government of the United States, and that could also have led us toward a certain degree of underestimation of the people of the United States. But this is not the result of a deliberate policy.

Maybe when you publish your book many of those who work in our press will also meditate on those questions. I, for my part, in conversations with them, can express those concerns and ask them to meditate a little on these themes. That for the sake of something you say which I think is true: that someday—which I do not at all believe will be immediate, but rather a great deal of time will pass—it will have to happen that better relations exist between our two peoples.

LOCKWOOD: It seems to me that we should try to lessen that time as much as possible, rather than to prolong it for unnecessary reasons.

CASTRO: I think that is reasonable. Let's go to lunch.

Volunteer women cane cutters in Oriente Province

Left, Above, and Following pages:
*Sugar-cane cutters at work at the
height of the harvest near Puerto
Padre, Oriente Province*

Castro, self-taught agronomist, explains his personal experimental sugar-cane station (Left) and inspects a recently planted cattle pasture (Right)

EDUCATION

One of the most conspicuously successful achievements of the Castro regime in the social area has been its massive education program. By the end of 1965, nearly 2,500,000 people, children and adults, were studying something (out of a total population of just over 7,000,000). Illiteracy, which had been over 23 percent before the Revolution, had been reduced to less than 3 percent (this figure includes the mentally retarded, those too old to learn, and 25,000 Haitians who speak only French). More than 1,000,000 adults were in some form of study, while over 150,000 youngsters were studying on full government scholarships. Currently, the government is conducting a campaign to raise each Cuban to at least a sixth-grade level of education. A recent UNESCO report designated Cuba as the country making the greatest effort in education in all of Latin America.

In mounting such an ambitious educational program Cuba's main problem has been to find enough primary and secondary grade teachers to staff it. To meet the need, a special teacher-training program was set up in 1959 by which young men and women learn to teach at the same time as they are completing their high school education.

The five-year program begins at Minas del Frío, a school camp located in Oriente Province high in the mists of the Sierra Maestra Mountains. Four thousand boys and girls who have completed sixth grade spend their first year of training here in total isolation. It is a life that is both physically demanding and academically rigorous. Classes are held outdoors, the students sleep in unheated dormitories, and since there is little else to do except study and go to classes, the level of achievement is generally very high.

The second and third years are spent at Topas de Collantes, another school camp in the Escambray Mountains. During their last two years, the students live and study in the more academic surroundings of the Makarenko Pedagogical Institute, near Havana. Here, they teach primary classes in Havana schools during the mornings, attend their own classes in the afternoons, and study at night.

It is an especially demanding course, since the students compress the normal six years of secondary school education into five, and at the same time they must acquire a basic knowledge of school curriculum and teaching methods. In spite of the harshness of the life, the long school hours, and the short vacations (ninety days per year), the discipline and the morale of the students are exceptionally high.

*Amid swirling mists of the Sierra Maestra, girl
students at Minas del Frío line up for lunch*

Above: *A student-teacher of Makarenko Institute conducts a class in ideology at a school for political prisoners undergoing rehabilitation. Topic: "The worker in capitalism and in socialism"*

A house in the Vedado suburb of Havana, once a middle-class home, now a school for scholarship students

Left: *Student-teachers at Tópes de Collantes going to early-morning open-air classes*

LAS GLORIAS DEL PUEBLO SON LAS GLORIAS DE TODOS

VICTORIA DE GIRON

Opposite and Above: *Scholarship students drilling at a maritime school near the Bay of Pigs. Poster commemorates the U.S. defeat: "The victories of the people are the victories of all"*

"Becados" (scholarship students) from the mountains in a music
school near Havana.

THE ARTS

Under the loosely administered patronage of the Revolution, the arts have flourished in Cuba and remained refreshingly free of the ideological influence and restraint common to other socialist cultures. There are no fewer than five dance companies, ranging from experimental and folkloric to the classical National Ballet directed by Alicia Alonzo, all subsidized by the government. There are six theatre drama groups in Havana, which offer a dramatic spectrum ranging from Sophocles and Molière to Ionesco, Miller and Albee, as well as plays by interesting Cuban playwrights, such as José Triana's *Night of the Assassins*. The ICAIC, Cuba's Motion Picture Institute, produces the most avant-garde weekly newsreel in the world. ICAIC's documentaries (*Cowboys of the Cauto, Now!*) and feature films like Titón's *Inconsolable Memories* and Humberto Solas' *Lucia* use modern film techniques and frequently win awards at European film festivals. ICAIC also imports a limited number of foreign films for Cuban audiences, such as *La Dolce Vita, Blow-up, Morgan* and *La Chinoise*. (U.S. films are, of course, prohibited by the American blockade.) The Cuban Book Institute (founded 1959) publishes twenty million volumes per year. These are mainly textbooks, but literary works by such diverse writers as Proust, Faulkner, Kafka, Sartre, Robbe-Grillet, Genet, Capote and Marcuse are published in handsomely designed editions of ten thousand and sell out immediately. So, too, do new works by important older Cuban writers such as Alejo Carpentier and Lezama Lima, and younger authors like Edmundo Desnoes, Heberto Padilla, Pablo Armando, Roberto F. Retamar, Lisadro Otero and Miguel Barnet. Desnoes and Barnet have been published in the U.S. The Casa de las Americas, which holds biennial competitions for Latin American writers in five literary categories, awards each winner one thousand U.S. dollars plus publication of his book. Perhaps the liveliest of all Cuban arts is painting. Lacking government subsidies, painters feel free to experiment with new styles and unpopular ideas. Raúl Martínez paints critical canvases in pop style utilizing multiple images of Fidel and Che; Antonia Eírez' giant expressionist canvases evoke a tortured world akin to that of Francis Bacon; Amélia Peláez and René Portocarrero are older nonobjective painters whose work is known internationally but who still live and work in Cuba. So far, Cuba has not attempted to coerce her artists to produce only such art as can serve as propaganda for the Revolution. Che Guevara wrote that socialist realism is a nineteenth-century art form completely obsolete for contemporary purposes. But the touchstone for all Cuban artists is the dictum set by Fidel Castro in 1963, at a time when the problem of ideology in art had become the subject of critical debate: "Within the Revolution, everything; outside the Revolution, nothing."

Students at new Havana modern dance school at Cubanacán perform their final examination

Aerial view of part of new Cubanacán art schools complex, located on grounds of former Havana Country Club. Architect Ricardo Porro used innovative Catalonian vault technique for supports because of shortage of building materials

Raúl Martínez, a "pop" painter of political portraits

Left: *José Masiques, a young abstractionist*

Antonia Eirez, an expressionist influenced by Francis Bacon, in her studio

Francisco Alea ("Titón"), a leading film director

Edmundo Desnoes, novelist, essayist and propagandist for the Party's "Council of Revolutionary Orientation"

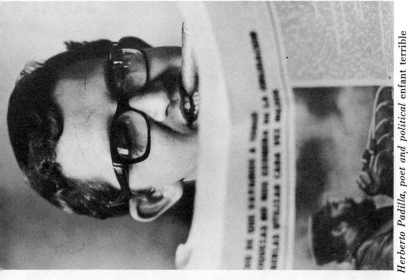

Herberto Padilla, poet and political enfant terrible

Roberto Fernández Retamar, poet and editor of Cuba's literary magazine, Casa

four:

Fidel's Fidel (interview— part two)

PERSONAL POWER

LOCKWOOD: It is a commonly held view in my country that you are a dictator with absolute power, that the Cuban people have no voice in their government, and that there is no sign that this is going to change.

CASTRO: I think we have to state the ideas a little more precisely. We are Marxists and look upon the state as an instrument of the ruling class to exercise power. What you people call "representative democracy" is, in our opinion, the dictatorship of the capitalists, and the North American state is an instrument of that class domination, from the domestic point of view as well as from the international point of view.

I believe that these are not simply theoretical positions. The ruling classes exercise power through the state and through all the means that they can depend on to defend their system. They depend not only on the state, its administration, and its armed forces for this purpose, but on all the rest of the instruments at the service of the system: the dominant political parties, which are completely controlled by those classes and take turns in power, and all the media of communication—the press, radio, television, newspapers, magazines, movies, publishing houses, technical and scientific societies, public education, the universities. All those media are at the service of a system that is under the control of the wealthy of the United States.

Naturally, you might tell me that in the United States it is possible to publish a book that is against the government or to write some critical articles. This doesn't at all threaten the security of the system. Anything that might threaten the system would be repressed, as has been proven. Even activities that constitute no danger at all to the United States have been persecuted; various personalities who were characterized, not by Marxist, but by progressive thought—in the movies, in television, in the universities, and in other intellectual media—have been investigated, have been imprisoned, have suffered persecution, have been required to appear before the Committee on so-called Un-American Affairs, with all the consequences that this implies. So, a real intellectual terror exists in the United States. The people who have the courage to express progressive opinions are few, out of fear of bringing down those consequences upon themselves. Criticisms are made in the United States, yes, but *within* the system, not against it. The system is something untouchable, sacred, against which only genuine exceptions dare to express themselves.

So I ask myself whether that isn't really a class dictatorship, the imposition of a system by all material and moral means? In the United States the people vote every four years for one of the candidates that the two parties choose, but that doesn't imply any change.

On the other hand, we think of the revolutionary state as an instrument of the power of the workers and peasants, that is, of the manual and intellectual workers, directed by a party that is composed of the best men from among them. We organize our party with the participation of the workers of all the centers of labor, who express their opinions in a completely free way, in assemblies, proposing and supporting those whom they believe should be members of the party or opposing those whom they believe should not be.

Our party is the representative of the workers and peasants, of the working class, in the same way that the Congress of the United States is the representative of the capitalists. So that our system is a class system too, in a period of transition. Ultimately, we will go even a little further and proclaim the nonnecessity of the state, the disappearance of the state with the disappearance of social classes. When Communism is a reality, that instrument will no longer be necessary as a coercive force by which one class maintains its domination over another, since neither exploiters nor exploited will exist. As Engels said, "The government over the people will be replaced by the administration of things and by the conduct of the processes of production."

You ask about power concentrated in one person. The truth is that, although I perform certain functions inherent to the offices that I hold within the state and the party, my authority to make decisions is really less than that of the President of the United States. If we are going to speak about personal power, in no other country in the world, not even under absolute monarchies, has there ever been such a high degree of power concentrated in one person as is concentrated in the President of the United States. That officeholder whom you call President can even take the country into a thermonuclear war without having to consult the Congress. There is no case like it in history. He intervened in Vietnam on his own decision. He intervened in Santo

Domingo on his own decision.* Thus, that functionary you call President is the most complete expression of the dictatorship of a class which on occasions exercises itself by conceding really absolute powers to one man.

Why don't you North Americans think a little about these questions, instead of accepting as an irrefutable truth your definition of democracy? Why don't you analyze the realities and the meaning of the words a little, instead of repeating them mechanically?

We honestly consider our system infinitely more democratic than that of the United States, because it is the genuine expression of the will of the vast majority of the country, made up not of the rich but of the poor.

LOCKWOOD: How do the majority express this "will"?

CASTRO: By struggling and fighting against oppression. They revealed it in the Sierra Maestra by defeating the well-equipped army of Batista. They revealed it at Playa Girón† by destroying the mercenary invaders. They revealed it in the Escambray in wiping out the counterrevolutionary bands. They reveal it constantly, in every public demonstration that the Revolution organizes with the multitudinous support of the masses. They have revealed it with their firm support of the Revolutionary Government in the face of the economic blockade, and by the fact that there are hundreds of thousands of men ready to die defending their Revolution.

LOCKWOOD: But if Cuba is not a dictatorship, in what way are your people able to effectively influence the leadership?

CASTRO: I believe that there is a mutual influence of the people over the leaders and of the leaders over the people. The first and most important thing is to have a genuine affection and respect for the people. The people can feel that and it wins them over. Sometimes the leaders have to take responsibilities on their own; sometimes they have to walk at the head of the people. The important thing is the identification of the leaders with the necessities, the aspirations and the feelings of the people. There are many ways of establishing this identification. The best way of all is to maintain the most immediate contact possible with the masses.

LOCKWOOD: Che Guevara, in his book *Socialism and Man in Cuba*, characterizes the manner of communication between the leaders of the Revolution and the people as "almost intuitive." Do you agree that there is this intuitive element in your leadership of the people?

CASTRO: At certain moments, under certain circumstances, when there is a great sense of confidence between the leaders and the

* *Castro is referring to President Lyndon B. Johnson.*

† *The Bay of Pigs.*

masses, yes. Especially in such a convulsive process as a revolution, the intuitive element can be necessary at the beginning, but not later on, when the revolution advances and is consolidated, because in such a process millions of men raise their political culture and their revolutionary conscience; thousands of capable men arise from the masses to take on the tasks of organization, of administration and of policy-making; and all this creates a developed culture, a powerful and organized force. Individual men begin to have less importance to the degree that the whole social task becomes more and more a collective undertaking, the work of millions of persons and the responsibility of tens of thousands of men.

LOCKWOOD: But do you feel that a kind of intuitive communication between yourself and the masses during these first years has kept you from making bad mistakes?

CASTRO: I don't know how a leader can arise or how a revolution can be led without a great sensitivity for understanding the problems of the people and without the ability, too, of formulating the means of confronting and resolving those problems. A revolution is not an easy process. It is hard, difficult. Great errors can cost the life of the revolution. Not only the leadership of the revolution, but its very life.

There must be not only intuition, an emotional communication of the leaders with the people, but there are other requisites. One has to find solutions, one has to put them into operation, one has to go forward, one has to choose the path correctly, the way of doing what has to be done. The leaders in a revolutionary process are not infallible receptacles of what the people think. One must find out how the people think and sometimes combat certain opinions, certain ideas, certain points of view which, in the judgment of the leaders, are mistaken. One cannot conceive of the leader as a simple carrier of ideas, a simple collector of opinions and impressions. He has to be also a creator of opinions, a creator of points of view; he has to *influence* the masses.

LOCKWOOD: Can you cite an example from your own experience when the leadership was in error about something and was so informed by the Cuban people?

CASTRO: Well, certain omissions or problems, rather than mistakes. For example, I remember visiting some regions of the Sierra Maestra where the peasants talked to me about the lack of credit. Also problems of the lack of roads, of medical services, a certain negligence on the part of the administrative leaders in certain regions. Cases like that occur often. But some particular error about which the leadership was informed by the people? Doubtless there must have been such mistakes, but offhand I don't recall any.

LOCKWOOD: Che Guevara, in the same book, says that whenever

revolutionary leaders are mistaken, the fact manifests itself in a reduction of the spirit of labor on the part of the workers, and in this way the leaders become aware that something is wrong. He gives the example of Aníbal Escalante.

CASTRO: Good. The example of Aníbal Escalante is a good example. Although, rather than an error, it could be considered as a wrong that developed in the course of the process, because at the beginning our movement was one force among many forces. It is true that ours was the most influential. A whole period of unification passed, of overcoming reservations and distrust, and in that period of union not everything was done in a harmonious way.

When you began to talk about this theme I thought you were referring to concrete mistakes of an administrative kind, but I see from the example you gave that you meant political mistakes that could affect the general course of the Revolution.

LOCKWOOD: But wasn't the problem created by Escalante potentially of great practical importance—?

CASTRO: Potentially it was important, because sectarianism was discouraging the masses and alienating them from the leadership. It was provoking discontent, encouraging opportunism, and creating a whole series of similar problems. And we had to overcome the problem without creating another kind of sectarianism, without making divisions in the ranks of the Revolution. There have been sectarianisms of different kinds which achieved greater or lesser influence, and we have actually always fought against all forms of sectarianism, no matter where they exist or what part or organization they come from. I believe they are all damaging.

But the case of Escalante is an example, indeed, of mistakes, of wrongs that appear in the course of a revolution which sometimes are not the mistakes of men but simply phenomena that appear and must be rectified. Often there are currents that get out of hand for which you cannot hold anybody in particular responsible.*

* Aníbal Escalante was Secretary of the Partido Socialista Popular (PSP), Cuba's pre-revolutionary, Stalinist-oriented Communist Party. When Castro came to power, the PSP was a minority party, somewhat discredited among the working-class for having collaborated with Batista. It remained so until the Bay of Pigs invasion in 1961, shortly after which Fidel formally espoused Communism. The PSP was then given the job of constructing the nation-wide party apparatus for the new Communist government. Escalante proceeded systematically to purge from high posts members of the 26th of July movement (Castro's revolutionary movement) and substitute them with PSP cadre. As Escalante's power grew, so did the complaints of Castro's ex-comrades-in-arms. On March 26, 1962, having remained above the battle as long as possible, Fidel finally intervened, delivering a scorching and humiliating denunciation of Escalante in a four-hour address on Cuban television. Escalante was exiled to the Soviet Union, relative moderation

Another example is excessive centralization, which is something damaging and negative. Why? Because it weakens local activities, the entire local life; it obstructs the possibility of overcoming many small faults; it impedes the initiative and action of communities for the solution of problems that are peculiar to each one of them. Once we became aware of this, we began the development of new local institutions, more decentralized forms of public administration.

But I think that on fundamental things our decisions have been correct. For example, to carry out an agrarian reform is a correct measure, but it is possible for many errors to be made later on in the practical execution of the reform. I explained to you the process through which we arrived at the idea of the people's farms, and how we could have committed a grave mistake by dividing up the land. That is one example of how, on the important questions, errors which could have had irreparable consequences later on have not been committed. Sometimes a measure may have been precipitous or premature; and sometimes it may have been late. There have also been occasions when the officials have managed things very subjectively, very capriciously, within the area where they were working. You must remember that each revolutionary leader or official very much imposes the stamp of his own ideas, his own personality, and his own points of view on the organization and the working methods of his respective department. Always one tries to choose the most able and competent men, and when it becomes obvious that somebody is not doing his job perfectly, he is replaced.

And in the end we still cannot set down precise rules about the revolutionary experience. We can talk about what we have learned up till now, but undoubtedly we still have a lot to learn and much experience to acquire before we're through.

LOCKWOOD: When does the revolutionary process end?

CASTRO: I think it has a long way to go yet. You could say that in its overall characteristics, in the essential matters, it has already

---

was restored to Cuban politics, and thus ended the so-called period of "sectarianism."

In 1968, Escalante was again in the news. Having been allowed to return to Cuba in 1964 as a private citizen, it was discovered that Escalante and a number of his friends were taking Moscow's side in the ideological polemic between Cuba and the USSR ("armed struggle" vs. "peaceful coexistence") and had been passing documents and information to Russia clandestinely. In an eight-hour, unpublished discourse to the Central Committee, Castro denounced Escalante and his "micro-fraction." A trial followed, largely secret, as a result of which Escalante and his collaborators received prison sentences.

The real significance of the case of Aníbal Escalante was the position it occupied in the dialectic between "old" and "new" Communists (and Communism) in Cuba, which has now been resolved in favor of the "new."

moved forward substantially. But many practical tasks still remain. There is a lot to be done. When will the revolutionary process end? When we arrive at Communism.

THE PARTY

LOCKWOOD: Is the party fully organized yet?

CASTRO: It is virtually organized at the base. The leadership cadres are being organized now. By the end of 1967 we will hold the first congress, with delegates elected by the members of the party throughout the entire country. Later on, we will be in a position to promulgate the constitution of the Socialist State.*

You must understand that during these years we have had first of all to defend the existence of the Revolution in a bitter struggle against a powerful enemy, the United States. We have not had all the time we would have liked to occupy ourselves with dressing the Revolution in its legal clothing. It was necessary first to survive, then to philosophize.

LOCKWOOD: When will the constitution be ready?

CASTRO: We have given ourselves a time limit:† before 1970. And certainly it will be long before that. We are also working on something else that is very important: the institution of decentralized local administrations. By the end of 1966 they will all be organized, and we will hold a kind of congress of local administrations that same year. It will be a great step forward.‡

LOCKWOOD: These local institutions will be administered by the party?

CASTRO: The party does not administer. The party, acting as a kind of parliament of workers, will select the local government officers, who will have to give an accounting of their administration to all the people every six months, in popular assemblies, with the participation of all the workers of the locality.

---

* On October 3, 1965, shortly after this conversation took place, the United Revolutionary Socialist Party of Cuba (PURSC) became the Communist Party of Cuba (PCC). More than 80% of the PCC's new 100-man central committee were former members of Castro's 26th of July or other non-Communist revolutionary organizations.

But the organization of the party on lower levels has progressed much more slowly than Castro anticipated. As of the end of 1968, the first party congress had been postponed indefinitely.

† By the end of 1968 the constitution was still being prepared, with no indication as to when it would be presented.

‡ Castro refers to Poder Local, "Local Power," also far behind schedule. The first Poder Local congress has yet to be held.

LOCKWOOD: And submit themselves to their questions?

CASTRO: To questions and proposals about all matters. And in the regions, there will be the same thing, an assembly once a year, before the delegates elected from the municipal districts.

LOCKWOOD: What is a region?

CASTRO: The level intermediate between the municipal district and the province.

We think it is going to be a great school of government. It will require the party to select competent officials, and it will require the officials to do their best work, because of the constant control that there will be over their activities. We believe that in this way we are developing entirely new democratic forms, and very effective ones.

LOCKWOOD: Would you explain what the party is and how it functions?

CASTRO: First, it is the revolutionary vanguard, the political organization of the workers who, manifesting the power of the state, mobilize the masses to the accomplishment of the tasks and functions of the Revolution. It educates them, it organizes them, it directs and controls the administration, it draws up the plans of work and controls the carrying out of those plans. It is, in short, the political power. There is no duality, neither of powers nor of functions.

When we hold the first congress we will be in a better position to map out all the tasks of the party; we will have a much better idea about what we have to do and how to do it. It will be a real congress which will discuss economic, social, and political problems, but it won't be an assembly of a formal character. We have always refused to fall into ceremonies and institutions of a formal type. For that reason we have chosen to go slowly and not to do things simply by formula in order to fill a vacuum without essential content. We could have drawn up a socialist constitution from the beginning, and it would possibly have been saturated with faults, with errors; whereas now, with the experience acquired during these years, we are in a position to work out a constitution that really is responsive to all the new realities of the Revolution.

CASTRO'S POLITICAL AUTOBIOGRAPHY

LOCKWOOD: Are you saying that you were already a Marxist-Leninist when you came to power in 1959, and that if you hadn't been busy defending the Revolution you would have drawn up a socialist constitution at that time?

CASTRO: Look, often things cannot be understood unless they are analyzed as a process. Nobody can say that he reaches certain political conclusions except through a process. Nobody reaches those convictions in a way, often not in a year. A lot of time has to pass before one reaches reliable political conclusions.

Long before I became a Marxist, my first questionings of an economic and social kind arose when I was a student at the university, studying political economy and especially capitalist economics, the problems posed by overproduction and the struggle between the workers and the machines. They aroused my attention extraordinarily and led me to turn my mind to these problems for the first time. How could there exist a conflict between man's technical possibilities and his needs for happiness, and why did it have to exist? How could there be overproduction of some goods, causing unemployment and hunger? Why did there have to be a contradiction between the interests of man and of the machine, when the machine should be man's great aid, precisely that aid which could free him from privations, misery, and want?

In this way I began to think of different forms for the organization of production and of property, although in a completely idealistic way, without any scientific basis. You might say that I had begun to transform myself into a kind of utopian socialist. At that time I had not read *The Communist Manifesto*. I had read hardly anything by Karl Marx. This was when I was a student in the second or third year of law. Later on, I read *The Communist Manifesto* of Marx and Engels, which made a deep impression on me. For the first time I saw a historical, systematic explanation of the problem, phrased in a very militant way, which captivated me completely.

Subsequently, as I went on studying labor legislation at the University of Havana, I had the opportunity to examine the political currents which have appeared since the French Revolution, the various theories that have tried to explain historical events and the development of human society. Without a doubt I found an extraordinary superiority in the Marxist point of view. It captivated me and awakened my curiosity, and in the succeeding years I read a number of works by Marx, Engels, and Lenin which gave me many theoretical insights. From the first moment, some of them seemed to me truly unquestionable: for example, the idea that society is divided into classes with antagonistic and irreconcilable interests.

That is a truth which is now widely accepted, even to a certain extent in the official channels of the capitalist countries, as when, for example, the governing circles of the United States talk about the desirability of developing a middle class in Latin America, complete and well prepared to govern. This is equivalent to accepting the Marxist viewpoint on the role which the bourgeois class plays in the capitalist state; although, of course, they refuse to believe that the dominance of those "well-prepared" bourgeois will inevitably disappear

155

by virtue of the laws which govern the development of human society.

This encounter with revolutionary ideas helped me to orient myself politically. But there is a big difference between having a theoretical knowledge and considering oneself a Marxist revolutionary. Unquestionably I had a rebellious temperament and at the same time felt a great intellectual curiosity about those problems. Those intellectual insights inclined me more and more toward political struggle. However, according to the method by which I then believed my ideas should be carried into practice, I still could not have been considered a true Marxist.

Then came the *coup d'état* of the tenth of March, when Batista took power.

At that time I already had some very definite political ideas about the need for structural changes. But before the tenth of March I had been thinking of utilizing legal means, of using the Parliament as a point of departure from which I might establish a revolutionary platform and motivate the masses in its favor—not as a means of bringing about those changes directly, however, because I didn't believe that my program could be realized in a legal, parliamentary way. I tell you in all honesty that already then I believed that I had to do it in a revolutionary way. I had acquired enough sense of reality to understand that.

Nonetheless, I was still in some ways ingenuous and deluded. In many ways I was still not a Marxist, and I did not consider myself a Communist. In spite of having read theoretically about imperialism as a phenomenon, I didn't understand it very well. I didn't thoroughly appreciate the relation that existed between the phenomenon of imperialism and the situation in Cuba. It is possible that I was then still very much influenced by the habits and the ideas of the *petit bourgeois* education I had received. When I graduated from the university I still did not have a very good political training.

Even so, one might say that I had advanced extraordinarily, since I had been a political illiterate when I entered the university. As the son of a landowner, educated in a Jesuit secondary school, I had brought nothing more than a rebellious temperament and the uprightness, the severe character which they had inculcated into me in the Jesuit school. Perhaps in that sense it helped me a lot to have chosen the career of law. Had I studied instead to become an agronomist—taking into account my present interest in nature and my vocation in agriculture—I might have remained ignorant of these problems. So, my mind had really evolved a great deal politically. In fact, my political consciousness was already much greater than that of the political party with which I had been associated during my student years.

That party, which had begun from very popular origins, had, over a period of years, been falling into the hands of landowners and opportunistic politicians. That is, in most of the country its apparatus was now in the hands of reactionary and rightist elements. In spite of this, there was always confidence among the people in what Chibás, the leader of the party, could do when he became President, and I myself was sure that the moment would come when he would have nothing to do with those people. I trusted his rebellious temperament, his personal honesty, and his feeling of obligation to the masses who supported him. While he lived, I always had some hope that a revolutionary movement could come out of that movement.

Then came the death of Chibás, and the party was left without a leader. By the very fact of his death—which happened in dramatic circumstances*—much of the population felt even more obligated to his party, even many who probably would not have voted for him when he was alive—a response typical of a profoundly emotional people like ours. So nobody doubted that the People's Party, as it was called, was going to win the elections and that those who held the key party positions—men whom I knew were incapable of producing any fundamental changes—would come to power.

For me it was unquestionable and a new disappointment that something even worse was now going to befall the country. I reasoned that when it did nobody would ever again be able to arouse a civic movement of the masses, because a general skepticism would take hold of the people.

In the meantime, in the bosom of that party, although completely outside the party machinery, I had gained some ascendancy among the masses, a certain influence that opened the path for me to candidacy and election as a deputy from the province of Havana.

I had worked out certain methods of political labor that proved to be very effective. There were many members of the People's Party who were not controlled by the machinery, especially in Havana Province. I concentrated my efforts on capturing these voters. I had succeeded in gathering almost eighty thousand addresses and, using the parliamentary mailing privilege, since I didn't have money for stamps, I sent out tens of thousands of letters every month. In this way I was able to gain enough support from the masses so that I was elected a delegate to the party assembly.

Already I was working with the fervent passion of a revolutionary. For the first time, I conceived a strategy for the revolutionary seizure of power. Once in the Parliament, I would break party discipline and present a program embracing practically all the measures that later on were contained in our Moncada program and which, since the victory

* *He committed suicide.*

157

of the Revolution, have been transformed into laws. I knew that such a program would never be approved in a Parliament the great majority of whose members were mouthpieces of the landowners and the big Cuban and foreign businesses. But I hoped, by proposing a program that recognized the most deeply felt aspirations of the majority of the population, to establish a revolutionary platform around which to mobilize the great masses of farmers, workers, unemployed, teachers, intellectual workers and other progressive sectors of the country.

I also understood the necessity of uniting a part of the armed forces to this movement of the revolutionary masses, and among the laws that I had in mind were some directed to capturing the support of the troops and of some of the newly appointed officers who had manifested certain political anxieties.

I already definitely believed in the need for seizing power by revolution, but at that time and in those circumstances, I thought this was only possible by relying upon the people and a part of the army. I was very far from believing then that such a revolution could be made a few years later with the people alone and against the entire army.

When the *coup d'état* of the tenth of March took place, everything changed radically. My idea then became, not to organize a movement, but to try to unite all the different forces against Batista. I intended to participate in that struggle simply as one more soldier. I began to organize the first action cells, hoping to work alongside those leaders of the party who might be ready to fulfill the elemental duty of fighting against Batista. In those circumstances I thought that the men with the most authority and prestige would put themselves at the front. As for myself, all I wanted was a rifle and orders to carry out any mission whatsoever. But when none of these leaders showed that they had either the ability or the resolution or the seriousness of purpose or the way to overthrow Batista, it was then that I finally worked out a strategy of my own.

We had no money. But I said to my associates that we didn't have to import weapons from the outside, that our weapons were here, well oiled and cared for, in the stockades of Batista. It was in order to get hold of some of those weapons that we attacked the Moncada Barracks.

To sum up: before the tenth of March I had already arrived at the conviction that it was necessary to organize a revolutionary movement, and to this end I was prepared to dedicate all of my position and my resources as a deputy. At that time, yes, I was thinking of organizing it and directing it myself.

But then when the *coup d'état* of the tenth of March occurred, creating new circumstances which demanded immediate action by men who were nationally known, my position was not that of acting on my own initiative, but rather that the struggle would carry itself out and the Revolution would make itself. I wore myself out talking with many people, insisting with many people, exhorting many people; in short, I spent a great deal of time looking for a chief.

My political ideas of that time were expressed in the speech to the court during the trial over the Moncada affair, "History Will Absolve Me." Even then I analyzed the class composition of our society, the need to mobilize the workers, the farmers, the unemployed, the teachers, the intellectual workers and the small proprietors against the regime. Even then I proposed a program of planned development for our economy, utilizing all the resources of the country to promote its economic development. My Moncada speech was the seed of all the things that were done later on. It could be called Marxist if you wish, but probably a true Marxist would have said that it was not.

Unquestionably, though, it was an advanced revolutionary program. And that program was openly proclaimed. Nobody can allege it was a fraud. Naturally it was a program with a wide basis, embracing the interests of wide sectors of the population, especially those sectors which fundamentally supported the Revolution.

In Cuba, people had been talking so long about revolution and revolutionary programs that the ruling classes paid no attention. They believed that ours was simply one more program, that all revolutionaries change and become conservatives with the passage of time. As a matter of fact, the opposite has happened to me. With the passing of time my thought has become more and more radical.

I have said that when we came to power I was somewhat idealistic and utopian, in the sense that I believed that everything we would do inside our country would have to be respected, both because it was just and because we had the full right to do it. I thought that nobody would dispute that right. But no sooner had we begun to carry out our revolutionary program, for which we had been fighting for years, than the phenomenon of American imperialism and its close connections to the problems of our country began to reveal themselves to us with full clarity. The contempt they felt toward the nation's affairs was manifested in a thousand ways. I well remember that when the U.S. ambassador arrived in Cuba, shortly after the victory of the Revolution, he came with the demeanor of a proconsul. I remember his words, his imposing attitude, and how our reactionary press received him almost as if the Savior had come.

The conflicts between all that the Revolution stands for and everything the United States stands for became clear immediately when they gave asylum to the worst criminals, individuals who had murdered hundreds of Cuban people. It was revealed by the campaigns they unleashed against the Revolution, and by their attempts to coerce us by every means.

That process completed my political education. With the passion that I felt for the Revolution, for the need to correct injustice, to eradicate exploitation, to wipe out privileges, with that same passion I collided with those who were opposed to all that, with imperialism and all that it represented.

And when I looked a little further, I saw what imperialism stands for in the rest of the world, that we were entangled in the same problem that peoples of other continents are entangled in. That is, I came to recognize the universal dimension that the problem has. And we all had occasion to learn of the solidarity of the Soviet Union and the Socialist camp, who were the only true allies of the effort to make a revolution within our country.

I have had a very interesting and very effective schooling. That is simply, more or less in general lines, the process which, from my first questionings until the present moment, made me into a Marxist revolutionary, which is what I consider myself today.

COMMUNISM

LOCKWOOD: If you had announced that you were a Marxist and openly espoused a socialist program while you were still a guerrilla leader in the Sierra Maestra, do you think you still would have been able to come to power?

CASTRO: That is not an easy question to answer. Possibly not. It would not have been intelligent to bring about such an open confrontation. I think that all radical revolutionaries, in certain moments or circumstances, do not announce programs that might unite all of their enemies on a single front. Throughout history, realistic revolutionaries have always proposed only those things that are attainable.

While we were in the Sierra Maestra, certain newspapermen came there—some of them seemed more like spies—to question us about some points of the Moncada program.* Their mission was obviously an inquisitorial one, and they reminded us a little of the Pharisee who asked Christ whether one should pay tribute to Caesar. Under such circumstances we replied more or less in the same way: "Render unto Caesar the things that are Caesar's and unto God the things that are God's."

In the Moncada program we had declared that we were going to nationalize some North American businesses, such as the electric company and the telephone company, and naturally we were in the middle of a struggle where it was not at all practical to say exactly

---

* The name given to Castro's original revolutionary program, set forth in his defense speech at the trial for his attack on the Moncada Barracks, Santiago de Cuba, July 26, 1953, and later rewritten by Castro during his imprisonment on the Isle of Pines.

what we intended to do with those businesses. So what we did was to treat them with all the cunning that was necessary under the circumstances.

You also remember, surely, the story of Lincoln, how it was only at the end of the Civil War that Lincoln proclaimed the freeing of the slaves. Possibly Lincoln wanted that from the beginning, possibly he wanted it even when he was just a candidate, and undoubtedly so did many others. But for a long time they didn't speak of it because they didn't think it was possible to do. Without doubt the proclamation of liberty for the slaves was a consequence of the Civil War.* In our case, to have stated a radical program at that moment would have resulted in aligning against the Revolution all the most reactionary forces, which were then divided. It would have caused the formation of a solid front among the North American imperialists, Batista, and the ruling classes. In the end, they would have called upon the troops of the United States to occupy the country. For Cuba, a small country, an island very close to the United States, with no possibility of receiving any outside help, this would have constituted a complex of forces difficult to overcome with the forces and means which we then had.

Furthermore, the degree of development of the people's revolutionary consciousness was much lower then than it was to be when we came to power.

In those days, there existed many prejudices against Communism. Most people did not know what Communism really was. I myself, when I was a secondary school student, had more or less the same prejudices as did any young man who had been educated in a parochial school, although I had little time to concern myself with politics, because at that age I was mostly interested in sports. I remember that I had the ideas which I heard in my own house, from parents, from my family, and which I heard from my teachers and professors.

Many people had no other idea of Communism except what the enemies of Communism told them about it. They endured misery, but they did not know the real causes of that misery; they didn't have, nor could they have had, a scientific explanation of these problems; they could not understand that they were problems of social structure. You must remember that more than a million persons in our country, adults, didn't know how to read or write. You could not have expected the great mass of the people to have had a level of culture high enough to comprehend those problems. Sometimes even when there is a high enough level of culture social problems are not understood.

* Castro is in error. The Emancipation Proclamation was issued September 22, 1862 (and had been presented by Lincoln to the cabinet early in the summer of 1862). The Civil War did not end until April 18, 1865, a few days after Lincoln's death.

Naturally, in these circumstances, to have said that our program was Marxist-Leninist or Communist would have awakened many prejudices. Besides that, many people would not have understood what it really meant.

At the same time that we were learning, the people were also learning. Through the same process that we, the leaders, became more revolutionary, the people became more revolutionary also. We have great confidence in the Cuban people, in their potential revolutionary capacity.

Nobody is born a revolutionary. A revolutionary is formed through a process. It is possible that there was some moment when I appeared less radical than I really was. It is possible too that I was more radical than even I myself knew. Ultimately, a revolutionary struggle is like a military war. You have to set for yourself only those goals that are attainable at a given moment. The fight depends on the correlation of forces, on a series of circumstances, and every revolutionary must propose for himself all the objectives that are possible within the correlation of forces and within the circumstances in which he acts.

If you ask me whether I considered myself a revolutionary at the time I was in the mountains, I would answer yes, I considered myself a revolutionary. If you asked me, did I consider myself a Marxist-Leninist, I would say no, I did not consider myself a Marxist-Leninist. If you asked me whether I considered myself a Communist, a classic Communist, I would say no, I did not consider myself a classic Communist. Today, yes, I believe I have that right. I have come full circle. Today I clearly see that, in the modern world, nobody can call himself a true revolutionary who is not a Marxist-Leninist. Just as in the time of the French Revolution to be a revolutionary you had to be a disciple of the ideas of Jean-Jacques Rousseau or of Voltaire, in the same way, today, if you do not subscribe to the theories of Marx and Lenin, you cannot consider yourself objectively a revolutionary. I have acquired a full understanding of that fact.

LOCKWOOD: Was Che Guevara in any way a political mentor of yours; did he help you to come to your present convictions about Marxism-Leninism?

CASTRO: I have told you the whole story of how I became a Marxist-Leninist. I didn't know Che Guevara when I attacked the Moncada, when I wrote "History Will Absolve Me," nor when I read *The Communist Manifesto* and the works of Lenin in the university. I believe that at the time I met Che Guevara he had a greater revolutionary development, ideologically speaking, then I had. From the theoretical point of view he was more formed, he was a more advanced revolutionary than I was. But in those days these were not the questions we talked about. What we discussed was the fight against Batista, the plan for landing in Cuba and for beginning guerrilla warfare. And in that situation it was Che Guevara's combative temperament as a man of action that impelled him to join me in my fight. Undoubtedly he was in sympathy with what we were doing, with our purposes and intentions. And no doubt he saw that I had a revolutionary position. But it really was action that occupied most of our time, not theoretical problems. There is no doubt, however, that he has had influence in both the revolutionary fight and the revolutionary process.

LOCKWOOD: Especially after 1959?

CASTRO: Both before 1959, during the armed fight, and after 1959, in the development of the revolutionary process.

You must remember, of course, that when I was in the mountains I was not a member of any Marxist party. We made an organization, and we started from certain positions. These positions were undoubtedly influenced, at least my ideas were very much influenced, as I have explained, by Marxist-Leninist theory. But I was not a Communist in the classical sense of the word, nor did I have obligations to any party—and in no way was I a disguised or infiltrated agent, or anything like that.

Neither was Che, whom I met in Mexico about a year and a half before the *Granma* landing, a member of any Communist party.

LOCKWOOD: Nor your brother Raúl, either?

CASTRO: Raúl, yes. Raúl, completely on his own, while he was a student at the university, had joined the Communist Youth. But it should be said that when he went to the Moncada attack he was not behaving in a completely disciplined way, properly speaking.

LOCKWOOD: You mean he broke party discipline?

CASTRO: Exactly.

LOCKWOOD: Was there anybody else in your original group that attacked the Moncada Barracks in 1953 who was also a Communist at that time?

CASTRO: Of those who took part in the Moncada attack, anybody else like that? Almost all of us young men who took part in the leadership of it—Abel Santamaria, Montané, Ñico López—were people of the left. We read books by Marx, by Engels, by Lenin when we had the time. During my trial they asked me whether it was true that we had books by Lenin, and I said yes, that we had read Lenin, and that I believed anybody who had not read him was an ignoramus. But members of the Communist Party? No. At that time Raúl was probably the only one among all of us, and he wasn't counted as one of the leaders of our movement. He went to Moncada as just another soldier.

LOCKWOOD: But when you did eventually announce that you had become a Communist, it took most Cubans by surprise. Isn't it true that many politically aware people who supported you while you were in the mountains, especially those from the middle and upper classes, did so on the basis of the program you had announced, and that they wouldn't have had anything to do with you had they foreseen that after only a few years in power you would announce that *fidelismo* was realy Communism?

CASTRO: I believe that all those middle-class and upper-middle-class people whom you call "politically aware" were already opposed to the Revolution before that date.

One of the first laws that the Revolution passed was the lowering of rents, and that law affected a good number of great property owners who lived off the rents they received from their houses. Of course, the Revolution compensated them, but the law affected them. Many of those people began to feel dissatisfaction with the Revolution.

That same year the Agrarian Reform Law was passed. Also many other laws were passed relating to mortgage loans, debts, etc.—a whole series of social laws which very much affected the interests of the middle class. Those laws were passed in 1959, but they had been announced in the Moncada program.

The fundamental laws of the Revolution had already been applied before my declaration [concerning Marxism]. All the structural changes, all the economic laws. So—they became disaffected because the Revolution made laws affecting their interests as an exploiting class, not because the Revolution made a political proclamation.

LOCKWOOD: But in your speech at the Moncada trial, you promised free elections, a free press, respect for private enterprise, the restoration of the 1940 Constitution and many other democratic reforms when you came to power.

CASTRO: Yes, that is true, and that was our program at that moment. Every revolutionary movement in every historical epoch proposes the greatest number of achievements possible. If you read the history of the French Revolution, you will find that the first aspirations of the revolutionaries were very limited. They even thought they would maintain the monarchy, but in the course of the revolutionary process they did away with it.

If you study the history of the Russian Revolution, you will find that the first programs of the Bolshevik party were not strictly socialist programs. At a certain stage, they even carried out certain conquests that were not socialist, because they didn't believe that the struggle for a more extensive program of socialism was in the order of the day. At the time of the Moncada attack our revolutionary goals were much more limited, and we would have been deluded if we had attempted at that moment to do more than we did.

No program implies the renunciation of new revolutionary stages, of new objectives. A program can set forth the immediate objectives of a revolution, but not all the objectives, not the ultimate objectives of a revolution.

Even now we have still not carried out an absolutely socialist program in Cuba. Many forms of property, many modes of production that are not strictly socialist still exist, and they will persist for a more or less extended time. That doesn't imply the renunciation of continuing to advance on the path to socialism.

At that moment, that program answered to the correlation of our forces. During the subsequent years of prison, of exile, of war in the mountains, the correlation of forces changed so extraordinarily in favor of our movement that we could set goals that were much more ambitious.

LOCKWOOD: Yes, but to return to my original question—wouldn't you admit that many of those who followed you because they believed in your Moncada program later had the right to feel they had been deceived?

CASTRO: I told no lies in the Moncada speech. That was how we thought at the moment, those were the goals we set ourselves, and all the changes that we proposed then we have since carried out. We have even gone beyond that program and are carrying out a much more profound revolution.

BATISTA AND THE MIDDLE CLASS

LOCKWOOD: How much do you think your victory in 1959 owed to Batista's ineptitude? Did he contribute to his own downfall?

CASTRO: I believe that it was both a military and political victory.

Batista was subject to a lot of antipathy and hatred. He was a representative of the military caste, of the corrupt politicians, of the big businessmen, of the huge landowners, and of the foreign companies. What could Batista do to win over the masses? The only thing he could do was defend those interests by fire and sword. He had no other choice than to use terror. As the struggle sharpened, he found himself obliged to resort more and more to committing barbarities. And while he was becoming more hated, we were developing more and more support among the population where we were fighting, and every day our victories were greater. Batista was militarily defeated, but he was also politically defeated.

LOCKWOOD: Could he have stayed in power longer if he had been able to maintain the support of the middle class, if he hadn't provoked them to disenchantment by antidemocratic methods and terroristic acts?

CASTRO: A resolute support from the middle class would have been able to prolong the battle, I would say, a few more months. It cannot be stated categorically that the middle class did not support Batista in a certain sense. The political parties of the middle classes were against the insurrection* and tried hard to evolve an electoral alternative to the formula of armed struggle. All those parties opposed our armed struggle for a long time. When the moment came when our propositions were triumphing and realities were proving us right, they fell into complete discredit, and the wealthy classes began to realize that Batista was incompetent. If Batista had shown the military capacity to put down the Revolution those people would have applauded him.

The middle class didn't fight against us, but it didn't participate actively in the Revolution either. It was never a decisive factor. Immediately after the victory, a certain interesting legend was created about the role of the middle class in the revolutionary struggle. Actually, only at the end, when Batista was already beaten, did this class participate in some acts of passive resistance. That very term defines it completely—passive resistance. While we had spent years in an active struggle against Batista.

This is very easy to prove. If you analyze the backgrounds of all the men who took part in the Moncada attack, you will see that they were far from being a representation of the middle class. Ninety percent of them were workers and farmers. If you analyze the men who landed in the Sierra Maestra, or especially the men who made up the rebel army, you will find that almost one hundred percent were workers and farmers.† If you analyze the economic assistance that we were able to collect from the middle class, you will find that it was practically nothing. Most of it came from collections we made in the working-class districts later on, when we established a system of taxation in the territories over which we had gained control. If only people would stop believing that a war can be won by passive resistance!

What part did the middle class play in the overthrow of Batista? Only a few of us came from the middle class, but we were not defending the interests of that class and we did not wage the war with the help of men of that class but with workers and farmers. These are absolutely historical truths that can be proven.

LOCKWOOD: If there had been active opposition from the Cuban middle class, could it have been decisive?

* Significantly, Cuba's Communist Party also opposed the insurrection on ideological grounds, adamantly withholding support from Castro's united front until October, 1958, less than three months before Batista capitulated.

† An exaggeration. Although Castro's original groups included a few proletarians, most of the 125 who attacked the Moncada and of the 82 who sailed on the Granma were young white-collar workers, professionals, students and middle-class intellectuals, including, of course, Fidel and Raúl Castro. However, many peasants and workers later joined Castro in the Sierra Maestra, making up a large part of the Rebel Army.

CASTRO: I don't think so. It would have been a longer struggle, more violent, keener from the beginning. But imagine the middle class actively supporting Batista in the fight against us! The Revolution would have broken out from the first moment as a violent class struggle, and we would have defeated them.

Of course, the middle class in Cuba was a social class with little political training and was extraordinarily passive. But even judging them as generously as possible, we, together with the poor peasants and the workers, would have overthrown Batista even if he had had their solid support. It must be remembered that Batista had the support of an important part of the middle class, that is, what could be called the upper middle class: bankers, businessmen, industrialists.

Don't forget that the day after the attack on the Palace* by the university students, after Batista was able to take command of the situation, the representatives of all the economic sectors went to the Palace to congratulate him. This was recorded in the newspapers of that day. The representatives of those classes, of those economic sectors to which you refer, offered him fervent support. The same thing would have happened had Batista succeeded in crushing the guerrilla bands in the mountains.

LOCKWOOD: Didn't you also receive help from this "upper middle class"?

CASTRO: Yes. When we had taken the territory where they had their sugar mills and their plantations, and we established a system of taxes supported by our military force, then we received large and immediate help. Even the American companies paid their taxes.

People in the United States occupy themselves with writing elaborate literary works about how the Revolution could have been prevented. This means that most of them think simply as counter-revolutionaries; they feel a genuine terror of revolutions and prefer intermediate formulas. We cannot agree with that point of view, which is conservative and reactionary. At the present time, the major concern of the United States seems to be to find a way by which revolutions outside of the United States can be avoided.

LOCKWOOD: Do you think that is because we Americans have nothing in our own background or experience to help us understand what a revolution is or what causes it?

CASTRO: Well, I understand that in some North American universities there are certain inquietudes of a political kind.

LOCKWOOD: Isn't it true that most young people go through a period of leftist orientation when they get to college? That is, that they discover radical ideas which lead them to a certain amount of political

* On March 13, 1957, a group of students who called themselves the Student Directorate made a bold attack on the Presidential Palace in Havana and nearly succeeded in assassinating Bastista. Only a few escaped.

167

reorientation, especially those who come from middle-class backgrounds.

CASTRO: In a certain sense that happened to me. But they will not come to Socialism by that route. However, it is a good thing that a new intellectuality is being developed in the United States, if not capable of doing revolutionary things, capable in some way of influencing the development of realistic points of view.

LOCKWOOD: There is a relatively large group of young people, principally students, who have been working in the field of civil rights, organizing marches, working with the Negroes in voter registration drives, etc. Some have even been killed. Wouldn't you call these revolutionaries, even if they are not Marxists?

CASTRO: Yes. Within the atmosphere that now prevails in the United States, to disagree with something that everyone else accepts is coming to deserve the name "revolutionary." The way U.S. policy is tending, it is becoming almost revolutionary just to be a liberal there.

LOCKWOOD: Getting back to our original discussion, what was the size of your army in 1959, at the end of the Revolutionary War?

CASTRO: It was small. At the end of the war, some three thousand men. We fought our decisive battles with three *hundred* men. In the last offensive, between May and August, 1958, Batista attacked us in the mountains with about ten thousand men. This isn't perhaps very well known. We had three hundred armed men. It is true that we had many more ready to join us, but they had no weapons. The battle lasted some seventy days. For about thirty-five days they attacked, and for thirty-five days we held the initiative, counterattacking. The outcome was that we destroyed the best battalions, and we captured five hundred men and some weapons: mortars, bazookas, and one or two tanks. That allowed us, now with eight hundred armed men, to spread out throughout the whole country, which caused a great demoralization in the enemy ranks.

After that came our final offensive. At the end of the war, we had fifteen thousand soldiers of Batista surrounded in Oriente Province alone. We had some twenty-five hundred men there, plus five hundred in Las Villas, a total of about three thousand men. Batista had armed forces of fifty thousand men. A large part of those troops were in the cities, guarding barracks, bridges, commercial installations, and strategic points. But his attack forces were completely destroyed.

LOCKWOOD: Do you think Batista could have beaten you if he had been a smarter military man, given his vast superiority of troops and armaments?

CASTRO: Unquestionably, if Batista had been a braver man, a man of different characteristics, he would have been able to instill more spirit in his soldiers. Instead, he tried to ignore the war, following the tactic of minimizing the importance of our force, believing that any gesture of his, such as visiting the front of operations, would have meant giving more political importance to our movement. By leading his troops better he could have prolonged the war, but he would not have won it. He would have lost just the same, and not long after. They had their best and only opportunity right at the beginning, when we were very few and inexperienced. Those were our most difficult moments.

By the time we had gained a knowledge of the terrain and had increased our force to a little more than a hundred armed men, there was already no way of destroying us with a professional army. The only way he could have contained us then would have been by fighting us with an army of peasants from the mountains where we were operating. For that it would have been necessary to obtain the genuine support of the exploited peasant class. But how could he have gained that support? Only a revolutionary movement can organize that force. Professional military men despise civilians, particularly the peasants. Furthermore, an army which served the landowners would never have been able to get the exploited farmers on their side. That is our thesis: that no revolutionary movement, no guerrilla movement that is supported by the peasant population, can be defeated. Unless, naturally, the revolutionary military leaders commit very grave errors.

CASTRO'S IMPORTANCE AS LEADER

LOCKWOOD: In all of this discussion of how your Revolution succeeded we have left out what is probably the most important single element—the effect that you as an individual have had on the whole process. What do you think might have happened to the Revolution if you had been killed while you were still in the mountains?

CASTRO: In the early moments it could have led to the defeat of the guerrilla movement. But as soon as our guerrilla force grew, and the second front in Oriente Province, directed by Raúl, was established, if they had killed me then in the Sierra Maestra, Raúl would have been able to carry on the war. He was perfectly prepared to lead it. He was a very good organizer and a very capable leader of soldiers.

I don't know, of course, whether he would have been able to overcome all the political problems. Not that he isn't capable in that field. But Raúl is five years younger than I am. At that time he was twenty-six years old. He had five years less experience, and he would have had to confront serious political problems. But my opinion is that he would have been able to handle them.

Why do I believe this? Because often men show what they are really capable of only when circumstances place a task before them. For example, when he faced the military task of directing a front which he himself opened with only fifty men, he had to make on-the-spot decisions and resolve great problems. He did this masterfully.

It is unquestionable that my main contribution was the conception of the way, of the strategy, of the adequate method for making a revolution. But once this was accepted by a group of men who had the same faith that I did, who were just as convinced as I was, the victory would have come even without me.

LOCKWOOD: Very few people would agree with you, I think. A revolution requires a leader of extraordinary abilities; not only military and political abilities, but someone who has within his personality a spark which excites men, which gives flesh to the idea and keeps the idea real from day to day. No one knew anything about Raúl Castro in 1959. Certainly he had no great mass support. He was known as your brother and as a brave soldier, but not particularly as a revolutionary leader.

CASTRO: Yes, but look: when I speak to you of Raúl, I forget completely that he is my brother. But this matter has to be talked about in complete fairness.

Many people know Raúl and know what he is like, and they don't need to be convinced of the truth of what I am saying. I have the privilege of knowing him better than anybody else. Though unquestionably my presence pretty much overshadows him, I can tell you that Raúl, from the political point of view, possesses magnificent aptitudes. But, what happens? He does not make decisions, because he knows it is not his right to do so. He is extraordinarily respectful. He always consults with me about all the important questions. I know him very well, and I am not conducting a campaign in his favor. When he came to the Revolution, he did it as one soldier more. I myself wasn't even capable then of understanding all his worth, as I have had the opportunity to do during the whole process since then.

Of course, under the present circumstances the constant presence of one outstanding leader tends a little to obscure the rest. That is a natural phenomenon, here or anywhere else. You see it, for example, in your own country. Sometimes a misfortune occurs, an accident; the President dies and suddenly another President comes to the fore. Kennedy was unquestionably a man of strong personality, and yet I have read many commentaries published in the United States in which the newspapers speak about certain abilities of Johnson which they didn't recognize in Kennedy; for example, his ability to manage the Congress and his ability to deal with certain diplomatic problems. None of those talents was recognized by the press before he became President. Individual men have their influence, that is undeniable. That influence is greater or lesser depending upon the circumstances. It could be said that a group of fortuitous circumstances determines the greater or lesser influence of individuals in revolutionary processes, often factors quite external to the virtues or the qualities of a particular man.

LOCKWOOD: You don't think that there are certain men who, appearing on the scene, are able, by their special vision or by the force of their personality, to influence events significantly?

CASTRO: Certainly that has always occurred. It still happens today but it will happen less and less often as the problems of government and administration become the tasks not of groups but of millions of men. Eventually millions of men will take responsibility for public problems of all kinds. In my personal experience, I see how much easier everything is done in Cuba today on account of the numbers of men who have acquired experience, who have broadened their intelligence in coping with problems. And it will increase more and more.

When a country is in a situation of great difficulty, oppressed, with a low level of culture and political education and lacking collective experience, the importance of the men who lead it is much greater. Certain factors determine that those leaders arise. Take the case of France. If there hadn't been the Second World War, if France had not been invaded by the Germans, probably De Gaulle would never have played the role he has played in the life of France. It was these factors, resulting from a series of circumstances, which made it possible for such a man to stand out. Nobody doubts that under normal circumstances this would not occur, even if you had men with the same character and talents as De Gaulle. Of course, there have been few men with the same character and talent as De Gaulle.

LOCKWOOD: Very few, and perhaps even fewer Fidel Castros.

CASTRO: I believe, yes, that there are not many such as me. Of all the boys who were born in the same year that I was, how many had the opportunity to go to school? In the place where I was born there were hundreds of children, children of the farmers and the workers, and the only one who had the social and economic opportunity to go beyond the sixth grade was me. The same thing must have happened with hundreds of thousands of children in all of Cuba. How many minds for all the branches of human activity must have been lost!

Certain circumstances favored me. First, economic circumstances allowed me to study. Second, the fact that I was born in the country, in a place close to the mountains, must have contributed to my trust in the land, to my belief in the possibilities of fighting in the mountains, even against a modern army. In addition, there were certain things peculiar to the geographical and social environment in which I grew up. Probably people born in the city would not have developed the same ideas.

It is not that I am trying, out of modesty, to diminish the role it has been my fortune to play. But I sincerely believe that the merits of the individual are always few, because there are always external factors which play a much more important role than his own character in determining what he does.

I have told you what I think about the problem of the counterrevolutionary prisoners. I think that the predicament of many of these men was predetermined by circumstances, and that such men, such offenses, will no longer exist here within twenty years. New circumstances will determine the future conduct of men. That is, I'm not trying to deny the guilt of those individuals or one's responsibility for one's own acts, but I do say that this responsibility is circumscribed by a relatively narrow circle of circumstances.

Therefore, I look upon the punishment established by revolutionary penal laws not as an end in itself, but merely as a means for the defense of the Revolution in a situation that offers no alternative.

LOCKWOOD: Apart from all that, you don't consider yourself a very unusual man?

CASTRO: (*long pause*): That is something that pertains to one's own conscience, to the opinion one has of oneself. I suppose that most men always have a good opinion of themselves. It would be hypocrisy for me to tell you that I don't have a high opinion of myself. But I say with all sincerity that I am also very self-critical.

LOCKWOOD: The Cubans consider you an exceptional man. The masses talk of you and cheer you almost like a savior—

CASTRO: Since you have got me onto this theme, I am going to tell you something, an opinion.

The masses bestow upon men a certain quality, perhaps out of necessity, perhaps because it cannot happen in any other way. There is a kind of mechanism in the human mind that tends to create symbols in which it concentrates its sentiments. By transforming men into symbols, they manifest a greater gratitude, they attribute to the individual what is not deserved by him alone but by the many. Often I think of the hundreds, even thousands of men who are working anonymously, making possible all those things for which the people are grateful. Recognition is not divided in an equitable way. It would be an error for any man—I say this sincerely—not to be conscious of this and to believe himself truly deserving of all that recognition and affection. One must have a proper appreciation of the things he has accomplished, but he should never consider himself deserving of the recognition that belongs to the many. I believe that that would be harmful to any leader.

LOCKWOOD: Do you think, then, that it was inevitable that some people who supported you earlier would become disenchanted with the Revolution after 1959, because their support was given for emotional reasons, and they didn't analyze your program?

CASTRO: I don't quite understand the question.

LOCKWOOD: Do you think that they idolized you as a savior who had beaten Batista and didn't ask themselves what it was you really stood for? What many of them really wanted and assumed you were going to give them was what you would call a petit-bourgeois democracy. Would you say that such people were blinded by emotionality as to what you really stood for?

CASTRO: Let me explain. Even in our own organization in those days there were many people who had prejudices, above all in the city. Even some of the leading officers of our movement, and very honorable people too, not at all opportunists. Nevertheless, one of the things that has given me the most satisfaction is to see how many of them have come to understand their limitations, their prejudices, their mistaken points of view, and how they have now been integrated into the Revolution in a devoted and sincere way.

One factor that at times created more problems than Marxism itself was sectarianism. This caused a lot of annoyance in some revolutionary people who thought they were being ignored or mistreated. Yet when the problem of sectarianism was overcome, many of these people were incorporated without prejudice and without reservation. Those were two evils that mutually produced one another: prejudice and sectarianism. That is, prejudice in favor of Marxism produced sectarianism, and sectarianism produced prejudices against Marxism.

THE EXILES

As for the people who left the country, there were different reasons. There were some people with a very clear class position who were in the forefront against any change of structure and felt themselves tricked when changes came about. Even though we had proclaimed them in our program, they didn't believe we would implement them, either because they had gotten used to changes never occurring or because they thought such changes would not be possible in Cuba because they would affect the American interests, and that any government that tried this was destined to be rapidly swept away.

Some also left out of fear of war or from insecurity. Others left out of opportunism, because they believed that if a great many of their class left, the Revolution wouldn't last very long.

There were even some people who left because, after a whole series of revolutionary laws had been passed, counterrevolutionaries spread a rumor that a law was going to be passed that would take away the rights of parents to bring up their children. This absurd campaign succeeded in convincing many people, especially those who already had a lot of doubts. They sent their children out of the country and later on left themselves. They had no other alternative; once their children were in the United States, they were not permitted to bring them back.

And there were also people who left out of prejudice, who had no need at all to leave, who could have lived much more happily in Cuba than abroad.

Many cases had nothing to do with politics. There have always been people who wanted to leave Cuba and live in a country like the United States which has a much higher standard of living. What happened is that before the Revolution many requirements were imposed on people in order to enter the United States, but after the Revolution everybody had a wonderful reason for being allowed into the United States—all they had to do was say they were against Communism.

Many people here worked for North American businesses like banks, refineries, the electric company, the telephone company—a certain working-class aristocracy with better salaries than the rest of the workers—some of whom were attracted by the North American way of life and wanted to live like a middle-class family in the United States. Naturally, that wasn't the case with those who did the hardest and poorest paid work for whatever North American or Cuban enterprise, like the cutting of sugar cane. It would be interesting to know how many sugar-cane workers have gone to the United States. You would find it very difficult to find any. Also among those who have emigrated must be counted the declassed people, *lumpen* elements who lived from gambling, prostitution, traffic in drugs, and other illicit activities. They have gone with their vices to Miami and other cities in the United States because they couldn't adapt themselves to a revolution that has eradicated those social ills.

PERSONAL POWER

LOCKWOOD: Going back to the mainstream of our discussion: would you say that when you took over the government you had what amounted to absolute power?

CASTRO: Look, in the first place, when the Revolution came to power, I was still full of certain illusions.

For example, as always in Cuba, there was distrust of the revolutionary leaders because personal ambition was always attributed to them, and that fact exercised on me a certain inhibiting influence. It was my wish that the things we wanted to do should be done without my occupying any fundamental office in the government or in the leadership of the country. Even when we were fighting in the Revolutionary War and making plans for a government that would replace Batista, I didn't plan to occupy the office of Prime Minister or President or any similar position.

However, there were many aspirants to the Presidency who were in exile. We repudiated them, because there were excellent people struggling and making sacrifices within the country who were not motivated by any kind of ambition or personal vanity. Then we, who didn't yet have enough force to raise a man from our own ranks, put forward a candidate for President who didn't belong to any party or organization and who didn't figure among the undisguised aspirants to the office.* It was our proposal to offer the greatest support to that President so that he might fulfill his offices perfectly.

What was my hope? That this man would be able to carry things out while I remained completely separate from power. That was really an illusion. In the course of events it turned out that neither was the man capable of doing the job nor was it possible for me to keep apart. Not because I didn't want to or wasn't inclined to, but because factors conspired to place me in a position where all problems came to rest upon me, inevitably, no matter how much I tried to evade responsibility. That situation came to a head at a time when the Revolution had been in power for several weeks and not a single measure had been taken, not a single thing had been done! This was beginning to create a certain very detrimental discontent. It was exactly then that it was proposed—not on my initiative—that I assume the office of Prime Minister. For my part, I made it a condition that I must have real authority to carry out the revolutionary program. Believing that things could have been done any differently was one of my illusions of those early days.

LOCKWOOD: In retrospect, then, you feel that you had to have the formal power in order to move your program forward? Because it seemed in those days that you had the nearly complete support of the people. After all, you were the leader of the Revolution, while Urrutia was someone about whom very few people knew anything—besides the fact that he had been the judge at your trial who spoke in your favor.

CASTRO: I am certain that things would have been very different if, instead of Urrutia, we had had the good luck to choose a man like Dorticós,† a truly competent and truly revolutionary man.

Even then, of course, I would always have had to play some role in

---

* Dr. Manuel Urrutia, now a bitter anti-Castro exile who resides in the United States.

† Osvaldo Dorticós, who has been Cuba's president since July, 1959.

the Revolution. I would have been able to help in many ways, whenever it was necessary, without having to hold any official office.

LOCKWOOD: Yet today you hold even more official titles than you did then: Prime Minister, Commander in Chief of the Armed Forces, Secretary of the Party, and head of the National Agrarian Reform Institute [INRA]. Why is that?

CASTRO: The office of commander in chief is held by all constitutional heads of state, and most of the administrative tasks related to the armed forces here are carried out by the Minister of the Armed Forces.* My office as chief of the Agrarian Reform Institute is related to the emphasis that the Revolution wishes to place on agriculture. My work there is fundamentally political, a kind of policy direction, not really the administrative work, which is carried out by a very competent associate, Curbelo, the vice-minister of INRA. And my office as Prime Minister is not strictly administrative, but a political office. The general administrative responsibility belongs to the President of the Republic.

LOCKWOOD: Certainly your activities as the head of INRA go far beyond the political—

CASTRO: Well, I have participated directly in working out many of the agricultural plans. But the Institute of Agrarian Reform is responsible for administering all the governmental agricultural centers in the country and many other questions related to agriculture, which it carries out through a well-organized apparatus and an efficient group of men.

LOCKWOOD: Even before you took over INRA, when Carlos Rafael Rodríguez was the head of it—

CASTRO: I also concerned myself with it, but not as much as now. And let me tell you that the principal reason why I again took over that office, which I had held at the beginning of the Revolution, was in order to mobilize the entire party to carry out in all the regions of Cuba the national agricultural policies which I set down.

I would also say that I don't think we were employing Carlos Rafael in the best way. Although he has unquestionable executive ability, his training and skill are superior in the field of economic planning, in which field he is now working and doing a very efficient job.

LOCKWOOD: But why should *you* have been his replacement? You already have more than enough to occupy your time.

CASTRO: Because before there was a little bit of overlap of functions when I participated in agricultural affairs Now, from the office of president of INRA, I can exercise complete supervision of the work that I was already doing in agriculture without any overlap of func-

* *Major Raúl Castro.*

tions or contradiction of my instructions by whoever else might occupy that office.

LOCKWOOD: A contradiction between your ideas and his?

CASTRO: It is not a question of ideas; it is a practical question. For example, here on the Isle of Pines, working on this agricultural plan, I am able to give all the necessary instructions to introduce the modifications I believe necessary, and to adopt all the measures here, as in any other part of the country, that I consider indispensable to carry forward the agrarian plans that today are the core of our national effort. These are functions that otherwise would belong to a minister whose sense of authority might be wounded. This is something plain.

LOCKWOOD: Isn't it likely then that a man who is placed in charge of a ministry or in some high position might feel inhibited about carrying out his own policies for fear that they won't coincide with yours, and that he might be removed, like Carlos Rafael?

CASTRO: No. And in addition, many problems are resolved without any participation from me, in consultation between the respective minister and the President of the Republic, who is also the Minister of Economy. There is a very thorough division of labor among the leaders.

In some tasks of the Revolution, such as those relating to agriculture and education, I have developed a special personal interest. But there are many other important fields, and numerous revolutionary cadres are concerned with them and act with a great degree of autonomy.

LOCKWOOD: Fidel, haven't you been overmodest in the assessment of yourself which you have presented? Don't you think especially that you have understated the amount of influence and power you personally hold in Cuba?

If we consider first only your *legal* power, it seems virtually absolute. As Prime Minister, you are the chief of state. In that capacity you lead the country and direct the government's foreign policy, and you are not restrained by any legislature or judicial authority or even as yet by a formal constitution. As Secretary of the party, whose highest echelons, including the directorate, are not elected but appointed by you, you occupy the seat of political power and you control all the means of political indoctrination of the people, including radio and TV, the press, and all other media for disseminating information. As president of the Institute of Agrarian Reform you have full responsibility for both initiating and supervising Cuba's agriculture—which is to say, Cuba's economy, since you have stated that the country's economic efforts will be devoted exclusively to agriculture through 1970. Lastly, you are the commander in chief of the armed forces. In your case this is much more than just a title, and logically so. As a revolutionary leader who came to power by fighting a military war with an army which you personally organized and led, it is natural for you to take the position of commander in chief seriously. For example, you personally commanded the military forces at the Bay of Pigs invasion, where you fought at the head of a column, and even did some shooting. This is certainly a much more literal use of the title "commander in chief" than most other heads of government exercise even though, as you say, they all hold it nominally.

In other words, in your hands are concentrated the four most potent sources of power: political, military, social, and economic. It is difficult to imagine what more legal authority one person might hold in Cuba.

Beyond all of that, you have a kind of personal power which may be even more significant: that is, the ability of your own mind and personality to inspire people, to convince them, to enthuse them, even to turn them into fanatics.

I personally have seen and heard evidences of this from people high and low, everywhere I've gone, all over Cuba. Everyone seems to agree that without the almost magnetic force of your personality there wouldn't have been any Revolution in the first place. Without you, there wouldn't have been any Moncada or any *Granma*, and the rebellion in the Sierra Maestra probably would have failed. Really, in January, 1959, it was you who brought the Cuban people to power, not the Cuban people who carried you to power.

Furthermore, it is difficult to give credence to your implication that it was the people of Cuba who decided for themselves that they wanted to be socialists, that they wanted a Communist society. Rather, it was you who concluded that this was the road they should take, and they followed you, not out of a theoretical conviction about Marxism-Leninism—in fact, if anything, they had a strong prejudice against Communism—but out of love and trust in Fidel Castro, their *líder máximo*.

There is no question that you are still the Maximum Leader of this country. One simple evidence of this is that throughout Cuba one finds displayed pictures of you, always in some heroic pose—of yourself practically alone among living Cubans. They range from small photographs that one sees hanging on the walls of the huts of most peasants in the mountains to gigantic images of yourself on posters and billboards that are to be seen everywhere, sometimes in the most unlikely places. One thinks especially of that enormous and rather ferocious picture of you that covers the façade of the Ministry of the Interior* headquarters building—it must be fifty feet high.

* *The Ministry of the Interior is the controlling agency for all of Cuba's intelligence and security apparatus. In a Castroless Cuba, it could be a strong base of political power.*

When you speak at a 26th of July or a May Day rally half a million people come to hear you. They come voluntarily, probably even happily. But it could be pointed out that Hitler and Mussolini used to get crowds of this size; they too came voluntarily and, to judge from the newsreels of those days, happily. Of course, I'm not suggesting that you are in a category with Hitler and Mussolini, though you have many enemies who would include you in that company. I think you are a man of greater vision, first, and secondly, I think you are motivated by a genuine desire for the well-being of your people. What I mean to suggest is that the ability to command the thunderous applause of huge crowds may be a sign that the masses support you, but not necessarily a sign that your policies are right.

Don't you feel that in having so much power, both real and potential, concentrated in the hands of one person, a potentially dangerous precedent is set? I wonder and worry what would happen, for example, if you were to die suddenly. It seems to me that it would leave an immense power vacuum.

Many things about you remind me of Lenin. He was also a charismatic revolutionary leader who held and exercised wide power. But Lenin died early, very suddenly. And his passing left a vacuum, into which, eventually, stepped a Stalin, and terror. Perhaps you believe that this could never happen in Cuba. But if you were to die tomorrow, whose picture would replace yours on the walls of the Ministry of the Interior, fifty feet high, and what would it signify for Cuba?

CASTRO: Fine. You have made statements that embrace so many problems, so many aspects, that it would be almost impossible for me to give you a complete answer to everything without speaking at too great a length. But I will do my best to improvise an answer.

In the first place, it seems to me that in what you establish as a basis for your question there is a somewhat distorted conception of the role of individuals in history.

I admit that individuals can certainly play a very important role in essential things, owing to a series of circumstances—some of which I referred to earlier—many of which are fortuitous and external to the wills of men. Actually your question seems to presuppose that a man can make history in a completely subjective way, or write a piece of the history of his country, and that really isn't true.

All men, whatever they do, have always acted within objective circumstances that determine the events. That is, no attitude is completely voluntary on the part of individuals, something that can come into being by the will or at the whim of men. I believe that the most a man can do is interpret the circumstances of a given moment correctly for a definite political purpose, and if that purpose is not based on something false, on something unreal, it can be carried out.

Of course, the role of the individual man is important, but this does not in any way mean that one can talk about absolute power. What is meant by absolute power? Power without limits, a power exercised by one person, without obedience to any norm, to any principle, to any opinion, to any program, to any objective. And that, truly, is not my situation.

Mine is not a hereditary power, or one manufactured by a governing class which could unlawfully hold onto that power. This power was created from the very beginning for the sake of and in close relation with the great majority of the people. They are really the masters and the creators of that power, as well as those who really constitute it.

I don't seek to deny the influence I have as the leader of these people, as their representative, nor the quantity of power concentrated in one person. However, it was not deliberately created. It did not constitute part of a philosophy. It did not constitute a concept of the state or of leadership. It was a result of the characteristics of the process, beginning with the time when we were a handful of men, until the end of the struggle, when we carried the whole population with us, or at least the vast majority of it. This situation arose in the relatively brief period of a few years, during which there was a constant struggle which did not allow the possibility of creating any other kinds of institutions.

The concentration of influence or power can be used for good or used for evil. But it would be much more serious if we took that concept as a definitive form of government, as the ideal way of creating and organizing a state or of ruling a country. Actually, this is very far from being my concept or that of the other leaders. It has been a transitional form, determined by circumstances. And we have lately been taking a series of steps toward the creation of another kind of leadership. These steps tend, without the need for waiting until an accident happens to me, and not on account of that fear but out of deep conviction, toward the establishment of institutional forms of collective leadership that include guarantees against precisely what you are concerned about. I realize that they are well-founded concerns, and you can be sure that they concern us too.

I am not thinking about the immediate present, because right now there are capable and very influential leaders, but about a future time when circumstances will not exist such that a man could acquire so much influence over events and people, a time when these forms of personal influence will be replaced by forms of institutional influence.

I have explained to you the efforts I made during the early days not to take on any official duty and the illusions I fell into of thinking I could maintain my distance from any kind of official function or power. I mentioned how at the time the suggestion arose—I can tell you exactly—do you know who proposed the idea? Miró Cardona. The suggestion to nominate me as Prime Minister came from Miró Cardona, who was then Prime Minister. He saw clearly that the government wasn't operating and took the initiative of making that proposition in the innermost council of the government. So I made one condition, and it was so stated to all, including President Urrutia, that if they named me Prime Minister they had to give me the power to take the initiative in the legislative and administrative fields, in order to carry forward the revolutionary program. At that time all authority was concentrated in the President of the Republic. I proposed that the authority be transferred and vested in the Council of Ministers and that the agreements passed by a majority of the Council should have the character of law. And that promise was fulfilled when I took over the office of Prime Minister. At that time, the party, properly speaking, had not yet been organized. What existed was a series of organizations, each with its own leadership and its constitution as a separate organism.

That was how I took the office of Prime Minister.

Now, it is true, as a matter of fact, that my influence has increased during the revolutionary process. But the growth of that influence has had a material and social basis, and that basis is the series of revolutionary laws that we have adopted, each of which, in one way or another, has produced advantages for the great majority of the people. That is, ours is not a magical power, ours is not a hypnotic power, but rather, an influence derived from deeds, from the deeds that the Revolution has brought into effect. And I have not brought them about alone; nobody could have done it if his ideas did not represent the active will of the great majority of the people. It is my understanding that my influence flows from a correct interpretation of the needs and aspirations and the possibilities of the people and from a correct interpretation of what things have had to be done.

Now, in leading the people, have I acted in a unipersonal manner? Never! All the decisions that have been made, absolutely all of them, have been discussed among the principal leaders of the Revolution. Never would I have felt satisfied with a single measure if it had been the result of a personal decision.

Furthermore, I have learned from experience that one must never be absolutely certain that the decision he takes or the ideas he has are always correct. Often, one can have a point of view which leaves out certain considerations or factors. And there is nothing more useful or positive or practical when a decision is going to be made on an important issue than hearing everybody else's opinion.

In the early days, decisions were taken in consultation with the different political leaders of the various organizations. Toward the end of 1960 all these revolutionary organizations were consolidated under a directorate, and never has a decision been taken without that group being in agreement.

It is true that the directorate was limited at the beginning, that it was not completely representative. And when the criticism of sectarianism was made, that directorate was enlarged and made more representative.

We are conscious that our leadership is still not sufficiently representative. We are involved at this moment in the task of organizing the party and its central committee. This is the next step, which we will take in order to establish in a real and formal way the broadest and most representative leadership possible.

So if you analyze the whole history of the revolutionary process, you see that, far from moving toward institutional forms of personal power, we have been taking more and more steps away from it: first uniting existing organizations; later, creating the organisms of leadership. And we will follow this course until we have finished creating, in a formal, institutional way, a method of collective leadership. We would not consider ourselves responsible men if these same concerns about the future were not present in all of us, and I believe that the statement you have made is, in that sense, very correct.

Concerning the question you raise about photographs, I don't know whether you are aware that one of the first laws that the Revolutionary Government passed, following a proposal of mine, was the prohibition against erecting statues to any living leader or putting his photographs in government offices. So you will see that in many places they have a small photograph in a little frame on a corner of the desk. In other places they don't have any photograph whatsoever. This can be seen by anybody. Furthermore, the same law prohibited giving the name of any living leader to any street, to any park, to any town. I believe that nowhere else, under circumstances such as ours, has a similar resolution been passed, and it was one of the first laws approved by the Revolution.

Also, notice that with regard to the very photographs which the people have, there is something curious. How have they been distributed? In an absolutely spontaneous way. No organism has been devoted to that activity. Where do most of the photographs come from that the peasants have? From magazines, from newspapers, from posters connected with some public meeting. There are photographs of all kinds and by all photographers, good ones and bad ones, an enormous variety.

Some people have even made a business from photographs, printing the ones they like and selling them in the street. What is absolutely true, and anybody can verify it, is that there has been no official initiative or policy regarding this situation. The fact that there are photographs in the houses has been a completely spontaneous thing among the people. We could have selected some photographs and printed hundreds of thousands of them and distributed them systematically, but this has not been done, because we are not interested in it.

LOCKWOOD: Perhaps the fact that it is done "spontaneously" on such a large scale illustrates the enormous personal influence which you hold with the masses, which in some cases takes on an almost religious aspect.

CASTRO: Yes, that is somewhat true, among the farmers principally, but in person they do not treat me like that. I visit many places, I talk a great deal with the farmers, and they treat me with great naturalness, which means that this mystical business doesn't exist. You yourself have seen how, when I visit the farmers, I talk with many of them, I go to their houses. They are somewhat accustomed to that and they treat me in a very familiar way. More than any mysticism, there is a certain feeling of familiarity.

And now, I don't believe that all the matters you raised have been answered yet.

In one of our informal conversations, I told you that generally twenty days or a month sometimes pass that I do not appear in the newspapers, when they don't publish news items or photographs or anything referring to my activities. Most of my activities are not made public. I mean that I do not have a press section organized so that people are constantly informed about everything I do, and I only appear in the newspapers when there is something important of a public nature. I carry on most of my work discreetly. You have been here for three months, and you can collect all the newspapers and can see how many times I have appeared in the press during that time. Occasionally, when I take a trip, some newspaperman goes along, but I do that very rarely.

LOCKWOOD: This is a relatively recent development, isn't it—that you can read the newspapers or watch TV for a month at a time without seeing your face or your name? How do you account for it?

CASTRO: Before, there were always a greater number of public meetings, and I generally appeared at each one of them. Today, people are much more involved in concrete work, so there is a lesser number of public meetings. Furthermore, there are now many more rallies in which other *compañeros* participate.

For any one of us, participation in these rallies is a strained and arduous duty. We have to resist many pressures, constant invitations to the meetings of each organization. They always want certain leaders there. I still have to speak at least three times a year at huge rallies.

LOCKWOOD: Do you prepare your speeches in advance?

CASTRO: Actually, I have ideas about the essential things, about the most important things, about those things I want to emphasize, but I never make any formal preparation. I have found that if you try to give a definite shape to your ideas, to give them a prior form, when you begin to speak you lose one of the finest influences that the public can exercise over the person who speaks, that of transmitting its ardor, its enthusiasm, its force, its inspiration to him.

Often, my speeches are conversations, exchanges of impressions with the public. Often, that interchange of impressions determines the need to stick closer to a subject, to a question, to some idea. It is much like a conversation; and really when you are going to have a talk with somebody, you cannot plan the whole conversation. Sometimes one doesn't know who is speaking, whether it is oneself or the people.

LOCKWOOD: Do you mean that you have the feeling that the people are speaking through you sometimes?

CASTRO: I remember a certain 26th of July celebration. The people did not go simply to listen; they went to manifest an attitude, a decisiveness, a state of mind, a happiness, a goal accomplished, a purpose regarding tasks that are not completed. It was a presence, a mobilization, and an action of the people in which they demonstrated their spirit, their support, their enthusiasm. The people manifest themselves in many ways in each of these meetings, especially in those that are not preceded by a parade.

LOCKWOOD: Many people in the crowds listening to you seem to have an experience similar to yours; they seem to have the sensation that they are speaking through you—

CASTRO: Yes! When something is said which seems like what they are thinking! Sometimes that happens. It is very strange. Our public has a great perceptibility, a great agility, a great capacity for understanding. In this, the levels of culture of the different regions can be appraised too. In some regions they have more capacity to understand rapidly, as if they sense what is going to be said, and in others they react with more sluggishness, although changes from one year to another are perceptible.

In the countryside, for example, people used to feel that they were inferior to the people of the city. Country people were called *campesinos* in a pejorative way. They were accused of being ignorant and uncivilized, and humorous stories were told about the *campesinos*. For this reason, when he went to the city, the peasant felt very timid and inhibited. That was in times before the Revolution. Today, the *campesinos* go to the city and feel another state of mind, another spirit. They are changing extraordinarily.

I like very much the atmosphere of the country. I enjoy myself very much when I go there. If it depended on me, I would always be in the country, in the mountains. I prefer it a thousand times to the city. The people are very healthy, very good.

It pleases me a great deal to visit the countryside, especially the mountains, and see the incredible change that has taken place in the spirit of the people, how universal the thirst for knowledge is, the happiness, and the optimism with which everybody—but especially the young people and the children—are looking to the future. Communism is not such a horrible thing!

You will find, if you analyze my speeches, that I do not try to create a faith among the people, but to teach them to meditate, to think, and to reason about the problems, the why of each thing. That is, we are trying to teach the people not to "believe," but to think. Nobody who carefully studied my speeches would be able to deny that there is a constant effort to get the people to reach certain conclusions by reasoning, by analysis, by conviction. If it were otherwise my speeches wouldn't have to be so long. You are aware that I have a certain reputation for making long speeches?

LOCKWOOD: Yes. But they've been getting shorter, haven't they?

CASTRO: A little shorter, exactly because I believe there is a much higher level of preparation, of understanding. Many of the things that I used to have to explain, to justify and to repeat are now well known. But fundamentally, my whole style has always been that of conversing and reasoning with the people. There is a great difference between our multitudes and the fascist mobs which you compared them to. Our multitudes are not fanatical. Rather, very firmly based convictions have been created on the basis of persuasion, of analysis, of reasoning.

The fascists brought together multitudes who seemed content. There is no doubt that those regimes had support in Italy and Germany, but their organization and mobilization of the masses was done by typically military means. They never had the character of spontaneity and, much less, the enthusiasm and the magnitude that our public meetings have. That is, we do not mobilize all the soldiers, all the militiamen, all the organizations; but the public is called together, and all the workers and their friends come, each one on his own. We offer facilities so that they can be brought to the meeting, but absolutely nobody is *required* to come. That is quite evident. Those who want to, come; those who don't, do not come.

And I'll tell you something else. If you consider the size of our population, barely seven million inhabitants, our public meetings are incomparably larger than those the fascists used to hold in Italy and Germany, in spite of Germany's enormous population. They are larger not only proportionately, but in absolute numbers.

Moreover, there is no comparison between the enthusiasm and the support generated by a revolution, which awakens feelings of noble generosity in man, and the enthusiasm that fascism generates, inspired by resentment, hatred, and the hunger to exploit and dominate other nations, races and men.

Our people have no egotistical feeling of any kind, they make no claim of superiority. The Revolution educates them in feelings of equality and brotherhood among all men and all peoples. It educates them in the ideal that one's own work, not the exploitation of others, is the just social way of earning one's living; in the idea of the right of each nation to the full enjoyment of its natural resources and the fruit of its labor, not the exploitation of some nations by others; in feelings of love, and not of hatred and discrimination between men. It awakens the faith of man in himself, the faith of peoples in a better life, the creative spirit of the masses. This is what generates the enthusiasm, this is what distinguishes our multitudes from the fascist multitudes, this is what also distinguishes socialism from imperialist capitalism.

And permit me to say, finally, that I don't experience any personal satisfaction whatsoever when I read or hear some of those flattering qualities which are attributed to me in the press. I have never spent a single second of pleasure over such things. I can tell you in all sincerity that they have no importance for me. And I think this is a positive thing. Because, as a general rule, power corrupts men. It makes them egotistical; it makes them selfish. Fortunately, this has never happened to me, and I don't think it will. Very honestly, I can say that nothing satisfies me more than seeing that every day things depend less and less on me, and more and more upon a collective spirit grounded in institutions.

One question must be asked: What importance can what a man accomplishes have if those accomplishments are going to last only as long as he lasts? If we really do love the Revolution, if we hope that the Revolution will always continue upon its road, and if we wish for our people the greatest happiness in their future, what value would all our good intentions have if we didn't take steps to ensure that they would not depend wholly on the will of only one man? If we didn't take steps to make it depend on the collective will of the nation?

We love the Revolution as a labor. We love it just as a painter, a sculptor or a writer may love his work. And, like him, we want our work to have a perennial value.

LOCKWOOD: You consider the making of a revolution a work of art?

CASTRO: Yes, I certainly do. Revolution is an art. And politics is also an art. The most important one, I think.

The Revolution is not made for the sake of revolution itself; it is made in order to create the best conditions for the development of the material and spiritual activities of the human being. That is, revolutions are only made with the postulate of creating a happier man. I believe that men have been concerned about this from the beginning of time, and I think that humanity has never been closer to being able to achieve it. Never before has humanity accumulated such a great quantity of scientific and technical resources for creating the best living conditions for mankind.

LOCKWOOD: Under the new constitution which you say will be promulgated soon, will the people have any electoral voice in determining who the collective leadership will be?

CASTRO: We will have a system of permanent participation of the mass of workers in the formation of the party, in the election of its members and in the replacement of such members of the party who do not deserve the trust of the masses.

That is, there will be a continuous election, a continuous participation of the masses in the formation of the political apparatus. The representatives of the working masses will be the members of the party. The party will be something like a combined parliament of the workers and interpreter of their will.

LOCKWOOD: And will that "parliament" in turn choose the directorate of the party?

CASTRO: It will be chosen by assemblies of delegates, who in turn are elected by the mass membership of the party.

LOCKWOOD: Will there be more than one slate of candidates among whom the people may vote?

CASTRO: It can happen that in the party congress there would be more than one candidate.

In your country, people are accustomed to think there is only one kind of democracy possible. I would say that there are two forms of democracy: bourgeois democracy and workers' democracy.

We think that our democracy is much more functional than yours because it is the constant expression of the true majority will. We think that the participation of our masses in political, economic and social problems will become infinitely greater than that which the North American citizen has in his bourgeois democracy, where he is reduced to voting once every four years for one of the candidates that only two parties designate.

We have to create our own forms of socialist democracy. And as I said before, one of the postulates of Marxism is the disappearance of the state as a coercive institution once the Communist society is established. To all those who are suspicious of the state, who fear it as the coercive instrument that it has been throughout history, we offer this ultimate prospect of a stateless society. I believe that we must continue working out that Marxist idea.

LOCKWOOD: Is Cuban Marxism going to be something quite different from all other forms of Marxism that have existed?

CASTRO: I believe that Marxism proposes that revolutionary ideas should be adapted to the concrete and specific conditions of each country. Character, tradition, an infinity of completely different circumstances take part in that process.

LOCKWOOD: What role do you expect to play in your government in the future, once the party is fully established and the constitution is in effect?

CASTRO: I think that for a few more years I will figure as the leader of the party. If I were to say that I didn't want that, people would think I was crazy. But you want me to speak sincerely? I will try to make it the least time possible. You know me very well, and you have seen how many other things I am attracted to which are not official activities.

I believe that all of us ought to retire relatively young. I don't propose this as a duty, but as something more—as a right.

LOCKWOOD: Can you really picture yourself as a retired "elder statesman"?

CASTRO (*laughing*): It is more difficult for me to imagine myself as an "elder" than as a retired statesman, because of the hardship it will be for me not to be able to climb mountains, to swim, to go spearfishing and to do all those things that please me.

But there is one thing which I am very much attracted to, and that is studying, experimenting and working in agriculture. I would then have the advantage that all my time could be devoted to that, and of course the disadvantage that I would not be able to put into practice with the same facility all those policies that have positive results.

But I am very much attracted by the field of study, and at the same time by nature, so that I don't think I will be bored. Well, nobody can say, because with time one's character sometimes changes too. Perhaps I will fall into the habit that comes to all of us of thinking that the younger generation is bungling everything. That is a mania characteristic of all old people. But I'm going to try to remain alert against it.

ATHLETICS

LOCKWOOD: You love athletics, don't you?

CASTRO: Yes, I really like sports very much. I always have, and I believe that they helped me a lot. For example, after a day of fishing I come back here and I feel much better. Above all one has to relax, because one becomes a little allergic to all these problems. I relax one day and return again, and thus my interest is always renewed.

LOCKWOOD: What other sports do you like besides fishing?

CASTRO: Well, I play handball a little. I like to go mountain-climbing, to swim, apart from fishing. Hunting I like somewhat, but not as much as underwater fishing. Basketball, too—when I was a student I played basketball. I like almost all sports. I like ping-pong. I like chess, although I don't play it very well; I play it very casually, but it seems to me more entertaining than dominoes. On rare occasions, like that time when you were with us when we were unable to leave the Sierra, I play dominoes a lot. When I was a student I also took part in track and field sports: eight hundred meters, fifteen hundred meters, the high jump, too, and the hop, skip, and a jump; but I never became a champion—at the scholastic level, yes—but I didn't practice much. For example, in the high jump I never learned very well the technique of doubling up. I also learned to throw the javelin pretty well, but here, too, I never succeeded in learning enough technique. And another sport I liked was football, what you call soccer.

LOCKWOOD: But spear-fishing is your favorite sport, isn't it? You went fishing today—next time I would like to go along and take pictures.

CASTRO (laughing): A day like today would have been good for taking photographs. But often when I go out I put on any kind of shorts, shirt, shoes, without worrying about color, size or age, and I like to do it without thinking about any public. The only thing I would like is a little bit of censorship over photographs of that kind. A little bit of right to censorship.

LOCKWOOD: Agreed.

CASTRO: And to know that we have finished. I imagine that until we have finished I will worry a lot. Today I have been fishing and, more than that, thinking about the book. I was beneath the water and thinking about the book. I have to free myself mentally from the subject.

LOCKWOOD: But it didn't seem to interfere with your fishing. How many pounds did you catch?

CASTRO: Four hundred and six pounds. In three hours and forty-five minutes. It was a great effort. I swam something like five or six miles.

LOCKWOOD: With aqualung, or just snorkel?

CASTRO: Snorkel.

LOCKWOOD: But you go very deep, don't you?

CASTRO: At times. The most that I have gone down was sixty feet, just once, trying to fish at the edge of the beryl—the beryl is the point where the depths begin, the border of the continental shelf. I was trying to catch a grouper, a fish that sometimes reaches three hundred and even more pounds, and I swam and swam and swam until I came up to it, and just when I got very close to it, it moved away. When I came back up to the surface I had a little blood running out of my nose. I had never gone down so far before, but it was also because I came up very suddenly. Usually I fish at depths between fifteen and fifty feet.

LOCKWOOD: Does the Prime Minister's doctor approve of your going down to such depths?

CASTRO (*laughing*): It was a wonderful proof of health. The doctor would have been much more worried had I not been able to do it.

LOCKWOOD: When are you going to take off your guerrilla uniform?

CASTRO: Possibly never. I feel good in it. It is the clothing I am now used to wearing, it raises very few problems, it's very simple, it's comfortable. . . .

LOCKWOOD: And the pistols that you all carry—why do you still wear them? Are they a symbol of something?

CASTRO: No, actually it is a custom, a habit, but a habit also based on the idea that at some moment it might be needed. At least I myself carry it for that reason. But fundamentally it is just a custom.

LOCKWOOD: But it's also a symbol of something, isn't it?

CASTRO: No. I don't take it to be a symbol. What could it be a symbol of? Of power? The pistol doesn't symbolize power.

LOCKWOOD: Not of power, perhaps, but of your attitude that there is a constant danger and that you are prepared to fight at any moment.

CASTRO: If one isn't ready to use it, one shouldn't carry it. I might need it for many things. The other day I killed a pigeon with my pistol; at other times I've had to draw it with the idea of making noise because a dog came toward me in a menacing tone, or because, passing through the fields, I encountered some aggressive cattle. Not with the intention of harming them, but just of making noise.

The custom is the result of many months of war, a revolutionary process characterized by unleashed passions, a struggle which takes on different forms at different moments. You don't know whether you will be going down a highway one day and run into an agent of the CIA. The possibility does exist, perhaps remotely, of having to use your weapon. For that reason there is a certain habit of not depending upon those who can come to your aid, but upon yourself.

LOCKWOOD: Have you ever had to use it to defend your life since you came to power in 1959?

CASTRO: No, never.

LOCKWOOD: There have never been attacks on your life?

CASTRO: Never any attacks; plots, yes.

LOCKWOOD: Don't you find it remarkable that there hasn't been even one attack on you in all this time?

CASTRO: There are several reasons, I think. One of them is that we have an efficient organization, a superb means of control and vigilance and of gathering information about the activities of our enemies. Also, although my style of working might make an attempt against my life easy because it takes me among the people a good deal and I don't take any special precautions, at the same time it could be that it also makes such an attempt more difficult.

The people who are with me are very effective, very efficient, and I think they command a lot of respect. There are also other circumstances, if you will, of a moral order. It seems to me that our enemies feel very demoralized. I am thinking of the defensive attitude they have always taken everywhere, that they have never taken an aggressive stance. Perhaps they have finally reached the conclusion that assassinating me would resolve nothing.

LOCKWOOD: But you only need to have one fanatic somewhere, such as the one who killed Kennedy—

CASTRO: But in the United States conditions are more favorable for the development of unbalanced people than in Cuba. It seems that the percentage of mentally disturbed people in the United States is very high, a proof perhaps of the degree of civilization, of the industrial development that the United States has achieved, and it seems to me also something appropriate to the system. From the time the individual gets up in the morning, he feels as if they were trying to influence his will in some way; he is a person pursued by a thousand pressures. For example, you can light a cigarette here and not see any advertising, or drink a soft drink, read a newspaper, go out into the street, turn on the radio. You can live somewhat more calmly. No one is trying to influence your will so incessantly, in every way. I think people in the United States live under a great strain, especially in large cities, and have great feelings of frustration. But I cannot expand very much on that subject. It belongs more properly to American sociologists and researchers.

"Everybody to Revolution Square with Fidel on May 1" (Havana street)

Right: *New apartment building in Santa Cla*

Above: *Children playing in Santa Clara*

"*If they want peace, there will be peace. But if they want war, we are not afraid of war!*" (*Havana suburb.*) *Missiles shown on poster are surface-to-air missiles donated by U.S.S.R.*

Outdoor café, Havana

Right, and Following pages: *26th of July celebration, Santa Clara*

Talking to construction workers at new Soviet thermoelectric plant, Santiago

Talking with workers in cement factory cafeteria, Santiago

Oil refinery workers listening to a Castro lecture

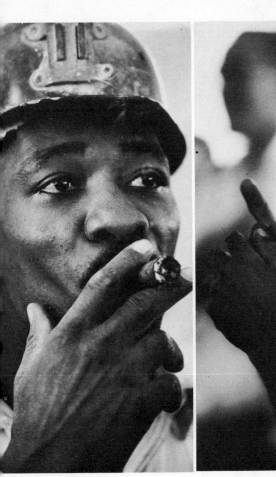

Castro speaks at midnight at a sugar mill in Oriente Province

Raúl Castro, Cuba's number two man, chauffeurs his big brother in a jeep around Birán (in the Sierra Maestra), their mutual birthplace

Brother vs. brother. As in everything else he does, Fidel plays baseball to win and complains loudly to the umpire upon losing a close call

five

Castro looks at the world (interview— part three)

THE UNITED STATES

LOCKWOOD: Thus far we haven't talked much about Cuba's relations with the United States. You were speaking earlier of some of the "illusions" you had when you first came to power in 1959. Was it one of your illusions that the Cuban Revolution and the United States were going to get along better than they actually have?

CASTRO: Yes. At that time, we believed that the revolutionary program could be carried out with a great degree of comprehension on the part of the people of the United States. Why? Simply because we believed in an illusory way that, because it was just, it would be accepted. True, we didn't think about the government of the United States. We thought about the *people* of the United States, that in some way their opinion would influence the decisions of the government.

What we didn't see completely clearly was that the North American interests affected by the Revolution possessed the means to bring about a change of opinion in the United States and to distort everything that was happening in Cuba and present it to the United States public in the worst form.

LOCKWOOD: You went to the United States not long after you came to power, didn't you—in April, 1959?

CASTRO: Yes, precisely in an effort to keep public opinion in the United States better informed and better disposed toward the Revolution in the face of the tremendous campaign that was being waged against us. When I went to the United States I had practically no contact with the government. It was with public opinion.

LOCKWOOD: You did meet with Vice President Nixon, though.

CASTRO: Yes. But my trip was not an official one. I had been invited by an organization of editors. But there were some—what I would

211

call—"acts of protocol," because diplomatic relations were being maintained. There was a luncheon with the then Secretary of State Herter and an invitation to speak with some senators. Nixon, too, wanted to talk with me, a long conversation. He has written his version of that talk, and he maintains that from then on he came to the conclusion that I was a dangerous character. At the time, I simply confined my self to expounding some viewpoints, to explaining the realities of our country, which I believed were similar to those of the rest of Latin America, and to demonstrating that the measures we were going to take, some of which affected North American interests, were just. More or less, if memory doesn't fail me, our conversation dealt with those themes.

At that time nobody in the United States talked about agrarian reform, nobody talked about the need for changes of structure; no kind of reform was mentioned. All that argumentation and all that vocabulary came much later, and then only in a demagogical way, not for love of the people, but for fear of revolution. In those days the words "agrarian reform" provoked terror in the Senate and amongst the political leaders of the United States. I am amazed at how there are so many people in the United States now talking about agrarian reform in Latin America, tax reform, the need for economic and social development, for education, medical services, highways and roads today, when hardly six years ago those words provoked terror. And when I went to the United States I explained to the North American people exactly why we had to do those things.

THE SOVIET UNION

LOCKWOOD: In 1960, when you nationalized the oil companies and the United States responded by withdrawing the Cuban sugar quota, do you agree that it was a decisive act on the part of the Soviet Union to step in at that moment, offering a long-term treaty to buy Cuban sugar? Wouldn't the bottom have fallen out of the Cuban economy as a result of the United States' action if the Soviet Union had not rushed in with aid?

CASTRO: In the first place, events did not happen in that manner. It is true that the cancellation of the sugar quota came when we took over the refineries. We took over the refineries when they suspended our supply of oil, and we nationalized American companies after the United States took away from us the remnant of the sugar quota.

But I certainly do consider that the purchase of sugar by the Soviet Union when the United States cut off the sugar quota was a decisive thing for the economy of the country.

LOCKWOOD: If the Soviet Union hadn't done so, what would have been the effect upon Cuba's economy?

CASTRO: The Cuban economy would have received a very hard blow. Maybe it would not have finished off the Revolution, but it would have forced us to live under almost primitive conditions for a long time.

LOCKWOOD: But you didn't know in advance that the Soviet Union would come to your aid, did you? So wasn't it a rather headstrong act to nationalize the refineries at that moment, since it was bound to elicit a retaliatory response from the United States? Did you perhaps underestimate the extent to which the United States would retaliate?

CASTRO: If we hadn't taken over the oil refineries and bought Russian oil, we would have been left without fuel. We had no other alternative. On the other hand, we did not underestimate the United States. I believe it was the other way around. The United States underestimated us.

LOCKWOOD: And it was as a result of this that Cuba entered into long-term agreements with the Soviet Union?

CASTRO: Yes.

LOCKWOOD: What are the economic ties that currently unite Cuba with the Soviet Union?

CASTRO: In the first place, the Soviet Union is the principal buyer of our sugar, in such large quantities and at a price that allows us to achieve the highest possible levels of production. The Soviet Union buys many other articles from us and could purchase many more if we produced them.

On the other hand, we receive from the Soviet Union fuel, factories, machinery, raw material, grain, and a series of articles which are indispensable for the economy. Moreover, during the years in which we were not able to send a sufficient amount of goods to pay for what we bought, they granted us sizable credits to purchase those products. Even at the present time, our imports have a greater value than our exports. We may be able by approximately 1967 or 1968 to have a balanced trade. By then our sugar trade with the Soviet Union will have reached its highest level.*

LOCKWOOD: In return for getting a premium price from the Soviet Union for sugar—over six cents a pound, which is triple the current world price†—do you pay a premium price for some Soviet goods, oil for example?

CASTRO: In reality, for the principal articles that we buy, petroleum

---

* An overly optimistic prediction. According to the Soviet press agency Tass, on March 21, 1968, Cuba and the U.S.S.R. signed a protocol to their standing commercial agreement calling for a new Soviet credit of $327 million to help Cuba finance the excess of her imports over exports in trade with the U.S.S.R.

† In 1965, less than two cents a pound.

and grains, we pay prices lower than what we used to pay to the United States.

LOCKWOOD: Yes, but in relation to the world market prices of these products, do you pay a premium price?

CASTRO: No. In our relations with the Soviet Union we have seen that they always try to avoid any policy of speculation in trade. There could be a case of some equipment on which, for reasons of cost, the price might be high. At other times, they are cheaper. And whenever we are not in agreement on prices, we discuss them. There have never been any difficulties. Remember, too, that the Soviet Union has given us all our military equipment free of charge, including not only weapons but means of transport, which are quite substantial.

LOCKWOOD: Did the fact that the Soviet Union came to your aid in 1960 and that military and economic links were subsequently established between Cuba and the Soviet Union influence or speed up the establishment of Marxism in Cuba?

CASTRO: They did not exactly bring it about, but it can be said that the connections with the Soviet Union very much matured the minds of both the people and the leaders of the Revolution.

LOCKWOOD: You think it made the people more receptive to socialism?

CASTRO: Undoubtedly it taught us something that we had not clearly understood at the beginning: that our true allies, the only ones that could help us make our revolution, were none other than those countries that had already had their own. We had an opportunity to see what proletarian internationalism was, that it was something more than a phrase; we saw it in deeds.

LOCKWOOD: Did the hostile actions of the American government have much to do with creating a receptive atmosphere for Communism in Cuba?

CASTRO: I think so, in the same way that the friendly acts of the Soviet Union also helped.

LOCKWOOD: Some observers have characterized your development as a Communist as having been largely a series of reactions on your part to a series of hostile actions by the United States. That is, that the United States in effect forced you and Cuba into the Communist camp.

CASTRO: I believe that the United States, with its imperialist foreign policy, constitutes part of the contemporary facts and circumstances that make revolutionaries out of people. It is not the only cause, but it is one of the many factors. It can be said that the policy of the United States is accelerating the process of radicalization of the revolutionary movements, not only in Cuba but in all parts of the world.

LOCKWOOD: But would you say, in a word, that you personally

would have become a Communist in any case, and that the United States' attitudes and actions only hastened the process?

CASTRO: It could be said that in the way that the United States was then and had to continue being imperialistic, we were destined inevitably to become Communists. Unquestionably, the United States today represents the most reactionary ideas in the world. And I think that they cause grave danger both to the world and to the people of the United States themselves.

LOCKWOOD: What do you mean—"reactionary ideas"?

CASTRO: I mean especially its role of world gendarme, its desire to impose outside its frontiers the kind of government system it thinks other states and other peoples should have.

CAPITALISM VS. COMMUNISM

CASTRO: I would say that the fact that the United States was at one time in the revolutionary avant-garde and had established the best and the most advanced political institutions of its time is one of the historical factors which greatly contributed to the eminence and development of that country. That, plus the natural advantages of being situated in an extraordinarily rich territory. But many North Americans still hark back to 1776, declaring that theirs is a progressive country. This is to pretend that the realities of the world and ideas have not changed at all in two hundred years. The fact is that they have changed extraordinarily.

Apart from this, although the United States arose as a nation based on the most revolutionary political principles of its time, this doesn't mean that its history has been characterized by a profound humanism.

Capitalist society deforms individuals greatly. It entangles them in an egotistical struggle for existence. What is the philosophical foundation of free enterprise? That the most competent, the most able, the most audacious will triumph. Success is the goal of each individual. And he has to achieve it in competition, in a war to the death with everybody else, in a pitiless struggle for existence. Capitalism presupposes that men are moved exclusively by material interests. It assumes that man is capable of acting rightly and correctly only when he can derive an advantage or a profit from it.

We Marxists have a much better concept of man. We believe that man is able to act uprightly out of reasons of a moral character, out of feelings of love and of solidarity with his fellow men.

I grant that in your country the majority of people have an opportunity to study and to work. But the majority do not have the *best* opportunities for study, the *best* opportunities for work or for participation in the direction of public affairs and the economy of the country. There are many who are born destined to be presidents of companies or already occupying privileged places in the society. Under capitalism there is a much higher productivity of work, a much greater social yield, and much better living conditions than there were under feudalism; but without the slightest doubt they are far inferior to the conditions of life which socialism permits.

For example, even though the northern part of the United States, led by Lincoln, struggled successfully for the liberation of the slaves, discrimination has endured there for a century and today still takes its toll in the blood of Negro citizens of the United States.

Why don't you ask yourself whether perhaps a relation doesn't exist between racial discrimination and the egoistic feelings that are developed under capitalism? Why hasn't the United States been able to eradicate discrimination? It is because racial discrimination and the exploitation of man by man are two things intimately joined. In Cuba, the exploitation of man by man has disappeared, and racial discrimination has disappeared too.

I am not expounding these ideas with the intention of hurting anybody or of wounding the feelings of the North American public. I am simply reasoning and meditating on this subject. I don't consider any people evil. What I do consider evil are certain systems that inculcate feelings of hatred in people.

LOCKWOOD: Are you predicting a socialist revolution in the United States?

CASTRO: No. I am a Marxist. As a Marxist I believe that revolutions are engendered by a state of misery and desperation in the masses. And that is not the condition of all the people of the United States, but only of a portion, especially the Negroes. And I do not believe that socialism can be imposed for purely theoretical or philanthropic reasons.

Only the masses can bring about a change of social structure, and the masses decide to make those great changes when their situation is one of desperation. Many years could pass without that happening to the masses of the United States.

In reality, the struggle between the classes is not being conducted inside the United States. It is being conducted outside the United States' borders, in Vietnam, in Santo Domingo, in Venezuela and in certain other countries, including Cuba. It is not the people of the United States who fight today against the North American capitalists, because United States citizens have a relatively high standard of living and they are not suffering from hunger or poverty. The ones who are fighting against the capitalists of the United States are the masses in the rest of the world who do live in conditions of hunger and poverty.

And just as I say to you that nobody can imagine a social revolution in the United States in the near future, in the same way nobody can deny that a social revolution is taking place in the rest of the poor and underdeveloped world against the North American capitalists. In all parts of the world you see that the most repressive and reactionary governments are backed by the political and military power of the North American capitalists.

LOCKWOOD: Is it your opinion that the United States capitalist system, in order to stay in power, needs to maintain what you call "reactionary colonial governments" in other parts of the world? If all of these governments you speak of were to fall, would the United States system still be able to maintain itself?

CASTRO: I sincerely believe so. What's more, it's possible that it would be strengthened, that there would result an even greater development of technology and of production and of the North American standard of living.

The foreign policy which monopolistic capital imposes is a ruinous one for the people of the United States. The United States had some thirty billion dollars in gold in its reserves at the end of the Second World War; in twenty years it has used up more than half of those reserves. What has it been used for? With what benefits for the people of the United States? Does the United States perhaps have more friends now than before?

In the United States many people proclaim that they are defending liberty in other countries. But what kind of liberty is it that they are defending, that nobody is grateful to them, that nobody appreciates this alleged defense of their liberties? What has happened in Korea, in Formosa, in South Vietnam? What country has prospered and has achieved peace and political stability under that protection from the United States? What solutions has it found to the great problems of the world? The United States has spent fabulous resources pursuing that policy; it will be able to spend less and less, because its gold reserves are being exhausted.

Perhaps the influence of the United States is greater now than it was twenty years ago when the war ended? Nobody could say so. It is a certainty that for twenty years, under the pretext of the struggle against Communism, the United States has been carrying out a repressive and reactionary policy in the international field, without having resolved the problems of a single underdeveloped country in the world.

LOCKWOOD: The United States views international Communism as one of the great problems of the world.

CASTRO: Why?

LOCKWOOD: To put it simply, our position is that international

Communism is a conspiracy to enslave peoples, not to liberate them.

CASTRO: That is an absolutely erroneous point of view. Look at the case of Cuba: the United States wants to "liberate" Cuba from Communism, but in reality Cuba doesn't want to be "liberated" from Communism. In order to "liberate" Cuba from Communism, the United States organized the followers of Batista, the most reactionary people of this country—torturers, conspirators, exploiters of all types, thieves. It organized them, trained them, and armed them in order to come to "liberate" the people of Cuba. None of those people had solved the needs of the people of Cuba in any way. They hadn't solved the problem of unemployment, ignorance, lack of medical care, the poverty and misery that existed in this country before the Revolution.

Tell me, for what purpose did the United States come to "liberate" us at the Bay of Pigs? To re-establish the power of the landowners, of the managers of its monopolistic businesses, of thieves, of torturers? In what sense can that be called liberty?

The United States says that it fights to defend freedom in Vietnam. Can anyone believe that if the people of Vietnam did not support the revolution they could have resisted as they have? What kind of freedom is that which the United States wants to impose on people at the point of a bayonet? What kind of freedom is that which the United States wants to impose in Santo Domingo, invading the country with its marines, violating the sovereignty of the country? What kind of freedom is that which the United States seeks to impose upon people against their will? And further, what right does the United States have to impose that kind of freedom on anybody?

It seems to me that those are simply words. Perhaps there are many people in the United States who believe them in good faith, but outside the United States nobody believes them.

LOCKWOOD: In your opinion, that is how most people in the United States think?

CASTRO: Yes, I believe so, because the people of the United States live well. They have few problems of an economic nature, they have a high standard of living, they haven't had much need to worry about these problems, and they don't have the experience needed in order to judge them. Historically, North Americans have developed under very favorable conditions, and they haven't had the opportunity to acquire the maturity and experience that other nations have.

LOCKWOOD: But you don't foresee the United States ever becoming a Socialist country?

CASTRO: Unquestionably, if the United States continues on the path it is following today it can reach socialism relatively easily. That is, by following a course contrary to its own economic interests which promotes the exhaustion of its financial resources: that of renouncing the possibilities of selling to the vast markets in the Socialist camp.*

And what is happening? The United States doesn't want to trade with China, so Japan increases its trade with China, England increases its trade with China, France increases its trade with China. The United States doesn't want to trade with the Soviet Union and one of the causes of the high level of the European economy, one of the factors that support the development of the European economy, is the increasing trade of Western Europe with the Soviet Union. In other words, the other capitalist and industrialized countries are taking advantage of the foolish United States policy to develop their own economies. A few years ago, countries went to war to gain markets. Today, what happens is that some countries, like the United States, are going to ruin by renouncing the possibilities of vast markets such as those of the Socialist camp and of the whole world in revolution.

I wonder whether the United States intends doing with the rest of the countries what it has done with Cuba, every time a revolution takes place? If so, the time will come when it will have to break off trade relations with actually the largest part of the world, with two or three billion human beings. I wonder whether it isn't really stupid that a country which has the enormous industrial possibilities of the United States gives up, as a policy, the market of those countries which could most use that machinery and food.

On the other hand, the role which the United States plays obliges it to exercise a species of international aid and to be the victim of all kinds of blackmail. In support of its repressive policy against liberation movements, it finds itself required to expend enormous sums. Often, the beneficiaries of that aid, understanding the United States' panic about revolutions, make the classic demand, "your money or Communism," without thereby resolving any of the problems of the world.

The only thing that can resolve the problems of hunger and misery in the underdeveloped countries is revolution—revolutions that really change social structures, that wipe out social bonds, that put an end to unnecessary costs and expenditures, the squandering of resources; revolutions which allow the people to devote themselves to planned and peaceful work.

What does an underdeveloped country need? It needs a revolutionary government and working tools, machinery and factories. A time

* *What Castro apparently means is that if the United States continues refusing to trade with Communist nations, the loss of these markets will eventually be so significant that our economy will collapse, creating the "objective conditions" for a socialist revolution.*

will come when the United States will understand that only those countries in which a revolution has taken place are in a position to fulfill their international financial obligations.

LOCKWOOD: If you were an American citizen with such feelings and convictions, how would you go about putting them into practice?

CASTRO: I don't think that's an easy question to answer. I have never put it to myself.

Among other things, one would have to place himself in an environment, in a university, in a youth organization, in a labor union, and set the imagination to work. A course of action? I think at best I would soon wind up in jail.

It is not easy to put myself within the character of the North Americans. They have a distinct idiosyncrasy, a distinct character, and a distinct sensibility and way of reacting to things. I know how Cubans would react to any given situation, but not North Americans. Sometimes the North American people give me the impression of having a cold temperament that is very insensitive and individualistic. In general they seem to me a people very different from ours. Not a people without virtues, not at all. They are very hard-working, enterprising, with a great capacity for organization and techniques. Without doubt, they are a people with many national virtues, but it is unquestionable that certain negative factors have influenced them.

AID TO OTHER REVOLUTIONS

LOCKWOOD: Is Cuba giving aid to revolutionary movements in other countries today?

CASTRO: I believe it is the duty of all revolutionary governments to help all the forces of liberation in whatever part of the world.

LOCKWOOD: What kind of aid does your country give to such movements?

CASTRO: Each country helps in whatever way it can. I don't think that anybody ought to say how he does it.

LOCKWOOD: Did Cuba help the revolution in Santo Domingo in any way, either before or during the fight?

CASTRO: Us? In what sense? If you ask whether the Cuban Revolution exerts some influence by its example upon the revolutionaries of other countries, I would say yes. The example of Cuba influences revolutionary events elsewhere. But we had nothing to do directly with the Dominican revolution, although we sympathized with the Dominican revolutionaries with all our heart. All our sympathies were with the Constitutionalists. We defended them in the United Nations and elsewhere but without having had any contact or relations with them.

LOCKWOOD: You must be aware that one reason for the United

States' intervention in Santo Domingo was supposedly in order to prevent the spread of Castroism—

CASTRO (*interrupting, chuckling*): Perhaps leaders would have appeared there who are not as bad as Fidel Castro.

LOCKWOOD: In a 1964 newspaper interview you said that one of the points you would consider as a basis for negotiations with the United States would be the question of Cuba abandoning its assistance to revolutionary movements in other Latin American countries. I gather that this is no longer your position.

CASTRO: What I said at that time was that our country was ready to live by norms of an international character, obeyed and accepted by all, of nonintervention in the internal affairs of the other countries.

I believe that this formula should not be limited only to Cuba. Bringing the concept up to date, I can say to you that we would gladly discuss our problems with the United States within the framework of a world policy of peace, but we have no interest in discussing them independently of the international situation. We are not interested in negotiating our differences while the United States is intervening in Santo Domingo, in Vietnam and elsewhere, while it is playing the role of repressive international policeman against the revolutionary movement. While this is going on, we prefer to run the same risks that all the other countries are running and have no desire to live in peace with the United States. We have no right to view our own problems independently of the rest of the world. Such a policy would greatly weaken the small countries which have problems with the imperialists.

What is the strategy of the Pentagon, that they think they can carry out that policy with impunity? It is the idea of nuclear equilibrium. Their hypothesis is that the outbreak of a thermonuclear war is impossible, given their massive destructive power and the inevitability of mutual annihilation, and that this leaves a margin for wars of another kind: conventional local wars, campaigns of limited repression, etc.

The United States believes that nuclear equilibrium leaves its hand free to develop these kinds of aggression without danger of nuclear war. In the same way, we revolutionaries believe that the revolutionary war can be developed without danger of nuclear war. That is, the only adequate counterpart of the present strategy of the United States, that of intervention, limited reprisals, and local war, is the policy of giving full support to the wars of liberation of all the peoples who want to free themselves from imperialism.

Before long, the United States will find itself required to disperse its forces in order to fight interventionist wars of a universally hateful nature against the revolutionary movements in Asia, in Africa, and Latin America. It will find itself increasingly alone, isolated, and repudiated by world opinion. The revolutionary movement will break out sooner or later in all oppressed and exploited countries, and if "nuclear equilibrium" creates a situation in which thermonuclear war would really be increasingly difficult, because neither side wants it, the United States will inevitably lose the fight against the revolutionary movement, simply because objective social and historical conditions extraordinarily favor that struggle of the underdeveloped peoples.

LOCKWOOD: Where else in Latin America do you look for revolutions to occur in the near future?

CASTRO: I think that there are many countries where objective conditions exist that are favorable for revolution, especially where the economic, political and social crisis is sharpest, where there are feudal conditions and the masses are living in conditions of hunger.

Revolutions depend not only on the objective conditions, but also on subjective factors, the degree of development of the revolutionary consciousness, the clarity with which the revolutionary leaders see the way and are willing to advance along it. If for the time being you except Chile and Uruguay—the only two countries which still maintain a legally established form of government and whose ruling classes do not maintain their hegemony by bloody and ruthless means as other countries have done—such conditions exist in all the countries of South America. The same can be said of Central America, if you except Costa Rica and Mexico. Although, naturally, I am not a prophet, knowing what might happen in any place at any moment. In Uruguay itself there is an evident danger of a reactionary military coup that can create conditions suitable for armed revolutionary resistance and even revolution.

LOCKWOOD: Why do you except Mexico?

CASTRO: In Mexico, although there are vast differences between the wealthy classes and the immense majority of the people, at any rate there did take place there an antifeudal revolution which created conditions favorable to the development of a national bourgeoisie and which also instituted certain measures of an anti-imperialist nature, such as the nationalization of oil and other measures in defense of the national interest. Mexico has had an undeniable economic development that has permitted a more advanced social development than in any other country in Latin America. But as I said, if those few countries are excepted, in all the rest of Latin America the objective conditions do exist for armed revolutionary struggle. I think, for example, that in countries like Brazil, Peru, Ecuador, and Colombia they exist in a very obvious way. There are certain countries, like Venezuela, where economic conditions, based on their income from petroleum, are better than in others, but where, nevertheless, there is a subjective factor which plays an important role—the revolutionaries are very eager to fight and the people have strong anti-imperialist sentiments, with a high level of political development—and where, unquestionably, alongside the great incomes that are received from the export of petroleum there exists a very great squandering of their resources and a fabulous extraction of profits on the part of the foreign corporations.

In Venezuela it has been demonstrated that the revolutionary spirit has deeply penetrated even the military institutions. It is the only country in Latin America where important pronouncements of a military nature, with clearly revolutionary ends of a leftist character, have taken place.

THE MISSILE CRISIS

LOCKWOOD: Since you brought up the subject of "nuclear equilibrium," perhaps we could talk a bit about the Missile Crisis of October, 1962. At what point was the decision taken, and upon whose initiative, to install Soviet nuclear missiles in Cuba?

CASTRO: Naturally the missiles would not have been sent in the first place if the Soviet Union had not been prepared to send them. But they wouldn't have been sent either if we had not felt the need for some measure that would unquestionably protect the country. We made the decision at a moment when we thought that concrete measures were necessary to paralyze the plans of aggression of the United States, and we posed this necessity to the Soviet Union.

LOCKWOOD: And the Soviet response was simply that the missiles would be sent immediately?

CASTRO: Yes.

LOCKWOOD: In retrospect, thinking about all that transpired as a result of that move, have you any regrets about the decision?

CASTRO: Actually, no.

LOCKWOOD: When the United States and the Soviet Union came to an agreement that the missiles would be removed, did Cuba have any power or influence by which she might have kept them here?

CASTRO: It would have been at the cost of a complete break with the Soviet Union, and that would have been really absurd on our part.

LOCKWOOD: But wasn't there great popular sentiment in Cuba for keeping the missiles?

CASTRO: We were all of us advocates of keeping the missiles in Cuba. Furthermore, the possibility that the Soviet Union would withdraw them was an alternative that had never entered our minds. That does not mean that we would have been opposed to the death to any solution whatsoever, but we would have preferred a more satisfactory solution, with the participation of Cuba in the discussion.

LOCKWOOD: What might have been an alternative solution?

CASTRO: At that moment we were advocates of confronting the events. We felt that we had a clear right as a sovereign country to adopt measures that were pertinent to our defense, and we were absolutely opposed to accepting the demands of the United States, which in our view curtailed the rights of our country.

As for the justness or not of our position, that will depend on whether or not the world succeeds in extricating itself from the threat of nuclear war. If that danger is definitely eradicated and the sovereignty and integrity of the little peoples is respected equally with that of the great, we will have no objection to admitting that our position was erroneous. In reality, we wish it to be so: that the world will never find itself involved in a thermonuclear war, that the integrity of the little peoples will be respected, and that the international repression of the United States will disappear. Then nothing would give us more satisfaction than to have been wrong.

LOCKWOOD: If that is so, perhaps you could explain in more detail why you felt that what was needed to defend Cuba was missiles with nuclear warheads in the first place. You say that you feared an American invasion—but there was no invasion of Cuba being mounted at that time; this was well known. And you must have realized that by allowing the introduction by the Soviet Union of nuclear missiles into Cuba at that moment you were creating a strong possibility of a nuclear conflict.

CASTRO: The danger of aggression existed, just as it now exists and will exist for a long time. Why did the missiles constitute security for us? Because the United States' strategy was, and is, based on nuclear equilibrium. Within that concept, the presence of missiles in Cuba would have kept us protected. They insured us against the danger of a local war, of something similar to what the United States is doing to North Vietnam, a war that, for a small country, can mean almost as much destruction and death as that of a nuclear war.

It was our understanding too at that time that the presence of those missiles in Cuba implied a strengthening of the Socialist camp as a unit.

I ask myself: what right did the United States have to protest against those installations here, if in Italy or in Turkey, in the vicinity of the Soviet Union, they had similar bases? Didn't that give Cuba and the Soviet Union the right to do the same? We were not only acting within our rights, but they were defensive measures similar to those which other countries take in other parts of the world.

LOCKWOOD: You felt that it made little difference whether Cuba was involved in a conventional war or in a thermonuclear war?

CASTRO: Conventional weapons with the employment of masses of airplanes are equivalent to the use of atomic weapons. We are certain that such an aggression by the United States against our country would cost us millions of lives, because it would mean the initiation of a struggle that would be indefinitely prolonged, with its sequel of destruction and death.

LOCKWOOD: And you are convinced that this is going to happen sooner or later?

CASTRO: I cannot be sure of what is going to happen sooner or later, but we are very much aware that the danger exists. If this were not so we would not spend so much effort and money in preparing our defenses.

LOCKWOOD: Can you state unequivocally that there are no ground-to-ground nuclear missiles in Cuba now?

CASTRO: I don't have to perform that service for the North American intelligence. They get enough information through their own channels.

LOCKWOOD: Then you might do it as a service for the American people, who don't have access to the reports of United States intelligence.

CASTRO: I do not want to make a declaration that might be interpreted as a renunciation of a right. But if this, as you say, can be useful to the North American people, for the sake of their tranquillity, I have no objection to declaring that those weapons do not exist. Unfortunately, there are none.

LOCKWOOD: Do you think that Khrushchev acted in a personal and highhanded manner in the Missile Crisis?

CASTRO: With regard to us, yes. Khrushchev had made great gestures of friendship toward our country. He had done things earlier that were extraordinarily helpful to us. But the way in which he conducted himself during the October Crisis was to us a serious affront.

LOCKWOOD: You had had close personal relations with Khrushchev?

CASTRO: Yes, I-had had very good relations with him, and we maintained those relations as much as possible afterward, because we believed, in spite of the wrong we had been done on that occasion, that the maintenance of the best relations with the Soviet state and people was vital to our Revolution. Khrushchev was still Prime Minister of the Soviet Union. On a personal level he was always kind to all of us. I have no doubt that he was sympathetic toward the Cuban Revolution.

LOCKWOOD: You mean that you think his actions toward Cuba during the Missile Crisis were well intentioned, even though you didn't agree with them?

CASTRO: He found himself in a great dilemma, facing factors related to peace and war, and those factors were what decided him. It was really a very grave responsibility that he had. In the end, it will be history that judges his decisions.

LOCKWOOD: What was your reaction when Khrushchev was removed from power in the Soviet Union? Were you surprised?

CASTRO: Honestly, yes. I had the impression that Khrushchev's leadership was stable.

LOCKWOOD: How do you think it happened?

CASTRO: I think it must have been brought about by a complex of circumstances, possibly of an internal character. It seems to be, also, that his methods of leadership had changed a lot and were becoming increasingly oriented toward a completely personal style. I might add that at the time Khrushchev was replaced, our relations with him had reached their lowest point.

LOCKWOOD: With him personally?

CASTRO: With him personally and consequently with his government. That situation improved considerably after the change.

LOCKWOOD: What do you mean? Why were relations at such a low point?

CASTRO: After the Missile Crisis, while the Soviet Union was pressing for the withdrawal of the remaining Soviet military personnel in Cuba, the subversive activities of the United States were growing increasingly frequent. In Central America a series of bases had been organized in order to promote aggressions against us. All of which, from our point of view, justified the position we had taken at the beginning of the crisis. Also, Khrushchev's attitude had changed, principally because of Cuba's position toward certain aspects of his international policy.

LOCKWOOD: Are you referring to the antagonism he was stirring up against Red China?

CASTRO: Not to that specifically, but to the general aspects of his policy, the whole of his foreign policy, beginning with the experience of the October Crisis.

LOCKWOOD: You thought he should have taken a tougher line with the United States?

CASTRO: Just that, essentially.

LOCKWOOD: But there was nothing else which he did that contributed to the weakening of relations?

CASTRO: I have mentioned the October Crisis and the subsequent climate of distrust, which could never be completely overcome.

LOCKWOOD: Distrust by Cuba of the Soviet Union?

CASTRO: I would say distrust between Khrushchev and ourselves.

LOCKWOOD: Has there been any diminution of the CIA's activities here since the Missile Crisis?

CASTRO: No, the CIA maintains its activities incessantly and with all possible resources. It works systematically with all the Cubans who are now in the United States, with the relatives and friends of the counterrevolutionaries who are there, trying constantly to organize webs of information, espionage, and counterrevolution. That is unceasing and daily. Much of the news related to the activities of the CIA we do not make public. Many times we know when agents come. We are always capturing agents, launches, boats, radio-communication equipment. We simply don't give out the news, in order to keep them in a state of the greatest insecurity and confusion.

They use different means. For example, they use mother ships to introduce speedboats full of agents. Later they come back to rescue them too. But because of our improved organization, that tactic has become more and more uncertain. They are now using the method of infiltrating people. When they come to pick them up, they don't come straight from the outside, but place a well-camouflaged launch at a place along the coast with the fuel and all the instructions concerning its handling and the route to follow written out. Later, they tell the people where they have to go to find the launch. We have captured quite a number of these launches. Proofs of the activities of the CIA? We have millions of proofs.

LOCKWOOD: What have been the effects of the United States blockade on Cuba?

CASTRO: The effect of the American blockade has been to require us to work harder and better.

LOCKWOOD: Would you say it has been effective?

CASTRO: It has been effective in favor of the Revolution.

LOCKWOOD: The blockade was intended to cut off Cuba's trade with the West. But aren't you now trading with France, Japan, Canada, England, Italy, and other western countries, and even planning to expand this commerce?

CASTRO: The United States utilizes all the pressures it can to cut off this trade, both against the governments of those countries and against the commercial companies that trade with us. But what happens? Why do all the other countries trade with us? Because they understand that a policy like that is a policy of suicide. Because those countries, far from following the United States in not trading with the Socialist camp, are trading more and more with it, and are filling the vacuum the United States leaves with its restrictive policy on such trade.

The Socialist camp is made up of more than a billion human beings. It is a gigantic market. It is absurd that any country which has maturity and experience should abandon such an opportunity.

LOCKWOOD: Apart from those which you've mentioned, what other points of physical conflict are there now between the United States and Cuba?

CASTRO: The provocations at Guantánamo Bay.

LOCKWOOD: They still continue?

CASTRO: Yes. That has a rhythm; at times they are more, sometimes less, but for some time now there have been no cases of injury or death. That is not because they do not shoot occasionally toward our territory, but what happens is that our emplacements now have better defenses, they are protected, whereas before they were out in the open.*

LOCKWOOD: And they are farther back from the boundary?

CASTRO: Yes, a little farther back, in more defensible positions.

LOCKWOOD: But Guantánamo isn't a real threat, is it? You don't expect an invasion from Guantánamo?

CASTRO: Concretely, we don't expect any invasion at any specific place or date, but we are conscious that a threat from the United States will always exist. For that reason, we see ourselves required to stay on guard, to devote a lot of our energy and resources to strengthening our defenses.

LOCKWOOD: Do you really think the United States will invade Cuba again?

CASTRO: The policy of the United States is modeled on interventionism and aggression. It is logical that we should always be very suspicious. On that account we have to behave as if that could happen any day.

We are also conscious, however, that it is not an easy thing for the United States to launch an attack against us. First, because they would have to employ large forces and to cope with a long war in our country, to become entangled in a struggle that would never end. In the second place, because it would expose them to very serious international complications, and they must know very well the things that can happen as a result of an invasion of Cuba. They would have much more to lose than to win, and in the long run they would not be able in so doing to stop the revolutionary movement in other areas.

* Since then there has been at least one incident of a Cuban soldier being shot to death in the Guantánamo perimeter. The United States claimed he had infiltrated into the American side; Cuba maintained that the man had never left Cuban territory and mobilized all its armed forces against a possible invasion.

LOCKWOOD: If that is so, why is there danger of a United States invasion?

CASTRO: The United States also knows how risky the intervention in Vietnam is, the disadvantages and the dangers to which they expose themselves in having to battle against an association of superior forces. Nevertheless, against all logic, contrary to the simplest common sense, and in spite of the advice of many of their allies, they have become increasingly engaged in that one-way street which is the war in South Vietnam. When a government behaves like that, what security can anyone have that they will not make a similar error in some other part of the world?

Many times in history measures have been taken because of an error in calculation. When Hitler launched the invasion of Poland and other countries, he undoubtedly thought that everything would come out well. Governments have been mistaken often. I believe the United States knows this—at least they ought to know it. But that doesn't mean that they will calculate correctly all the risks or complicatons that could arise uncontrollably.

They ought to know, too, that our relations with the Soviet Union are good. They ought to know that the leaders of the Soviet Union have a very definite, very firm standpoint regarding Cuba.

LOCKWOOD: At the end of the Missile Crisis, one of the points of the accord between the United States and the Soviet Union was a pledge by the United States that it would not invade Cuba. That agreement is still in effect, is it not?

CASTRO: That is indisputable. The agreement is a matter both of fact and of legality. The United States has since alleged that because we haven't permitted inspection there is no such agreement, but *de facto* they accept it. They acknowledge that the Soviet Union has fulfilled its part of the bargain. Thus, they are required to fulfill theirs. On more than one occasion they have made declarations that the agreement doesn't exist. But that agreement exists *de facto*, and I can say to you that even *more* agreements exist besides, about which not a word was ever said. However, I don't think this is the occasion to speak about them. I am not writing my memoirs; I am a Prime Minister in active service. One day, perhaps, it will be known that the United States made some other concessions in relation to the October Crisis besides those which were made public.

LOCKWOOD: In a written, signed agreement?

CASTRO: It was not an agreement in accordance with protocol. It was an agreement that took place by letter and through diplomatic contacts.

LOCKWOOD: But it exists in some written form?

CASTRO: Why do you worry so much about whether it's written or not, when the English, the forefathers of the North Americans, were the ones who originated the idea of the "unwritten law"?

LOCKWOOD: Are the U-2 flights continuing over Cuba?

CASTRO: The U-2 flights, yes, continue over Cuba. Not only the U-2 flights; they take photographs too from their satellites. As a matter of fact, there is in the world today a kind of universal space observation. I don't think there is any place on the earth that is not perfectly depicted. I imagine that the United States is also perfectly photographed, but this is, of course, only a supposition of mine. But I believe that there is not a place anywhere in the world beyond the reach of photographic cameras. It's getting difficult for the ladies to take sunbaths!

LOCKWOOD: You have the ability to shoot down the U-2s, don't you? Why don't you do it?

CASTRO: Really, in a certain sense, the flights of the U-2 planes over Cuba are one consequence of the October Crisis. We never agreed to permitting the U-2 flights, and there came a moment when we felt that they had to be halted at all costs. But the ground-to-air missiles were not in our hands at that time.

Later, Cuban personnel were instructed in their use, and on the occasion when the projectiles were turned over to Cuba, we made the pledge not to use those weapons except in a case of strict necessity, for the defense of the country in case of aggression. Since we don't want to appear in any way as provocateurs, desiring a conflict, we have strictly abided by that pledge, although the missiles are now in our hands.

POLITICAL PRISONERS

LOCKWOOD: How many political prisoners are there at the present time?

CASTRO: Although we usually do not give this kind of information, I am going to make an exception with you. I think there must be approximately twenty thousand. But this number comprises all those sentenced by revolutionary tribunals, including not only those sentenced on account of counterrevolutionary activities, but also those sentenced for offenses against the people during Batista's regime, as well as many cases that have nothing to do with political activities, such as embezzlement, theft, or assault, which because of their character were transferred to revolutionary tribunals. Many of these sentenced are undergoing a process of rehabilitation and do not properly belong in prison. They receive regular permission to leave for periods up to a week, and they are on the verge of enjoying complete liberty.

LOCKWOOD: Would you describe how the rehabilitation plan for counterrevolutionaries works?

CASTRO: There are two kinds of rehabilitation. One is for the cases of persons living in rural areas who collaborated with the counterrevolutionary bands which were operating in the Escambray Mountains. These cases were not sent to prison; they were transferred to agricultural work for a period of one to two years on *granjas* [state farms]. During the period of time between their arrest and their release, the Revolutionary Government has taken care of all the needs of their families. Upon their release, they have been and are being relocated as agricultural workers, and they and their families are given new living quarters built for them by the government.

The other type of rehabilitation has to do with cases of persons under sentence for offenses against the people during the time of Batista's tyranny, as well as with those sentenced for counterrevolutionary offenses from 1959 onward. Their rehabilitation has three stages: first, the participation of the sentenced person in agricultural work, study, and other activities; a second stage in which he is allowed to visit his family periodically; and a third stage when he is paroled.

Unfortunately, we are going to have prisoners for counterrevolutionary reasons for many years to come. This is not easy to understand unless social and historical events are analyzed with scientific rigor, and above all unless the widespread support which the Revolution has among the people is kept in mind.

In a revolutionary process, there are no neutrals; there are only partisans of the revolution or enemies of it. In every great revolutionary process it has happened like this: in the French Revolution, in the Russian Revolution, in our Revolution. I'm not speaking of uprisings, but of processes in which great social changes take place, great class struggles involving millions of persons.

We are in the middle of such a struggle. While it lasts, while the counterrevolution exists and is supported by the United States; while that country organizes groups for espionage and sabotage, tries to form bands, infiltrates hundreds of people into our territory, sends bombs, explosives, and arms; while the counterrevolution has that support—even though its force will grow weaker and weaker—the revolutionary tribunals will have to exist in order to punish those who undertake such activities against the Revolution.

It would be a good thing if the citizens of the United States would think about the great responsibility which the CIA and the United States government bear toward those prisoners.

In the case of the invasion at the Bay of Pigs, the Revolution was kind to the invaders. It executed only those who had committed crimes in the past, individuals who had carried out an infinity of crimes and tortures against revolutionaries during the struggle against Batista, and who later joined the mercenaries. Against them, the most severe law was applied. As for the others, we could have kept them in prison for twenty or thirty years. However, on the initiative of the Revolutionary Government, the formula of indemnity was established. For us, this was not a vital thing; it was, in a certain sense, a moral act, obliging the United States to pay an indemnity for the damage they had done us.

LOCKWOOD: Was the indemnity fully paid?

CASTRO: No, actually something happened there. A bad precedent, I would say, because they didn't pay the whole of the indemnity, neither in quantity nor in quality. Trusting in the seriousness of the Red Cross, we assumed certain risks in giving freedom to all the prisoners before they had finished paying all the indemnity. We even gave freedom to some North Americans who weren't included in the negotiations. Donovan* asked particularly that we free them without waiting until the indemnity had been fully paid. And afterward it turned out that Donovan didn't have enough power to fulfill his commitments. I don't blame him, but I do blame the government of the United States, because they did something very bad, and it will go against other North American citizens who might one day find themselves in a similar situation. I think that they have lost more than we have.

LOCKWOOD: What has not been paid?

CASTRO: We have calculated that they paid a total of forty million dollars out of a total of sixty-two million that was promised. A lot of medical equipment was not sent. And they didn't keep their word about many of the medicines, neither in quality nor in quantity.

For that reason we have refused to listen to any proposals intended to help other people imprisoned for crimes against the Revolution. It must be remembered that the government of the United States is accountable not only for those who came in the invasion, which was a very clear and very direct involvement, but also for thousands of men who are imprisoned because they had enlisted in the organizations of the CIA. Of course, these people will come out of prison only by virtue of the Revolutionary Government's rehabilitation plans, since the United States itself is unable to offer them any hope of freedom.

LOCKWOOD: You once stated that if the United States government would agree to cease trying to foster counterrevolution in Cuba, you would consider freeing the majority, if not all, of your political prisoners. Has your position changed on this matter?

CASTRO: That was a proposal we made because we believe that the

---

* *James B. Donovan, New York lawyer who, acting "unofficially," negotiated personally with Castro for the release of the Bay of Pigs prisoners. Agreement was concluded December 21, 1962 (about one month after the Missile Crisis).*

counterrevolutionary activity directed and encouraged by the United States is the fundamental cause of the existing tensions and, therefore, of the measures that we find ourselves obliged to take. I am certain that without the support of the United States there would be no counterrevolution. If the counterrevolution ends, the necessity of keeping many of the counterrevolutionaries in prison will end too.

We are not worried about the counterrevolution. We are used to it, and we have developed the means to fight it with absolute efficiency.

LOCKWOOD: How many of the twenty thousand political prisoners are in some form of rehabilitation plan?

CASTRO: I think at least half. But that is my own personal estimate. Here on the Isle of Pines, where prisoners under sentence for the most serious crimes are kept, about 40 percent are participating in rehabilitation.

The idea of organizing technological education among the prisoners is an idea that came up recently, and the first steps are already being taken. We may possibly organize here two technological instiutes, one for cattle raising and another for citrus fruits. It could happen that counterrevolutionary prisoners who go into prison with a relatively low level of education will leave with technical training and a job, even having graduated from the university, depending on their educational level when they were captured.

I believe that this is a unique program, and we are very satisfied with the measures we are taking. I have no doubt that many of these men will come to be revolutionaries.

LOCKWOOD: Is that your purpose—to make revolutionaries out of them?

CASTRO: No, no, our basic purpose is to solve a specific social problem. The socialist state cannot consider the destiny of any man as being outside its concern. If a man is in prison for whatever cause, even for conspiring against the state, the Revolution has to try, in all possible ways, to make him useful in some way, to offer him some opportunity, some possibility of integrating himself into society so that he can work and live a decent life. I believe that some will sincerely become revolutionaries. Although that isn't the purpose, when it happens we will be pleased, of course.

LOCKWOOD: To what extent is political indoctrination a part of their rehabilitation?

CASTRO: Well, there is a revolutionary instructor with them. He lives together with them, he eats what they eat and endures the same regimen, and he is charged with explaining to the prisoners the work of the Revolution and its philosophical foundations and historical causes. If these arguments are sound and convincing, all those who have lacked certain elements of judgment will be able to judge events in a correct way. That is, they are offered the facts that permit them to make a better analysis of the Revolution. For instance, they are offered access to books on political questions.

LOCKWOOD: What kind of books?

CASTRO: Different kinds. Some historical works. Of course, we give them books on Marxism, but also books by authors who are not Marxists and who write on different questions of political or human interest.

We admit that we do not offer them detective novels or cowboy stories or stories about Tarzan. But good books, in general. It would be senseless to offer them books that weren't of good quality. A simple book of propaganda has no effect on anybody.

"We must cut off the hands of Imperialism in Vietnam!"

Top: A Soviet anti-aircraft battery, manned by Cuban soldiers, Oriente Province, evidence of vast armaments donated by the U.S.S.R. Similar batteries are in action in North Vietnam

Bottom: "Maximum speed, 40 km/hr." A Russian speed sign on a road inside a Cuban military airport near Camagüey is a memento of the Missile Crisis

Castro liked The Invisible Government *(an exposé of the CIA) so much that he had it translated into Spanish and published in Cuba (the edition sold out within two weeks)*

242

Top: "And for the 10th of June we will have six megatons of sugar!" Bottom: New Lenin Hospital near Camagüey with all equipment Posters throughout Cuba depict Uncle Sam as the arch-enemy of the donated by Soviet Union Revolution. Other sign urges Cubans to fight creeping bureaucracy

Top: *A Russian radar-dome "weather ship" sails into Havana harbor*
for servicing

Bottom: *Control center of huge, fully automated thermoelectric*
plant in Pinar del Rio, one of two such plants donated by the Soviet
Union

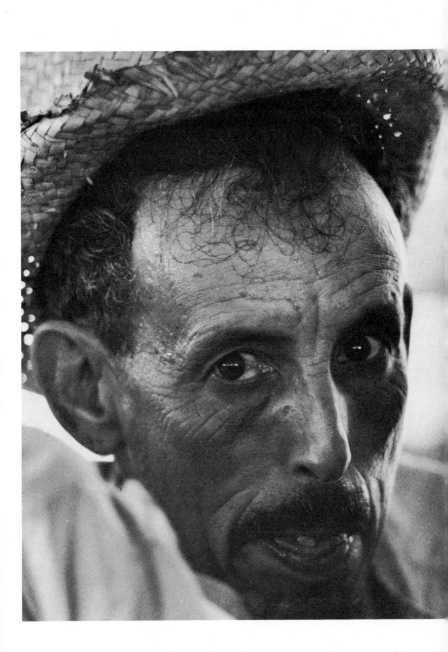

political
prisoners

Fidel Castro has often said, "In a revolution there are no neutrals." One of the stickiest problems Cuba's revolutionary leaders have had to face is the question of what to do with the political prisoners and their families. By mid-1964, the number of men interned in government jails and prison camps for political crimes or "errors" was listed officially at over fifteen thousand. One year later, Castro indicated that the number was now closer to twenty thousand and still growing; this in spite of the fact that counterrevolutionary activity has been slackening gradually ever since the Missile Crisis. In proportion to the total population, this would be equivalent to having six hundred thousand men in jail for political reasons in the United States. Such a large increment of able-bodied men out of circulation represents an extremely heavy burden upon the young Revolution, economically as well as morally.

The majority of the internees are not, as one might assume, men of urban backgrounds, but *campesinos*—peasants of the mountains and the outlying rural areas. Most are serving terms ranging from two to twenty years, according to the gravity of their crimes. Not only must they be housed, fed, and maintained by the government, but so must their families as well. *Campesinos* traditionally have very large families. The fecundity of Cuba is as characteristic of its populace as its soil, and in the countryside, where the act of procreation is often the main form of recreation and birth control almost unknown, a peasant wife may bear as many as fifteen children. When the head of such a large household goes to jail, the state must assume the support of his wife and those children who have not yet attained their majority. This alone produces a staggering economic load on the Revolution. Moreover, it is an outlay for which no productivity is received in return.

Furthermore, the removal of so substantial a number of laborers from the national work force for a period of years is a loss an underdeveloped nation can ill afford at a moment when it is making every effort to stabilize its economy by developing its agriculture. Poor in machine technology, Cuba still must rely on mobilizing its manpower (and even woman- and child-power) to do the main work of sowing and harvesting. Though the enormous sugar harvest of 1965 of over six million tons was a socialist *tour de force* (third largest in

247

Cuba's history), it was possible only because large segments of the nonagricultural population were organized into "volunteer battalions" which spent from two to four months wielding machetes in the cane fields at the height of the harvest, while soldiers, office-workers, intellectuals, women and children cut cane on weekends. The progressively larger harvests now planned will create an even greater need for able-bodied men at least through 1970.

Finally, a certain moral problem is inevitably posed in a small nation when so many men are in jail for political reasons. Counting both prisoners and their families, the total of those directly involved comes to nearly three percent of the entire population. This means that there are few Cubans who do not have at least one relative or friend incarcerated for a political crime. Moreover, a high percentage of those prisoners were jailed for committing very minor "errors." Many, it appears, were the victims of overzealous revolutionary tribunals which, in the aftermath of the Bay of Pigs invasion, meted out justice with a vindictive severity reminiscent of the Reign of Terror in revolutionary France.

For such a combination of reasons both practical and humane, Fidel Castro was prompted to seek out a way by which the largest possible number of Cuba's political prisoners could be reintegrated into society as speedily as possible. Beginning in 1963, a rehabilitation program was begun which has evolved, through a process of trial and error, into what is probably one of the most original and effective methods for dealing with counterrevolutionaries yet conceived.

Because of the extreme sensitivity of the subject, there has been until now an almost complete blackout on information regarding prisoner rehabilitation in Cuba. I was the first journalist, foreign or Cuban, given an opportunity to visit the prisons and the rehabilitation centers and to photograph and talk with the internees.

According to Castro, at least one-half of Cuba's political prisoners are currently in some kind of rehabilitation program. All are eligible for rehabilitation "except those under sentence for the gravest crimes," e.g., murder or treason. There are several different plans which vary from one another in certain details, but most of them follow the same basic three-stage formula: prison, rehabilitation center, and "conditional liberty." The largest of the plans, the "Special Plan for *Campesinos*," differs from the others in that it "rehabilitates" the prisoners' families simultaneously with the men themselves.

From the time a man enters jail, his record is reviewed periodically by a committee of prison authorities and plan officials. When they have determined that he might be suitable for rehabilitation, he is approached by a representative of the plan, who explains the advantages of the program and advises the prisoner that he is now eligible to enter. That is all that is said about it. No pressure is brought on a prisoner to join. He must request it himself, when he is ready, the theory being that if the individual is given time to make up his own mind and enters the program highly motivated, his chances for successful rehabilitation will be much greater.

The second phase is that of a *reeducando,* "one who is being reeducated." The prisoner is moved from the jail to one of several prison camps in the interior of Cuba. Here, though he still wears a convict's uniform (blue now, instead of jail yellow) and lives behind barbed wire, the conditions of his life are infinitely improved. Instead of in a cell, he sleeps in an army-style barracks with fifty or seventy-five other men. Part of the day he works on a *granja,* one of the huge state farms, as an agricultural laborer, planting trees or milking cows or harvesting fruit or cutting sugar cane, depending on the season and the type of crop in the region where he is located. If he has a special skill that can be used, he is put to work at it immediately. If, as in the majority of cases, his background is that of a simple farm laborer, if he shows an aptitude for something better, he will eventually be trained and given more responsibility.

At least three hours a day, five days a week, he goes to school—usually after lunch, when the sun is hottest and it is difficult to work—in classrooms in the camp. If he is a peasant, he probably has little education or none at all. He is taught the same primary school curriculum which all uneducated Cubans are now studying under the government's massive effort to raise its citizens to at least the sixth-grade level. If he is illiterate, he is given extra hours of instruction in reading and writing. Once he passes the sixth grade, he may, if he has the aptitude, continue his education through high school, and some go even further.

After school, the prisoner goes back to work again until dinnertime. Evenings are generally free. Lights are out by nine-thirty or ten o'clock, since he must rise at five in the morning. On Sundays, relatives are allowed to visit him in the camp.

Once every forty-five days each prisoner is given a pass to go home and spend three days with his family. Since his home town can be as much as eight hundred miles away, the prisoner is given enough traveling time to ensure that he will have the full three days; thus he may be gone from the camp as much as a week. These trips are made on the honor system, entirely unsupervised; a prisoner is simply given money for his round-trip fare and his meals and is told to be back in camp by a certain day and time. Castro told me that as far as he knew not a single man had ever failed to return on time.

According to Castro and other officials to whom I talked, the ulti-mate aim of the rehabilitation program is not to transform counter-revolutionaries into Communists, but to "neutralize" them politically to the point where the government can be reasonably certain that they won't resume their activities against the regime upon their release. The main effort, they said, is to convince these men that the Revolu-tion is really working to ameliorate social conditions for all Cubans, to demonstrate to them that in opposing the Revolution they erred out of ignorance. "Once they understand this firmly," said one plan offi-cial, "they can be restored to society in a frame of mind which will inspire them to work productively. We do not try to indoctrinate them. Most of the internees have such a low level of political under-standing when they come to us that they would not understand it if we did. We try to give them examples rather than words to prove that we are right, and then let them make up their own minds."

Nonetheless, the distinction between the words "indoctrination" and "instruction" may be little more than a semantic one. One class which every prisoner attends is called "political studies." This is basi-cally a course in Cuban history, together with a smattering of elemen-tary economics and sociology, all taught from a stridently Marxist theoretical point of view. The texts, which I have had an opportunity to study, are identical with those used for political science instruction in the armed forces. They contain liberal doses of Marx, Engels, and Lenin, as well as speeches and theoretical writings by leading Cuban Communists, including, of course, Fidel Castro.

The introduction to the textbook for the "political studies" course indicates the astringently dogmatic world view which Cuban ideolo-gists hope will be absorbed by the *reeducandos*. Some excerpts:

"Humanity has traversed a long and complete road, stretch-ing from the primitive community, through slavery, feudalism, and capitalism, to the socialism of today, formed in the power-ful Socialist camp. . . .

"In order to carry out the great, historical fight which our country is leading in Latin America, it is necessary to under-stand the real causes and motivating forces of historical events and the laws of development. . . .

"Historical materialism was born in the decade of the 1840's, created by Marx and Engels, great sages and thinkers, teachers and guides of the working class. The appearance of historical and dialectical materialism represented the most magnificent practical revolution in science. . . .

"Bourgeois sociologists and politicians declare as accidental and unnatural an event so in accordance with the laws and necessary from the historical point of view as the Great October Socialist Revolution, only because that revolution and that socialist state system contradicted the interests of the bourgeois . . . society. Just as the triumphs of the anti-imperialist and anti-feudal revolution in China and of our own socialist revolution ninety miles away from the international gendarme of reaction are considered by reactionary leaders as "abnormal" and "unnatural" phenomena. . . .

" 'History can be made. The people make it, the masses make it. . . . History is something alone and it is impossible to come subjectively and remake it. All subjective histories which are remade then have to be unmade all over again, in order to clear the way for objective history, real history.'

"So spoke our Commander in Chief, Fidel, indicting history in his testimony of March 26, 1962. Under these principles let us study this book, taking from each of its chapters the doctrines of the development of our society, of its characteristics, of the role of each class or group according to its interests, and thus we will be able to see and understand how men do not create history according to their will but in conformity with objective material conditions."

Since the language of this introduction is so pedantically obscure as to make it almost incomprehensible to a literate reader, one may doubt that it makes much of an impression on the peasant *reeducandos*, even with the help of an instructor. But its point of view is clear enough: "bourgeois imperialism," especially the Yankee variety, is "the arch-foe and arch-exploiter of the working classes." In other words, when a worker enlists in the service of a counterrevolutionary movement, he is, in effect, cutting his own throat.

Indoctrination is not limited merely to "political studies" class but finds its way into history, geography, Spanish and everything else, even mathematics. An example from a lesson on multiplication:

In the semi-colonial colonies of Latin America about 4 people die of hunger, curable disease, or premature old age every minute. How many people die in Latin America every 3 minutes under the social system of exploitation which imperialism has established?

Let us multiply $3 \times 4 = 12$.

Answer: The result of multiplying the number of people who die every minute by 3 minutes gives us the number of Latin

Americans who die in our continent every 3 minutes and would not die under a just social system.

Or another example from a Spanish lesson, which begins with a two-page, impassioned recounting of the Bay of Pigs invasion:

Use the following words. Look up their meanings in the back of the book:

antepenultimate
sterile
fervor
CIA

But probably more effective than all of this in reforming the prisoners' political attitudes are the Cuban newspapers, which daily print a one-sided, ponderously didactic version of world news that chimes in strict unison with the party line (the Cuban, not the Russian, party line) and also carry the full text of all speeches by Fidel Castro and other top Cubans. The prisoners receive one paper a day, *Granma*, the official party organ, and devour it with an avidity which, from a journalistic standpoint, is totally undeserved. Twice a week in the evening, the resident instructor in each barracks holds an informal seminar, in which the latest speeches or news accounts appearing in *Granma* are discussed and explained in thorough detail.

There is no question but that all this constitutes something more than mere instruction; it is indoctrination. But it is not brainwashing. There is no coercion. No individual is forced, either physically or psychologically, to change his views about anything. I have personally verified this fact in conversations with dozens of prisoners in different parts of Cuba. A few of them said they realized that they had been mistaken before and now favored the Revolution. More often they would frown and indicate that they really didn't know what they thought about it. But all agreed that nobody in the prison camp was telling them what they should think and say as a means of obtaining their freedom sooner. The fact is, I found that without exception the prisoners with whom I talked were peasants who had only a rudimentary understanding of political matters and even less interest in them, regardless of how long they had been interned. Some had been out of circulation as long as five years.

They were all interested in only one thing: getting out and going home. Quiet men, somewhat timid and gentle of disposition, the mere question "Where do you come from?" immediately conjured in each of them a look of profound, melancholy yearning for home. Inquiries as to the nature of the crimes they had committed usually brought only the vaguest, most unlikely responses, indicating that many of them were still somewhat bewildered as to exactly why they were in prison. "A man came to the door and asked for my name. So I gave it." (This from a prisoner with a sentence of two years.) "I gave two pair of shoes to my friend because I thought he needed them, only instead he took them to the bandits." (Three-year sentence.) When I asked whether they didn't think these sentences were extremely unjust for such minor infractions—you couldn't call them crimes—most of them seemed not to know what to answer. A plan official who accompanied me on one such occasion told me that the peasants always minimize their crimes when talking about them, mainly out of embarrassment.

To each barracks there is assigned a "revolutionary instructor" from the Ministry of the Interior, the agency responsible for all of Cuba's prisons. This man, who eats, sleeps and lives with his charges, is carefully selected for his intelligence and understanding. Often, he is himself a former peasant. He is to his men a combined barracks sergeant, ideological mentor and father-figure to whom they bring all their problems. It is his main responsibility to mark each prisoner's progress, and it is primarily his reports which determine when a man is ready to return to the outside.

A prisoner may be eligible for release after serving at least one year in the plan and a minimum of 25 percent of his total sentence. Exactly how much longer he serves depends on his conduct, his work record, and his progress in developing a "neutral" (i.e., positive) attitude toward the Revolution.

In order not to create jealousy among the other prisoners, a *reeducando* about to be released is not informed until the night before he is to leave. Then he is issued a suit of new clothes and some "mustering-out" pay and wished good luck by the authorities. Like any man on parole, he is technically still liable for the balance of his sentence should he fall into trouble again. In practice, however, he is a free man. There is no surveillance and no parole board to report to. He can live anywhere in Cuba.

Prisoners serving in rehabilitation centers on the Isle of Pines or other areas where there is a shortage of agricultural labor are encouraged by the government upon their release to bring their families and settle on the same *granja* where they have been working. As an inducement they are offered a new, completely furnished house, a good salary and other benefits. But the choice is voluntary, and most of the peasants prefer to return to their native villages rather than stay to put down roots in a new place.*

* *This does not apply to those in the "Special Plan for* Campesinos" *(see following).*

It seems likely that some of these people should not be in jail in the first place and that many others were given sentences far out of proportion to their transgressions. In a sense, as Fidel Castro himself admits, they are casualties of the revolutionary process. The Cuban Revolution, like all others, is radical and uncompromising, especially in times of crisis, engendering extreme measures whose results are sometimes deplorable. For the thousands of peasants who are political prisoners, the rehabilitation plan is at least a step in the direction of redressing the imbalance. Throughout their internship they are treated with unusual respect and even understanding. They do not live in cells under armed guard or march in formation or perform dirty menial tasks. Their life is healthy, they eat well, they obtain an education, learn an occupation, and they are allowed to go home unshepherded every seven weeks. They are set free after serving a fraction of their sentence. And a genuine effort is made to see to it that they are reintegrated into society without prejudice.

SOME PRISONERS

Following are notes on conversations I had with prisoners in rehabilitation centers in Miramar, Pinar del Río, and on the Isle of Pines.

Man with a horse, Sandino, Pinar del Río. He came originally from Las Villas Province. Sentenced for two years, now already at liberty. "I was taken because I saw a man who was a counterrevolutionary, he had fled, and I didn't report it." His family lives in a new house in Sandino City. He likes life there so much that he gave up another, better job as head of a dairy because it would not have permitted him to live in Sandino.

In the prison. Man seated on underneath bunk. He is from the Escambray Mountains, an illiterate. His sentence is for five years. Has been in rehabilitation camp twenty-three months.

"What was your crime?"

"My problem was that I gave dinner to three bandits in the mountains. I didn't know them and I didn't know who they were, but afterward I found out they were counterrevolutionaries."

"Don't you think your punishment is unjust? That seems like a very small crime."

"Well, they treat me very well, but I think it was unjust for what I did. But at least I see my family in Miramar every forty-five days."

"Do you consider yourself a revolutionary now?"

"*Bueno*, I don't consider myself a revolutionary or not a revolutionary. I don't know anything about politics. I am here twenty-three months, and I don't know anything about the Revolution now any more than before."

"What kind of work do you do here?"

"I work planting maize, also on the tobacco farm. In the mountains I was a coffee worker."

In a prison, man writing letter on top bunk.

"How do you like it here?"

"*Bueno*, very well, I feel fine, I am treated well. As long as I am doing work I feel all right. The only thing is being separated from my family."

"How many children have you?"

"Five, señor."

"Whom are you writing to?"

"My sister."

"Where are you from?"

"Pinar del Río Province—San Juan y Martínez."

"What is your sentence?"

"Five years."

"What did you do that was wrong?"

"I joined a counterrevolutionary movement. I didn't do anything though, I just joined. It was only that a man came up to me and said, 'Would you like to join this thing?' And I said, "No, *chico*, I don't want to have anything to do with political things,' and he said, 'No, wait a minute—you don't have to worry, there's nothing to do, all we need is your name and your father's name.' So I gave him my name, and later it was found, and I was taken and I was given a trial and a sentence, and that is how I am here."

"Don't you think that five years in jail is a pretty stiff sentence for doing only that?"

After thinking it over a while. "Well, I was guilty. I gave my name. I think my sentence is a stiff one, but I'm healthy, that's the main thing, and I'm working. I mind being away from my family though. That's the unfair thing. It's hard."

"Do you feel any differently now about the Revolution than before you were taken?"

"Yes. We read a book which explains everything."

"Why did you join the counterrevolution in the first place? What did you have against the Revolution?"

"*Bueno*, sometimes you do things without thinking. Things seem much clearer to me now, and now I feel myself in favor in the Revolution. I have learned the true background of how things are."

A doctor from Oriente Province. He was working as physician in the camp dispensary, also helping out at a nearby hospital.

"What was your crime?"

"I was a doctor in Puerto Padre, in Oriente. My problem was that my wife left me and went to Canada, taking my daughter, and I went a little crazy. I tried to go to the States from Oriente in a small boat, and they caught me. I was sentenced for five years."

"How long have you been here?"

"Twenty-seven months. I am going to be leaving in a few days, I don't know when. Now I have a fiancée in Puerto Padre, and we are going to be married two weeks after I get home. I feel as though I have been given a chance at a whole new life. It's an amazing experience."

"Do you feel any differently about the Revolution now than you did when you went to jail?"

"Look, I never was a counterrevolutionary. The Revolution never touched me with a rose petal."

"Do you consider yourself a revolutionary now?"

"Not now, but perhaps some day. I know now that the Revolution has benefited the majority of people in Cuba."

The doctor didn't know it yet, but he was going to be released the next morning. Moreover, he had invited all the officials of the prison to his wedding, and, although Puerto Padre is at the other end of Cuba, all those who could be spared actually attended the ceremony three weeks later.

One afternoon while I was staying with Castro at his house on the Isle of Pines, he made a spur-of-the-moment jeep tour of some of the *granjas,* in the course of which he stopped for about half an hour at a prison camp. He went into one of the barracks where the men were resting (it was a Saturday afternoon) and held an impromptu conversation with them.

Speaking, besides Castro, are Tarrado, the prison camp administrator, and various prisoners. Fidel, who does not know in detail how the rehabilitation program works, has been asking Tarrado questions about working hours, study time, and passes. At this point one of the prisoners breaks in.

PRISONER: The pass is the best reward that a *reeducando* can get!
FIDEL: Which pass? The pass for the street? [Castro, himself an ex-prisoner, is using convict slang. "The street" is the same as "the outside" in United States prison jargon.]
TARRADO: Yes, that of the street. He can go in the street to see his family.

PRISONER: That is the greatest thing!

FIDEL: For how long?

TARRADO: It depends; for example, to Santiago de Cuba we give them one hundred and twenty hours.

FIDEL: Every how often?

TARRADO: Every forty-five days.

FIDEL: When they go, the expenses are paid by . . . ?

TARRADO: We pay the travel expenses.

PRISONER: Some men just came back from pass.

TARRADO: This one just arrived. Where were you?

PRISONER (*very excited*): In Matanzas!

TARRADO: What was your impression of Matanzas?

PRISONER: No, no, fantastic! The street is just the greatest! (*The other prisoners laugh.*)

TARRADO: How long was it since you had been in Matanzas?

PRISONER: Five years—I thought I was going to die!

TARRADO: And your family—?

PRISONER: My family—*Ave María! Bueno*, to tell the truth I'm a little nervous. (*Laughter.*)

FIDEL: How did you feel, having contact with the street for the first time?

PRISONER: No, no, very well, the people very happy and all.

FIDEL: How are they treated?

PRISONER: Well! Well! Now I'm thinking of getting married! I brought a letter for El Señor Director of the Plan.

FIDEL: Yes? But a fiancée from before, no?

PRISONER: Yes, *Compañero Comandante*. For years I have everything arranged, and now on my second pass I'm thinking to get married. Maybe they'll give me seven days, or whatever.

OTHER PRISONER: You weren't supposed to be back until nine o'clock tonight!

PRISONER: Yes, I wasn't supposed to get back till nine o'clock tonight, and I've been here since this morning! (*Laughter.*)

FIDEL: This was your first time out?

PRISONER: The first time, yes. But listen to me, the street—it's terrible! Look, I'm not allowed to drink in the street, but—all the beer you could drink, and sandwiches, and the people with their little bags for the beach! I came back here with regret, sincerely! (*Laughter.*)

FIDEL: I'm going to tell you something. There still aren't many things, but there will be, because what is going on here on the Isle of Pines is happening all over the country. The abundance we are going to have of milk and food—

PRISONER (*interrupting*): I said, "Well, Fidel talks about bourgeoisie, and what we have in the house is bourgeoisie." (*Laughter.*) I saw meat, I saw rice, I saw crabs, they gave me crabs in my house and eggs and everything, milk too. And the way it was there, they didn't give me just a little of anything. I filled myself up and had a quantity of things.

FIDEL: But there still isn't enough. There will be more, because we're just getting started. In this country we still don't produce enough so that everyone can eat. That's what we're after.

PRISONER (*philosophically*): Well, we'll have what we'll have.

FIDEL: I'm going to give you people some idea. For instance, we are going to put forty thousand cows on the Isle of Pines. . . . [Castro goes on to cite figures on how milk production on the island is to be expanded.]

What we want—I think that you will understand it in time; it will cost a little more effort—what we want is the best solution, a solution that can be useful both for yourselves and for the country. I think that ever since we began we have been occupied in improving all the plans, because men who are in jails create nothing.

ANOTHER PRISONER: What's not good for one is not good for everybody else.

FIDEL: Now, the living conditions here are much different. Here one lives a little more comfortably than they live back there in the *circular*.*

PRISONER: No, what—in the jail? It's terrible in there!

FIDEL: And also the work. It's not the same there as being here in the countryside, really working now, and making progress. When one sees that he is learning, that he's advancing—he was in the second grade before and now he's in the sixth, and his buddy has gone even further—he knows that there is a prospect for the future which is good both for yourselves and for the country. And that's what we're after.

I think some of you could get to be technicians or engineers. We'll give you the same facilities we give to a worker who wants to study. We have ten thousand workers in technological institutes now. An adult man studying hard can get from the second grade to the eighth grade in two years, studying all the time and working at the same time. . . .

In any event, you have to adapt yourselves to reality. You were thinking in a way different from ours, you were thinking different things, and time will tell who is right. What has been created in the midst of the struggle, as a result of the Revolution, you will under-

* *Colloquial name for the notorious, centuries-old circular prison on the Isle of Pines.*

stand better in time. But this is a way out, a way out of a situation.

A man here can, by studying hard, make himself an engineer and go on to a much better future with much more personal satisfaction than the man who gets hold of a boat and takes off for Miami. Positively, positively, what I'm saying is so. How are all those people who left doing now? Only those who had money don't have any problems. You have a copy of the book *Bajo Palabrea?* *

PRISONER: Here's somebody who has it.

OTHER PRISONER: They loaned it to me.

FIDEL: Doesn't it explain pretty well how things are over there?

OTHER PRISONER (*after a long pause, apologetically*): I came this morning from the street, and I'm still nervous.

FIDEL: Put the idea in your head that you are a student. From now on, don't think like a prisoner, but get the idea into your head that you are on a scholarship, that you are a student.

Men who improve themselves, who acquire a technical education here, I am sure they are going to be treated with great respect out in the street. . . . People esteem the man who improves himself, who comes with a second-grade education and leaves with a level of precollege technician. This produces admiration in everybody in the street, and people are going to take that more into account than the fact that he was a prisoner. Anyone who treats you badly is not a revolutionary, but a counterrevolutionary. . . .

ANOTHER PRISONER JUST RETURNED: When I was going down the highway, from one side to the other all I could see was *marabú*, *marabú* [a kind of cattle pasture], and *malanga, malanga, malanga*, and I said: "What is this, *caballero!*"

FIDEL: But it isn't enough, because people are eating more than what there is.

PRISONER: How they eat!

FIDEL: This is a poor country, not a rich one. It used to have a rich façade, but what did the worker who cut cane and produced the money actually have? . . . The workers didn't share the profits that came into this country, and they still have little, because those who now have the most are the people of Havana: amusements, possibilities for study.

There are still many shacks. What are we going to do? There isn't enough cement. People in the countryside now have work all year round, but they still go several years without having their own homes. . . . Now we are going to build a brick factory on the Isle of Pines,

---

* A book about the life of Cuban exiles in Miami as seen through the eyes of a woman, Marta A. Gonzalez, who lived there three years and then returned to Cuba.

and we are going to start constructing two thousand cottages a year for those who want to stay here and work, including those who are in the rehabilitation plans.

PRISONER: This is voluntary?

FIDEL: Of course.

PRISONER: Because I don't want to stay here and work.

FIDEL: You are from the city?

PRISONER: No . . . from Carlos Rojas, in the country.

FIDEL: We're not trying to convince anybody to stay. Only if he falls in love with the idea. The only ones we want to stay here are those who fall in love with it, just as you did with your fiancée. (*Laughter.*) We're not going to make a campaign to keep people here. There are many soldiers who have stayed, they've gotten married. They look for the wife and build the house.

OTHER PRISONER: *Comandante*, I promise that when they give me liberty, if they give me the materials I promise to build my house.

FIDEL: You can go wherever you like.

THE SPECIAL PLAN FOR CAMPESINOS

Of all the rehabilitation plans, the most interesting and by far the most ambitious is that known as the "Special Plan for *Campesinos*," which works simultaneously but separately with both the prisoners and their families. While their husbands are in jail or prison camp, the wives and children, under the Special Plan, are moved from their rural villages to a series of houses in a suburb of Havana. Here they stay, also undergoing a form of "rehabilitation," until the husbands are set free.

The Special Plan, or "Plan Number Two" as it is also called, had its genesis as a result of Castro's campaigns to wipe out the counter-revolutionary bands which operated in the mountain regions of Las Villas and Pinar del Río provinces from shortly after the Bay of Pigs invasion until mid-1963. Because of the remoteness and inaccessibility of these regions, the "bandits" were able to survive for a long time unscathed, preying on the local peasantry for food, money and clothing. To flush them out, Castro finally took the expedient of methodically depopulating the areas adjacent to where the counterrevolutionaries were hiding. With their sources of supply thus dried up, the bands were gradually eliminated, and the peasants who had collaborated with them were tried, sentenced and sent to prison. To solve the problem of what to do with their now homeless families, Plan Number Two was created.

The unlikely geographical headquarters of Plan Number Two is Miramar, an elegant, sprawling suburb which stretches along the sea westward from Havana. Once the exclusive property of Havana's wealthy and fashionable upper middle class, its classic boulevards are straight, long and wide, lined with royal palm trees and divided by grassy malls landscaped with spreading shade trees and thick shrubbery manicured in odd shapes, like poodles' hair. Its secluded side streets are luxuriantly wooded with tall old trees: acacia, locust, Spanish oak, and others more exotic, indigenous only to Cuba. Its homes, many with their own swimming pools, vary in size from the comfortable to the sumptuous; in architecture, from neoclassical Roman to modern American; in taste, from elegant to ostentatious. Many are ornate replicas of Mediterranean villas.

Most of the former inhabitants of Miramar, "lackeys of imperialism" and "exploiters of the working class" as they are now remembered in postrevolutionary Cuba, have long since fled to the United States or abroad, ceding their property to the state. Their yacht clubs and private beaches, once the epicenter of the gayest and chicest party society of antebellum Havana, are now recreation clubs for workers and their families. The mansions of the moneyed have been transformed into dormitories for scholarship students and dwellings for more than one thousand *campesino* families of Plan Number Two for Peasants.

The houses of Plan Number Two are called *albergues* ("shelters"— undoubtedly there is intentional revolutionary irony in so naming them) and are scattered over a 160-block area of Miramar. The area is divided into seven zones, each containing between fifteen and twenty-five *albergues*, depending on their size (an *albergue* may house anywhere from thirty to one hundred fifty people). An effort is made to put people who come from the same village or region together in the same *albergue* or at least one nearby.

Plan Number Two is strictly a female society. Boys, upon reaching grade school age, leave the *albergue* to become *becados* (scholarship students) and are boarded in another part of Miramar. It is also administered by women, specially selected and trained members of the Federation of Cuban Women, a militant revolutionary organization whose founder and national president is Vilma Castro, the wife of Fidel's brother, Raúl.

For a peasant family coming directly from a mountain village where they have spent all their lives to the sophisticated environs of Miramar, the Plan is in itself a revolutionary experience and sometimes a traumatic one. Plan officials take great pains to ease the shock of transition from the moment of their arrival. After moving into an *albergue*, where they are introduced to the other residents and given a room of their own—two if they need it (the average family number in an *albergue* is four, but may be as high as ten)—the entire family is taken to the Plan's clothing supply store. There each member is issued a complete outfit of clothing—dresses, underwear, shoes, sneakers, even toys for the children. All of this is given free. The supervisor of their *albergue* and the leader of the zone in which it is located are both on hand to help the women overcome their shyness and to see to it that they and their children try everything on. Because there are so many things that the peasants haven't seen before—brassieres, for example, are examined with expressions of puzzlement and doubt— this process usually takes several hours. After a timid beginning, helped and encouraged by Plan officials, the women eventually succumb to the apparently universal feminine delight in shopping for new clothes.

The director of Plan Two for Peasants is a bright, vigorous woman of thirty-two known simply by her first name, Lucy. Like Castro and many of the Revolution's leaders, Lucy is from Oriente Province, the daughter of a middle-class family who rebelled against her background and has become a dedicated Marxist revolutionary. With the help of a staff of competent and fiercely loyal women assistants, many of them volunteers, Lucy runs Plan Two with an organizational efficiency rare in Cuba. She herself works a normal eighteen hours a day and is in continual motion, moving from one *albergue* to another, supervising everything, checking on problems, hearing complaints, and explaining the philosophy of the plan to the peasants in simple, understandable words imbued with an apostolic fervor. Wherever she goes, the women flock around her and greet her with hugs and kisses which she returns with unfeigned tenderness. In her sense of total commitment and selfless dedication, Lucy personifies many of the best qualities of the Cuban Revolution.

From the moment they enter Plan Number Two, the mountain women spend most of their time being educated in one way or another. They are given careful instruction in how to dress themselves, in cooking, washing, housecleaning, hygiene for themselves and their children. They are taught how to put on make-up. There is a beauty parlor where they have their hair done (free) once a week. Each day, while the children are in school and the toddlers in special nurseries, the women attend primary grade school classes in one of two separate schools for adults. There are special literacy classes for those who cannot read or write. In the afternoon they study. Just as in the prison camps where their husbands are, once or twice a week in the evenings a Plan instructor conducts an informal political discussion with the women of each *albergue*. The text, usually drawn from the newspapers, is often a recent speech by Castro. These ideological discussions are rudimentary and not very effectual. The wives have even less interest in political matters than their husbands.

As in other plans, the husbands come from the prison camps to visit their families once every forty-five days. (Those still in jail do not have that privilege until they get to the prison camp.) There are special *albergues*, called marital pavilions, where husbands and wives spend the nights together. During the days, they stay at the *albergue* with their families, taking all their meals with them there. Every three months, Plan families are taken back to their villages in the mountains for a week-long stay with their relatives. Relatives can visit them in Miramar whenever they wish.

The goal of all the women, of course, is to leave the Plan and be reunited with their husbands. Unlike the other plans, under Plan Number Two, families who complete rehabilitation may not return to their home towns but are resettled in a new city in Pinar del Río Province called Sandino City. Each family is given a new home with two to four bedrooms, furniture, linens, dishes, kitchenware, a ten-day supply of food, even pictures for the walls. The husbands work at jobs on neighboring *granjas*. The wives are also given jobs in Sandino if they are able to work.

The wife is made to understand that she can help her husband (and herself) to be released sooner through her own efforts. One way is by joining the Plan branch of the Federation of Cuban Women. In fact, since practically all the women belong to it, she can scarcely avoid joining. (At the time of my visit there were 1,500 women in the Plan, of whom 1,000 belonged to the Federation.) The *federadas* have a good time, participating in activities and skits and cheers and songfests much like those one would find at an American girls' summer camp. There is also, amid the gaiety, a great deal of slogan-shouting and ideological word-parroting in Federation assemblies—a fact which I found disquieting. I doubted whether more than a handful of the *guajiras* whom I heard singing "The International" at the top of their lungs really understood what the words meant. Subsequent conversations with some of them confirmed that suspicion.

"We know that the motive of the majority of the women who join the Federation is to help get their husband out of prison and go with him into a new house," Lucy told me. "But we take advantage of that fact. We feel sure that they will eventually be wholehearted members of the Federation and supporters of the Revolution."

Each month, the status and behavior of both husband and wife are reviewed by the respective authorities for signs of progress. Egress from the plan comes, on the average, after 25 percent of the sentence has been served, although a family must spend a minimum of one year in the Plan.

At the time I visited Sandino City about four hundred families had already moved in. The city was still very much under construction;

some of the main buildings, such as the school and the assembly hall, had not yet been completed. Hundreds of additional homes were also in the process of being built, and new streets were being graded and tarred. The houses, of cement-block construction, seemed well built, if rather plain. The families I visited seemed happy enough in their new environment, although there were some exceptions, older people who badly missed their mountain homes. I noticed too that, despite all the careful training the women had been given in such matters as cleanliness and grooming during their stay in Miramar, many had already reverted to the habits of their former rural life. Some wives had already stopped doing their hair and shaving their legs, others seemed no longer to care how neat their clothes or their homes looked, and there were young children running around outside without any clothing on at all.

Political prisoners planting citrus trees, Isle of Pines

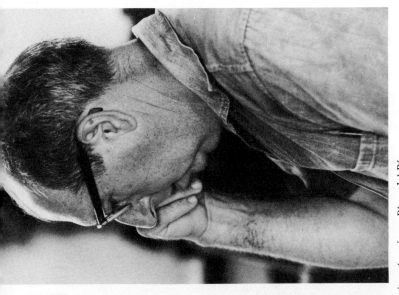

Political prisoners in the barracks of a prison farm, Pinar del Río

Dropping in unexpectedly, Castro holds an impromptu discussion with prisoners undergoing rehabilitation in their Isle of Pines barracks

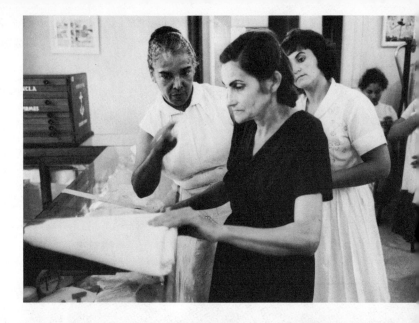

A new family enters the Plan. Coming from the mountains of Las Villas, they have never been to a city before. At the Plan's commissary, Mercedes (Right), their zone leader, helps the mother pick out cloth for a dress she will make, while two of her children (she has six others) play in dazzled excitement with their new toys

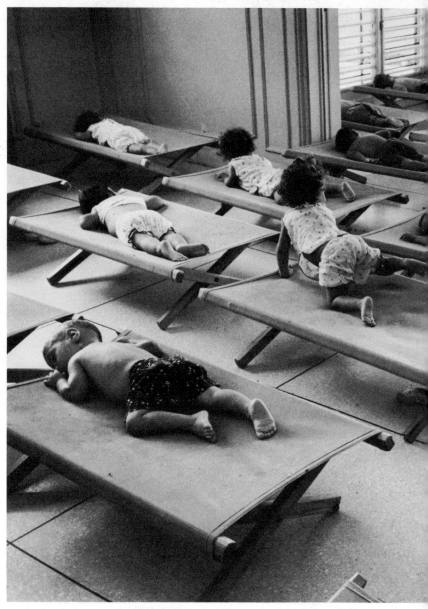

Nurseries for infants run by the Plan free the mothers for work and study

Nursery school in Plan Number Two. Similar centers for toddlers and infants are operated by the government throughout Cuba for working mothers who pay only nominal fees

The bedroom of a Plan Number Two wife

The Plan makes an undisguised effort to imbue the women with revolutionary fervor. The area of Plan Number Two is divided into six zones, which compete for the highest percentage of membership in the Cuban Federation of Women—a militant, nationwide organization headed by Vilma Castro (Raúl Castro's wife)

A common wedding. Formerly, most mountain couples in Cuba did not marry. Today, the state encourages them to legalize their relationships (and, often, their large families) by providing, on certain holidays each year, special communal weddings for all who wish them. There is no religious service, only a registration ceremony. The state also provides a wedding cake, drinks and entertainment, new clothes, and a three-day paid honeymoon. For these separated couples of Plan Number Two, this is an added attraction

After completing rehabilitation, prisoners are reintegrated into Cuban society. Left: A "parolee," reunited with his family, works as a cowpuncher on a granja in Pinar del Río. Right: Although Plan Number Two women are taught hygiene and other civilized ways, many revert to customs of the mountains. This child in Sandino City has clothes, but wears only his new sneakers

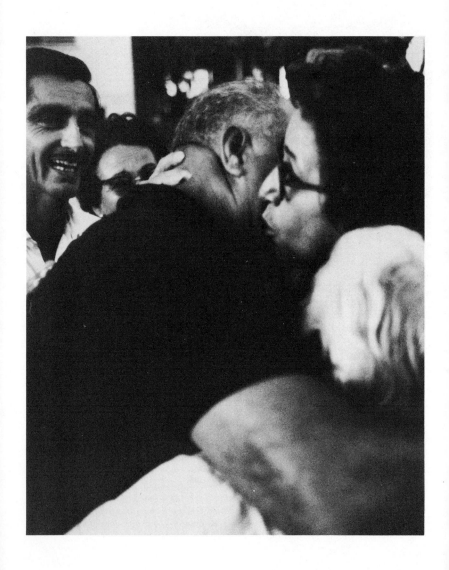

seven

Camarioca and the exodus

I had left Cuba in late August. At the beginning of October, Fidel Castro suddenly announced his willingness to be rid of all Cubans who wished to leave the country. In a move that caught the United States by surprise, Castro opened the small port of Camarioca as an emigration center to which Cuban exiles in America were invited to come in small boats to pick up their relatives and friends, and he announced his desire to negotiate with the U.S. Government for regular air lifts between Varadero Beach and Miami to take out the bulk of the refugees.

So, only six weeks after I had returned to New York, I was once again on my way to Cuba to report on the exodus for *Life* magazine.

This time, I had no problems about establishing contact. The evening I arrived, I had a late dinner with some friends and was getting undressed at about 1 A.M. when there was a knock on my door. It was Comandante Vallejo. He urged me to get back into my clothes and hurry downstairs; Castro was waiting in his car in front of the hotel to say hello.

I got into the back of his blue Oldsmobile next to Fidel, who greeted me cordially, and we drove toward the home of Osvaldo Dorticós, Cuba's President, with whom Castro had an appointment for an all-night working session.

As we rode through the nearly empty streets, Castro talked contentedly about the exodus, which had already begun from Camarioca, where hundreds of boats had arrived. Negotiations with the United States for the airlift, he said, were going "well but slowly," and it would be several days before one could expect any resolution. He personally was conducting the negotiations with Ernst Stadelhofer, the Swiss ambassador to Cuba, who represents United States' interests there. He was pleased to note that the exodus idea had had "a substantial echo" both within and outside Cuba.

At Dorticós' house we shook hands, and he got out, giving orders for the chauffeur to return me to the hotel. As he and Vallejo went up the walk, I saw lights being switched on inside the darkened house—apparently President Dorticós had taken the precaution of getting a few hours of sleep beforehand. Next day, Vallejo told me that Dorticós and Fidel had worked until 8 A.M.

For the next ten days I divided my time equally between Havana and Camarioca. Havana, like all Latin-American capitals, has a normally high decibel-level of nervous conversation, but now there was an atmosphere of heightened excitement, a genuine buzz in the air. In the streets, at the coffee stands, everywhere, people seemed to be talking about Camarioca, about the negotiations, about leaving. There seemed no fear of reprisal, for many families were openly making plans to go, so many in fact that Camarioca jokes had become the vogue of Havana. One morning, as I was setting out for Camarioca in a taxi rented from my hotel, another hotel cabbie pulled up next to us at a stoplight and admonished my driver, shaking a seriocomic finger at him: "Now, Paco, don't forget to come back!"

At the "International Port of Camarioca," a small fishing village located on a tiny inlet about seventy miles east of Havana, and not far from the beach resort of Varadero, things were, for Cuba, unusually well organized. Somehow, the harassed, overworked officials were managing to register and care for the Cuban exiles arriving on incoming boats, contact the relatives they had come to get, process them through once they arrived, and turn away others who wanted to go but had no authorization. They did so with a combination of unremitting politeness and gentle concern, in spite of an almost total lack of sleep and telephones that wouldn't stop ringing.

The scenes of reunion which I witnessed at Camarioca were such a heartbreaking combination of grief and joy as to make an outsider feel embarrassed to be watching, let alone photographing them. Cuban families, when they are separated, do not merely miss one another; they *hunger*. I saw many who had been separated four, five, and six years: fathers who had come for children whom they had left as babies and now found as tall boys and girls; sons returning for aging parents whom they had already given up hope of seeing alive again. These scenes were made all the more poignant by the realization that most families would still remain partly divided, for among them were numerous brothers, sisters, parents, or children who for one or another reason chose to stay in Cuba but had come to say a last, unexpected hello and good-by. One man who had come for his whole family discovered that none of them wanted to leave; he filled his boat with others. Another man left with his three children but without his wife.

But there was no lack of passengers for any empty spaces on the rickety boats that were leaving for Miami. Men, women, and children, from infants-in-arms to the halt and senile, passed docilely through the processing lines, let themselves be inspected for jewels and money, and clambered gratefully onto the boats without a word, blindly fearful that some official might change his mind and order them back. Once on the boat many women pulled crucifixes out of their bosoms and exposed them defiantly on their dresses.* Some fingered rosaries, mumbling the words through their tears. One old man of ninety-seven who was practically moribund with arteriosclerosis had to be carried on board his boat in a chair hoisted by four Ministry of the Interior officials. His condition was so bad that the Camarioca authorities felt obliged to announce over the loudspeakers the man's name, age and disease and that the Cuban government, having tried to dissuade him from sailing, now took no further responsibility for his welfare. His daughter, who had come from Miami to get him, said to me, "Better that he should die on the ocean than stay alive here in this lousy country." The old man was too ill to say anything.

For other Cubans not personally involved, Camarioca was little more than a spectacle. Every day, thousands of exodus-watchers stood four and five deep on the sidewalk of the bridge overlooking the harbor or lined the far bank, opposite the camp. Each time a boat arrived, they cheered. Each time a boat left, they cheered even more loudly. Their voices bubbled gaily; for all their festivity, they might have been spectators at a regatta. The fancier the boat that came in, or the more passengers it carried, the louder their cheers and applause. On weekends, families brought their children and picnic lunches and stayed all day.

The only official comment made by the authorities on the scene was a large billboard set in the bank of the harbor at a point where it had to be seen by all boats passing in or out. On it, in bright red letters, was printed a quotation from a Castro speech about Camarioca:

"In the years to come, how many will hope, how many will be weeping to return, to set foot again on the land which they betrayed and which they looked down upon."

Ten days passed before I again saw Castro, on a Tuesday, when I photographed him greeting U.S.S.R. Foreign Minister Andrei Gromyko at Havana's airport. Fidel held several talks with Gromyko that day and the next, most of them in private. The longest began before midnight on Wednesday and lasted until seven o'clock Thursday morning. The same morning, Castro rose after three hours' sleep,

---

* Though why they should have done so I don't know, since it is quite commonplace to see women wearing crucifixes in the streets in Cuba.

read the cables, had lunch, pitched a strenuous nine innings of baseball, met with some officials, and went at eight o'clock to the Havana soccer stadium to preside at the opening of a week-long convention of the Cuban Union of Young Communists, to which I also went separately as a photographer.

It had been raining intermittently all day. As the delegations of youthful athletes and gymnasts from the various provinces exercised and maneuvered in unison on the field, earnestly emulating a ritual that has become *de rigueur* for Communist youth groups all over the world, the rain began to fall in torrents again. By the time Castro left the stands and descended to the field to address the crowd and a national TV audience, the deluge had knocked out the loudspeaker system. For fifteen minutes Castro and a dozen other high Cuban officials were required to stand unprotected on the platform in the center of the field while the trouble was being located and fixed.

It was too wet to take pictures, so I left early with a Cuban photographer who was fortunate enough to have a car. He took me to his penthouse apartment in Vedado which he, his wife, and their two children shared with his parents and a friend. We dried off and sat watching Fidel on television (barely visible in the rain) while we drank up a few bottles of Czechoslovakian pilsner beer. In the next room, I could hear members of his family and their friends discussing plans for going to Miami.

It was 1:30 A.M. when I returned to my hotel. There was a note in my box from Vallejo saying to be ready, a car would be coming to pick me up. I went to my room. A few moments later the phone rang.

"Lee, I am one of Vallejo's men. I have the car for you; we are waiting in the lobby."

I explained that my cameras were soaked, and that if there was no hurry I would like another five minutes to finish drying them.

"Okay. Take your time—there's no hurry," the man said. "We will be waiting."

Ten minutes later I emerged from the elevator into the cavernous lobby, deserted except for the two bodyguards in green fatigues lounging against the bell captain's booth. I stopped and slapped my head in dismay.

"What's the matter?" one asked.

"I left my damn light meter in the room. Do I have time to get it?"

"Sure. There's no hurry—go ahead," the guard said, lighting a cigarette.

On the tenth floor, as I was unlocking the door to my room, the phone began to ring.

"Lee," said the same voice. "Hurry up."

"I'll be right down, but you said there was no hurry."

"I said that. But Vallejo says that there *is* a hurry," the guard answered matter-of-factly.

"Vallejo? Why didn't you tell me Vallejo was there?" I dropped the phone, found the light meter, and raced for the elevator.

The two guards escorted me quickly through the glass doors. Outside at the curb was not one, but the entire fleet of Oldsmobiles lined up, headlights dark and motors idling. As we approached, the drivers flashed their beams on one after the other and revved the engines. Vallejo stepped from one of the cars and held the door for me. In the back was Fidel, calmly puffing a cigar. I had unknowingly kept him waiting twenty minutes.

He seemed not to mind. As we drove down the driveway ramp of the hotel and headed for the suburbs, he began talking about how hard it had rained earlier, during his speech. Afterward he had gone home to change into dry clothes and have something to eat. "Now," he said, "we are on our way to pick up 'El Suizo'" ("The Swiss," Castro's more or less affectionate title for the Swiss ambassador).

"Tonight we are going to have our most decisive meeting. El Suizo has his instructions from Washington, Cuba has prepared all her points concisely, and I think at last we are about to reach an agreement."

The only problem, Castro went on, rubbing his chin, was that he couldn't decide where the meeting ought to be held. "We don't know exactly what to do with El Suizo. He will certainly invite us into the embassy or the residence and offer us something to eat and drink. But we would rather not do that . . . it is not Cuban ground. On the other hand, we could take him to my office in the Ministry, which would be logical from the standpoint of protocol. But I don't like protocol very much. So the question is, what to do with him? And I was thinking, perhaps the best thing would be something very friendly and informal, such as going somewhere to have a cup of coffee, or perhaps just riding around in the car like this, and talking, riding around Havana. . . ."

I put in, "Well, if it doesn't make any difference to you, from the standpoint of photography I would certainly prefer a cup of coffee in some restaurant to a ride in the back of a dark car."

Fidel thought it over. Finally, he said, "Yes . . . you know, I can see that that would make a very interesting photograph." He began to imagine it as if he were a picture editor sending me off on an assignment and telling me what to look for. "The two of us just sitting there in public . . . in a public restaurant . . . very inconspicuous . . .

2 A.M., still a few people around . . . a peaceful conversation set in the ambience of a typical Cuban place, very relaxed . . . yes, it could be an important picture. I must first ask El Suizo if he agrees, of course."

Ambassador Stadelhofer, an affable, pigeon-shaped man with the suave equanimity of the professional diplomat, approved of the idea at once and looked pleased. I got into another car, while he took my seat beside Castro. For a few minutes we circled around Marianao, the posh Havana suburb in which most of the embassies are located, looking for a restaurant open at that hour. Finally we swung across the avenue and halted in front of an all-night pizzeria. It had a dining terrace, open on all sides but covered by a red canopied roof. The décor was modern and pleasant. There were perhaps two dozen people sitting at various tables. They seemed singularly unruffled at the appearance of the Prime Minister, hardly looking up from their beer and pasta as the two men walked through to the rear and sat down at a table. Members of the bodyguard unobtrusively took up positions at other tables at a respectful distance from them, while others kept watch outside the restaurant.

Both men drew papers from their inside pockets and laid them on the table. Immediately, as if on cue, they began talking with serious expressions and earnest gestures. Each drank a cup of coffee. Castro smoked one long cigar, which outlasted half a pack of Ambassador Stadelhofer's Marlboros. The conversation lasted about an hour and a half. The pizzeria's name, appropriately, was Il Mare Aperto—"The Open Sea."

Later, riding home from the ambassador's residence, Castro confirmed that the negotiations had gone as he had planned. "This meeting has been decisive. All obstacles for the flights are now disposed of." He seemed happy and also, at last, a bit tired. A little after 4 A.M., he dropped me off at my hotel and went home to sleep.

Just twenty-four hours later I accompanied Ambassador Stadelhofer, at his invitation, to a small military airport at Baracoa. After being twice misdirected to wrong sections of the airport, we found the ambassador's plane, a four-engine Russian transport with Cubana Airlines markings. It was still in its hangar, being readied for his flight. El Suizo stood watching the airport workmen pulling the chocks from the wheels and rolling the gangway up to the Ilyushin's high door and sighed: "Here I am, the Swiss ambassador to Cuba. But I represent the interests of the United States here, and now I am getting onto a Russian plane to fly to Nassau, a British island, where I will be met by an American jet which will take me to Washington. Ach, what a crazy world!" With that, he shook hands correctly with each of his assistants and boarded the plane.

Sunday morning, a car picked me up and took me to a ball park at an army camp outside of Havana where Fidel was playing. There were about a hundred spectators, mainly soldiers and their wives or girl friends, watching delightedly as Castro, in gay spirits, pitched and batted and jockeyed raucously from the bench and clowned hugely with players and audience alike. Though Fidel takes baseball seriously (like everything else), it is not one of the sports at which he is most talented. He throws sidearm, with good control but with not very much on the ball. There isn't much difference between his fast ball and his curve. Both are what the players call "fat pitches," and this time, as on every other occasion I have seen him play, he was clobbered unmercifully. Yet he stayed in there—what manager would dare yank Fidel Castro? At the end of nine innings his team was behind by something like 11 to 2, so he pitched two more innings. Ramiro Valdez, the short, compact, sinister-looking G-2 chief of Cuba, whose wispy, pointed beard gives him the appearance of a large gnome, ragged the *Jefe* from the sidelines and begged him to let him pitch. Castro pretended to ignore him. "Come on, Fidel," Valdez called. "Let me play. I'm a much better pitcher than you are!"

After the game I rode back in an abbreviated caravan to Castro's apartment house, a heavily guarded, four-story building on a side street in Vedado. With him and Vallejo, I climbed the three flights to his apartment, the closest thing to a home that he has anywhere. It was a suite of rooms of modest size, fairly modern, functional and airy, but rather spartanly furnished. The walls of the main room were covered with blond wood paneling. Halfway up to the ceiling a platform had been constructed, with access via a wooden ladder, on which could be seen a desk and a chair. This was meant to be Castro's office, but, Vallejo told me, he has never used it. A few chairs and tables, a small dining area, some shelves laden with books and bric-a-brac, and one or two prints on the wall completed the trappings of the Prime Minister's home. A door from the dining room led out onto a large, square open terrace which was obviously the Prime Minister's exercise area. The floor was covered with wooden planking, and a regulation basketball net with a backboard was hung on the wall at one end. At the other end there was an impressive array of physical fitness and sports equipment: weights, dumbbells, a rowing machine, a trampoline, a rack containing baseballs, bats, and gloves, etc. Most of it had the appearance of frequent use.

Fidel motioned me into a chair and himself collapsed into a reclining posture chair upholstered in the skin of some spotted animal, a leopard perhaps. The hide was worn thin, and the footrest had been broken and then badly repaired, so that his boots rested on it slightly askew. Fidel unbuttoned his fatigue shirt. He was still perspiring and breathing heavily from the exertion of the game. On the wall directly over his head was a framed color print of one of the startling Keane portraits of children: a little girl in a flowing dress with huge, round, inky, haunted eyes.

LOCKWOOD: Why have you suddenly decided to allow Cubans to go to the United States?

CASTRO: The Cuban government has always had the same policy since the beginning of the Revolution of allowing those who want to leave the country to do so freely. Under that policy, tens of thousands of Cubans left Cuba every year, from 1959 until 1962. Right after the Missile Crisis of October 1962, the United States government canceled daily flights between the United States and Cuba and refused to re-open them, although we protested, because it created an abnormal situation. At the time of the cancellation there were about one hundred thousand applications for visas to go to the United States. Many others had already received their visas from the United States. These were families who had one foot in Cuba and one foot in the United States. Some had part of their relatives here and part there. Some had sent their children, expecting to follow. Others, who had visas, had already given up their jobs when the flights were canceled and now they couldn't go to the U.S.A.

The United States not only canceled flights between Miami and Cuba, it also exerted all kinds of pressure on Mexico and Spain to cancel their air service to Cuba. These were the only ones that continued, in spite of the pressure. During the last three years as many people have been leaving Cuba by these routes as there have been flights and seats for them. So we categorically deny that we are instituting a new policy.

LOCKWOOD: But why right now? What is the reason for the timing of your opening Camarioca and proposing an airlift to the United States?

CASTRO: There's no special timing. I want to explain something very important. In the beginning after the Revolution, America did everything possible to encourage the highest number of people to leave Cuba, both as a propagandistic move against the Revolution and to drain the country of its technicians and qualified personnel.

Apparently, the moment came when the United States felt this was no longer a good policy. After the October Crisis, they decided it was a better policy to prevent people from leaving, based on the hope of an internal uprising taking place in Cuba. This was a change in tactics, not to try to solve the Cuban problem from outside but from within. It was accompanied by intensive activity of trying to organize counterrevolutionary movements inside Cuba, as well as introducing tremendous amounts of arms and weapons.

Now, after three years, that policy has been a complete failure. The fact that the United States has accepted Cuba's proposal for an airlift is related to the fact that their hopes of fomenting an internal uprising here have now been abandoned. So it is not Cuba who is changing her policy, but the United States who is changing her policy, for the third time.

LOCKWOOD: Do you think that among those who are leaving now are many who are potential counter-revolutionaries?

CASTRO: No. The activity of the counterrevolution has pretty well diminished. Undoubtedly, a portion of those leaving could potentially be used in this kind of service. But many others of those leaving are not at all against the Revolution. There are cases of people who have relatives in the States and see no alternative but to leave the country. There are cases where influential members of a family are counterrevolutionary and take with them people who in some way depend on them, but these don't go to the United States happily. There are some cases where the wives are counterrevolutionary and exert tremendous pressure on their weak husbands to go. Sometimes it is the reverse. And there are cases of people who remain neutral, although in a revolution there are very few people who remain neutral. In such cases, the preoccupation that takes them there is economic. Maybe they have always dreamed of going to the United States but couldn't do it before. Before, many people wanted to go there to make more money. You can't pretend that the United States is not a highly industrialized, economically developed country, and that this is not the case with Cuba. The U.S.A. uses immigration from Cuba as a political weapon. However, historically, the United States has always been forced to establish restrictions, since people from many countries with lower living standards would like to go there as immigrants. And I can tell you one thing: if before the Revolution the United States had permitted free entrance of Cuban citizens without restrictions, a much larger number would have gone then than the total of all those who have left since the Revolution or who will in the future. To what other underdeveloped country in this hemisphere has the United States offered its citizens an opportunity to immigrate freely? Any other Latin-American country to which it made such an offer would empty out overnight.

LOCKWOOD: What kind of people have already left Cuba, from 1959 until now?

CASTRO: They were not those whom we consider to be among the best citizens of the country. Of course, many who would not otherwise

291

have left had to do so because of the Revolution, those who belonged to the richest element of the population. In addition, many have gone who couldn't adapt themselves to the Revolution—self-employed people, people with economic ambitions, small businessmen, and also many who were "parasites," making their living from gambling, drug traffic, and prostitution. And also some technicians who were concentrated in Havana and wouldn't have worked in the interior of the country. Their departure had little effect. But those who formerly lived the worst here have not left: the sugar-cane cutters, for example, those who do the hardest work and also the most productive. There are a few exceptions, of course.

LOCKWOOD: How many people do you think will leave under the new arrangement?

CASTRO: We have our data and the Americans have theirs. Ours is based on the number who had requested permission to leave when the flights to the United States were canceled after the October Crisis. I would say that the number—depending of course on the propaganda, because if we made a big campaign here to influence as many as possible to leave, the number would of course be greater—I would say between one hundred thousand and one hundred fifty thousand people. That is, between one and two percent of the population. In any case, the number they are talking about in the United States of three hundred fifty thousand is exaggerated.*

LOCKWOOD: But suppose that it turns out to be a much larger number than you expect. Would you take steps to keep some people from leaving?

CASTRO: Ah, you can be sure that if it should be two hundred thousand, three hundred thousand, half a million, or even a million, we will adhere to our stated policy, because it is based on a revolutionary conviction we have always had about what we want to do in this country, that is, to have a society of free men and women who desire to live here voluntarily under a new social form. We are Marxist revolutionaries, and as such the frontiers of our feelings are not determined by geographic boundaries. We conceive of society as divided into classes . . . men are divided into the exploiters and the exploited. Those who are exploited are our compatriots all over the world; and the exploiters all over the world are our enemies. We feel more sympathy for a poor, exploited Negro in the South of the United

* By mid-1968, approximately one hundred thousand Cubans had arrived in the U.S. via the Varadero-Miami airlift. At least another one hundred thousand, and perhaps twice that number, were on the list and awaiting clearance to leave. A recent ruling compels all able-bodied men and women to work in agriculture while awaiting their turn to leave.

States than for a rich Cuban. Our country is really the whole world, and all the revolutionaries of the world are our brothers. That is our conviction.

There are some people who have some illusions about the Cuban Revolution because tens of thousands of people have chosen not to live under socialism. What they forget is that millions of our citizens will never leave their country or change their way of life. The idea of going to the United States has always been a big attraction for a certain number of people because it is the wealthiest nation in the world. However, in spite of the fact that we are still poor and under-developed, the overwhelming majority of our men and women will never abandon their country. So—we'll see. I will not say that all who stay will be with the Revolution. But something which no one can deny is that the great majority of the population supports the Revolution. They are prepared to make great sacrifices, to give their lives for the Revolution. I would ask you how many who live in the United States would be willing to give their lives for capitalism or for representative democracy?

LOCKWOOD: Is the fact that you have initiated negotiations on this particular question an indication that you desire to have better relations with the United States in general?

CASTRO: Really, it shouldn't be interpreted that way. We cannot be idealists or illusionaries. The tensions that exist between the United States and Cuba are based on facts and circumstances much more profound and can't in any way be influenced by this particular situation. It might establish some sort of formal precedent. But at bottom the differences between us are based on the policy that the United States is carrying on all over the world. As long as that policy doesn't change, the tensions between Cuba and the United States cannot be lessened.

LOCKWOOD: Do you enjoy negotiating with the Swiss ambassador?

CASTRO: The Swiss ambassador is a skillful diplomat, intelligent, tenacious; and I think he's a very well-intentioned man. He always does his best on a matter he considers useful and positive.

LOCKWOOD: In other words, a professional diplomat.

CASTRO (*laughing*): Yes. The Swiss have a long tradition in diplomacy, to be sure. One must not forget that the ambassador is a Swiss ambassador, with all the diplomatic skills which Switzerland has developed through the centuries. . . . I think El Suizo represents the United States' interests in Cuba much better than any of the former American ambassadors. In my opinion, he's much more intelligent than the American ambassadors whom I have known. Above all, he discusses things objectively, the opposite of the Americans, who have a tendency to speak with a certain air of superiority. Maybe it would be a good idea for the United States to let the Swiss be their ambassadors everywhere. They'd be more successful, probably.

As we were saying good-by, I asked Fidel if he would autograph something for me.

"Certainly," he said. "What is it?"

I handed him a one-peso note of Revolutionary scrip, printed in red and black, the colors of Castro's now-defunct rebel 26th of July movement. During the time he was in the mountains, his underground had printed and sold such currency to raise money for the Revolution.

He looked at it with astonishment. "Who gave you this?" he asked.

"No one gave it to me. I bought it for a dollar, in 1958."

Fidel flattened it out against the wall with his left hand and signed and dated it. "You'd better be careful and not show this to anyone when you get back to the States—they're liable to accuse you of having given money to support a Communist revolution."

"But I didn't know that it was going to turn out to be a Communist revolution when I bought it," I replied.

Fidel laughed and handed me the bill. "You know something?" he said. "Neither did I."

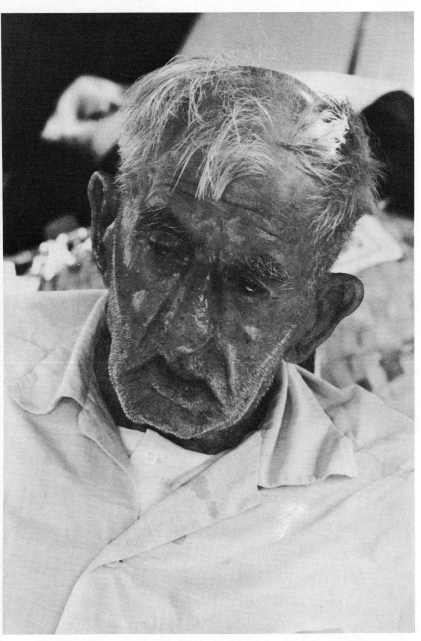

A ninety-seven-year-old man with arteriosclerosis is one of the passengers

For those who are leaving, the worst part is the waiting

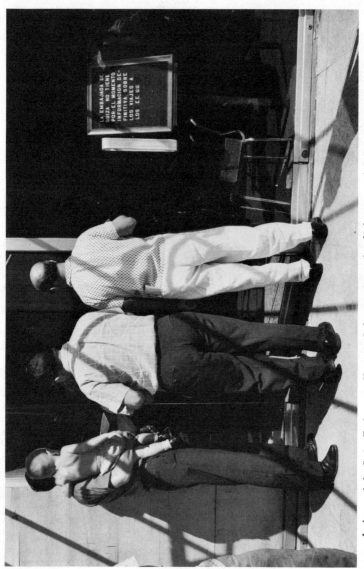

In front of the Swiss Embassy in Havana, Cubans wait anxiously for news of flights to the United States

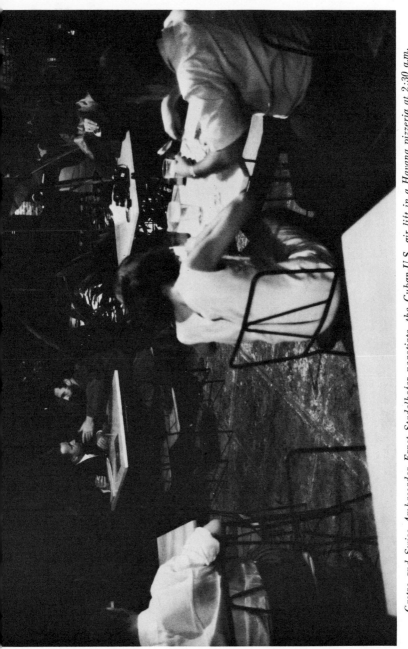

Castro and Swiss Ambassador Ernst Stadelhofer negotiate the Cuban-U.S. air lift in a Havana pizzeria at 2:30 a.m.

eight:

Portfolio: images of Cuba

315

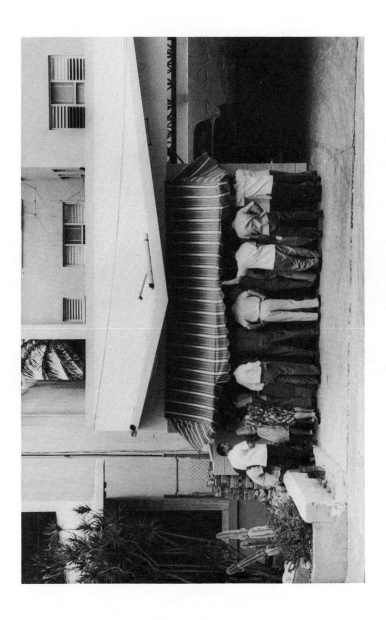

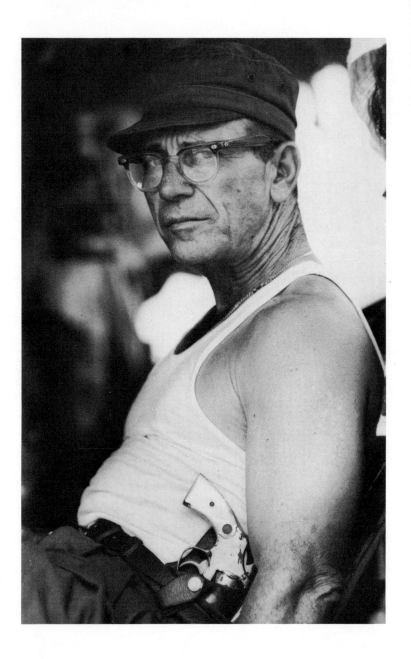

nine: conclusions

The author of a book always gets to say the last word. This is probably unfair to Castro (but fortunate for me), since his disputatious mind would surely find some plausible reply for each criticism I offer. However, my real purpose is not to debate Fidel but to balance his view of Cuba with my own observations, leaving it to the reader to remember that the last word in a book is not necessarily the last word on the subject.

Not unexpectedly, Fidel Castro has nothing but warm words for his current relations with the Soviet Union. Even if there are, as is quite likely, strong tensions running behind the façade of Cuban-Russian socialist solidarity, it would be unthinkable, given Cuba's preponderate economic and military dependence on the U.S.S.R., for Castro to voice them to an American writer. Likewise, on the subject of Cuba's role in aiding other revolutionary movements in Latin America, he is tactically (and predictably) evasive. Nor is there any doubt that when talking about the United States he often uses the opportunity to indulge in a little propagandistic exaggeration. Castro always knows when he is speaking for publication. Foreign policy considerations aside, however, I believe that Fidel made an effort to respond honestly and often with impressive candor throughout the long interrogation. Instead of doubting the sincerity of his words, I consider it much more fruitful to question the validity of some of the interpretations which he makes.

Like all converts to Marxism, Castro displays a tendency to rewrite, or at least revise, history according to the tenets of his adopted faith. Employing the pseudo-scientific jargon of dialectical materialism, he now looks back upon his dynamic and oft-shifting revolution as a "process" in which the "objective factors" of the "class struggle" successfully worked themselves out.

In this effort to fit his revolution historically into the Marxist theory of class struggle, it seems to me that Castro attributes an exaggerated importance to the role played in it by the peasants and workers of Cuba, while at the same time demeaning unfairly the support he obtained from the middle classes. The fact is that Fidel's victory, more psychological than military, was a mass, not a class, phenomenon, and largely personal in nature. So compelling was the force of Castro's personality, and his ability to project it, that he succeeded in cutting across class lines and appealing to the growing numbers of

325

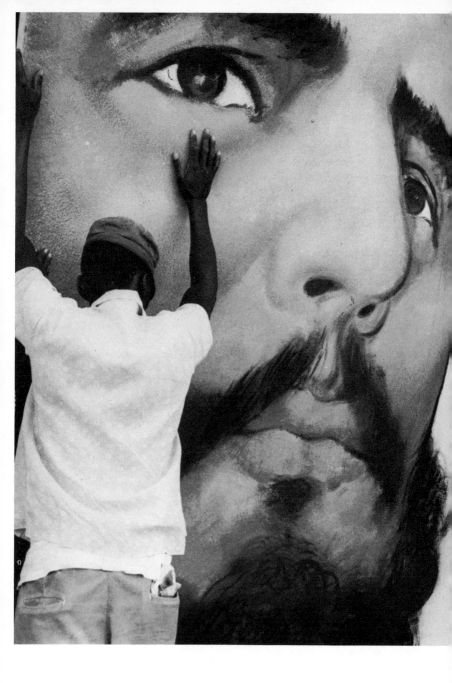

326

disaffected citizens in all sectors of Cuban society during the final years of Batista's rule. There is no questioning his assertion that the *campesinos* supported him. In the mountain areas where his guerrillas were fighting, their aid was important and even, in the beginning, crucial. But the majority of the peasantry in Cuba—as in most countries, historically—was basically apolitical. If many of the peasants were with him in spirit, few were in a position to render him any real assistance.

Just as Castro's was not a peasants' revolution in the classic sense of that term, it was not a workers' revolution either. Cuba's labor movement played a passive role in the revolutionary struggle at best (and at worst, to its discredit, a reactionary one). Even the Communist Party, which before 1959 controlled about 25 percent of Cuba's laborers, adamantly refused its support. In April, 1958, when Castro called for a nationwide general strike, which many observers feel could have brought the Revolution to power six months earlier if it had succeeded, the Communists torpedoed the effort by refusing to call out their men, and the strike failed. Not until late 1958 did the Communists change their minds and decide to back the insurrection, too late to be of significant help to the rebels, who by this time had gained the decisive upper hand.

Much more telling was the support gained from the middle class. Most of the Revolution's leaders, including Fidel himself, were of bourgeois origin. So, too, were many members of the 26th of July underground, which throughout the war carried on a successful campaign of sabotage and harassment, effectively extending Castro's presence from his mountain isolation into the cities. It also collected and passed along to him quantities of money, arms, and soldiers and kept him supplied with information. The underground fought bravely under conditions of severe danger and suffered more casualties by the end of the war than all of Castro's armed forces.

It is my belief that a large part of Cuba's middle class was not "passive," as Castro says in the interview, but actively *for* the Revolution, and that their support ultimately became one of the decisive elements in its fortunes. It is also possible that the systematic demolition of the Cuban middle class in the years following Castro's accession to power may ultimately prove one of the essential tragedies of the Cuban Revolution. Undeniably, this class included many elements that could only have gotten in the Revolution's way: "parasites" and "*lumpen*," as Castro calls them, as well as others, such as wealthy landowners, businessmen, shopkeepers, etc., who could not have put up with the loss of income and social status for very long, or older people too set in their ways to be able to adjust to the rigors of a radical revolution. These would have fled in any event. But one looks back over the seven years in vain for evidence of any real attempt to achieve a *rapprochement* with that segment of the bourgeoisie that might have contributed positively to the new state: the doctors, lawyers, teachers and other professionals, the agricultural and industrial technicians, the artists and intellectuals. No segment of the middle class welcomed Castro more enthusiastically in 1959 or remained more open-minded in attempting to integrate themselves into the Revolution as it veered rapidly toward the left during the early years. Most of them departed, finally, in dismay at the increasingly unyielding demands placed upon them by Cuba's inexorable march toward Communism. That their absence is sorely felt has been reflected in the industrial chaos and agricultural mismanagement which subsequently plagued Cuba's economy, and in the deficiency of the quality of instruction in the government's crash program to educate the masses—to cite only two examples.

Fidel Castro undoubtedly would deny this criticism with some heat and argue that these people could have stayed had they wanted to but left because they lacked a "revolutionary conscience." Admittedly, for a man who is accustomed to the comforts and privileges of the bourgeois life to transform himself into a socialist revolutionary requires considerable sacrifice and perseverance, acts of will of which not everyone is capable. Yet it must also be said that Castro and other revolutionary leaders (notably Che Guevara) often seem to be animated by a deep-seated prejudice against the bourgeoisie, reinforced by the teachings of Marx and Lenin, which impels them to condemn everything middle-class with a stiff-backed sense of morality—partly, perhaps, in overcompensation for their own bourgeois origins.

Castro continually minimizes his own role in the revolutionary process both before and after 1959. Here again, I feel he is motivated less by false modesty than by a determination to place himself at the service of Marxist theory. "An individual cannot make history. The masses make it, the people make it," says Castro, echoing Marx. But it seems undeniable that Fidel has been at once the creator, motor force, guide and spokesman for the Revolution from its first attack in 1953 until the present moment. Today, under the theoretically "collective" system of Communism, he holds more real power and is more indispensable than ever.

This view is, in fact, shared by most Cubans. In October, 1965, a few weeks after Castro triumphantly announced that the party would soon be fully established throughout Cuba, with a politburo, a one-hundred-man Central Committee, and party cells on every level, I had lunch with a *comandante* who is one of the closest members of Fidel's inner circle. To him I remarked that the new system was very neat on paper, but that it seemed to me the whole structure still depended completely upon Castro, whose power and importance remained undiminished. "Sure," said the *comandante,* "you're right—without Fidel the whole thing would just fall apart. We'd have nothing!"

Another potential cause of anxiety is what seems to me Castro's rather sanguine attitude toward the deliberate suppression of criticism in Cuban society and the demand that all media of expression adhere uniformly to the party line. While admitting that this is organically not a healthy situation, he defends it as a necessary evil to be endured so long as the Revolution is in a "situation of emergency and strain" in the fight against imperialism. "Naturally, when we no longer live under these circumstances, the causes that necessitate severe measures will disappear," Castro says. Yet one might question the assumption that the state can raise or lower the level of freedom of expression as easily as it can, for example, regulate the production of eggs. Censorship as an instrument of the state has a way of getting out of hand. Historically, once a climate of restriction has been established in other Socialist societies, it has tended to persist, like a stain. In China, where the Communist regime has long been stable, the "hundred flowers" which Chairman Mao said might bloom were cut down by an early frost, and the intellectual climate has continued oppressive. In the Soviet Union, where the third generation of Communists is now in school, individual expression is scarcely any less constricted, in spite of sporadic attempts by the government to "liberalize" the atmosphere.

"I believe in the free man, I believe in the educated man, I believe in the man able to think, in the man who acts always out of convictions, without fear of any kind, and I believe that ideas must be able to defend themselves. . . . A people sufficiently educated, capable of making a correct judgment without fear of coming into contact with ideas that could confound or deflect them. . . ."

If Castro is sincere in proposing this as one of the main goals of his revolution—as I believe he is—it would seem a good idea to begin working toward it now, while the new society is still in a formative state. Cuba, geographically and politically almost isolated from the world of ideas, truly needs all the criticism and dissenting opinion it can get at this moment. Cubans are by nature a free-thinking people, impulsively uninhibited in expressing their views about anything to anybody, including Fidel himself. That ethnic characteristic is one of the intangible causes for hope for the future of Cuba's Revolution. But already the virus of suppression has begun to infect the intellectual atmosphere. In a future Cuba without Castro, should a new generation come to power schooled in Communist double-think, confirmed in the belief that it is more important that the state survive than that the individual be able to question freely, the infection could become fatal.

Linked with this is another potential cause for alarm: that there is around Castro himself, as far as I can ascertain, a dangerous lack of criticism and debate. The people closest to Castro are without exception those who adore him or, at the least, defer to him completely. Most of them are ex-guerrilla comrades from the mountain days who still react to Fidel's every word like soldiers obeying their commander. Such discipline is commendable, perhaps even indispensable, but it should not be all. Equally important for a leader with so much power and so much at stake in how it is used is that he have near him men of intellect and imagination who are capable of generating original ideas, and who are unafraid to express them, even when they run counter to doctrine.

Granted, this is not easy. The constant demands and responsibilities of great power tend to render a leader hypersensitive to criticism, however well-intentioned. But difficult though Castro might find it to abide the goads of dissenting minds, they could provide a liberating influence, an important ballast against the creeping dogmatism that is an inherent danger in all monolithic governments. Che Guevara was perhaps the last Cuban leader of sharp intellect who was always willing to argue a difference of opinion with Fidel. He is missed. *"Comandante en Jefe—Ordenes!"* ("Commander in Chief—we await your orders!") is a slogan one sees inscribed everywhere in Cuba these days to rally popular support for the Revolution. But in Orwellian fashion, it also symbolizes the prevailing attitude toward dissent.

It is clear that today, after seven years, we still cannot talk about the Cuban Revolution without Fidel Castro. He dominates it utterly, from top to bottom. There is no one anywhere in the society who can rival him in power or influence, for the real source of his strength is his ability to communicate directly with the people and to dominate them with his personality.

Two things about Cuba were especially in Castro's favor when he took power. One was its relatively small size, which has allowed him to keep in personal touch with everything of importance happening anywhere on the island. Castro is constantly on the road, usually without an itinerary, showing up at the most unexpected places. There are few Cubans who do not have the opportunity to see him in the flesh at least once a year. Moreover, he genuinely loves to meet people, to talk to them, ask how things are going, listen to their complaints or debate their ideas. In this manner Fidel, who has an innate distrust of written reports from the field, is able simultaneously to inform himself at firsthand, give the local workers a boost in morale, and keep his subordinates on their toes.

A second unique advantage which Castro inherited was Cuba's modern, fully developed, American-style mass communications system. Today in Havana alone there are still three TV and five radio stations, and every other large city has ample, well-equipped facilities. The per capita distribution of TV sets in Cuba is still higher than in any other socialist nation (and far superior to that of the Soviet Union or China). Through the use of nationwide hookups Castro is able, in effect, to convene the entire populace whenever he has a report to make or a new idea to put across, or, as happens frequently these days, in order to rally the people to make some extra effort or sacrifice.

It should be said, however, that no amount of personal appearances or television addresses by even so persuasive a speaker as Castro could have much effect after seven years did he not enjoy the genuine support of the majority of the populace. Unquestionably, they do support him, as I have personally witnessed on innumerable occasions. The constant talk one reads in the American press of the growing popular disenchantment with Castro is almost entirely the product of editorial wishful thinking. Certainly there is grumbling to be heard inside Cuba about such things as the shortage of goods, the long work hours, the bureaucratic inefficiencies of the socialist administration, etc. But one should not confuse grumbling with unrest. Even when Cubans feel they are being victimized by injustice or inequity at the hands of some lesser official, they are apt to complain, in their bitterness, "This would never happen if Fidel knew about it."

Why do the Cuban people support Fidel Castro?

For most, the answer is a combination of hero-worship, faith in his personal honesty, and appreciation of the practical accomplishments of his Revolution. A large minority also backs him because there is no foreseeable alternative.

First, of course, there was his fairy-tale victory over the dictatorship of Fulgencio Batista, the most repressive and terroristic regime which Cuba had ever known in a long history of iniquitous governments. Since coming to power, Castro has given the country for the first time a government virtually free of corruption and abuse. He has eradicated graft, gambling and prostitution and abolished the use of position for personal privilege, deep festers from which Cuban society formerly suffered with resignation. Fidel's insistence that his associates continue to wear their guerrilla uniforms and to live a comparatively Spartan existence is a tacit way of demonstrating that the leaders are at the service of the people, not the other way round, as under former governments. Moreover, every Cuban knows that no matter how hard people are working, no one is working harder than Fidel. At sugar harvest time, for example, when thousands of city people are recruited as "volunteers" to go to the country and help cut the cane, Castro (dragging with him practically the entire administration) spends two weeks in the fields slashing away with a machete. Of course the propaganda values of the situation are obvious, and he is filmed and photographed from all angles and even interviewed while he works. But when the reporters and cameraman have packed up and departed for the city, Castro goes on cutting cane, eight, ten, twelve hours a day, and everybody knows it.

Secondly, the Castro Revolution has instituted sweeping social reforms which have given the masses, notably the peasants, many real benefits they did not have before. Among these are the agrarian (land) reform, the abolition of racial discrimination, free education and medical care for every citizen, and, more practically, the building and staffing of hundreds of new schools and hospitals in the rural areas. A successful mass literacy campaign has been followed by another drive to educate every citizen at least to the sixth-grade level. The peasants also now have a generally higher standard of living than before the Revolution. There is virtually no unemployment in the nation. In the cities, the Urban Reform Law has cut dwelling rentals to a fraction of a worker's salary, and thousands of families now pay no rent at all. All of these were elements of Castro's original revolutionary program, and he has carried them out.

Thirdly, Cubans are pleased that Fidel has managed to give Cuba a place in the sun, to make it count for something on the international scene after centuries of colonial domination. They take special and almost perverse pride in what they see as the courage and the strategic brilliance with which he has handled the "Colossus of the North"— the United States—thwarting us at every turn. First he took over the United States oil refineries, the American business interests and the huge American landholdings and got away with it. When the United States canceled the sugar quota, and fiscal disaster seemed imminent, he arranged for the Soviet Union to finance Cuba's economy. When we shifted our tactics and tried a military operation, Castro personally led the counterattack that routed the "Yankees" at the Bay of Pigs, simultaneously shaming the United States in the eyes of the world and extracting a huge ransom for the CIA prisoners he captured. As a deterrent to further invasions, he talked Khrushchev into installing missiles, and for a brief time at least, little Cuba was theoretically* a nuclear power. Khrushchev backed out under United States pressure, but the price of the insult to Cuba was enough matériel to equip the largest and most modern military establishment in Latin America. Now he has even dared to denounce the leadership of Communist China as "blackmailers" and "pirates." Who else but Fidel could have done all this? And what will he do next? Cubans say fondly, "Life under Fidel may have its problems, but it is never dull!"

Recently, after several hectic, exciting years of living in the present, Fidel Castro has turned his attention to the fact of his own mortality and taken steps to institutionalize the Cuban Revolution. The form he has chosen, the instrument by which he hopes to perpetuate his movement, is Communism, Soviet-style. It is much too early to speak with any certainty about what effect this will have on Cuba's future. The machinery has been delivered, but it is still being unpacked. For the time being, however, my own hopes, like those of the *comandante* quoted earlier, repose more with Castro than with Communism.

To me, Communism remains, after fifty years of development, a system that has yet to prove itself. Despite its acceptance by a large part of the world, in which it has succeeded in raising the material and social levels of the masses to a large extent, it has failed consistently in what is perhaps the most important area of all, that of individual human liberty. In every case where the Marxist system rules, the freedom of the individual has been sublimated to, and in most cases harshly suppressed by, the state. There is no reason for assurance that this will not also happen in Cuba. Cubans have already voluntarily ceded a good deal of their personal prerogatives in the name of Emergency (the "irreconcilable threat of Yankee imperialism"). One may only hope that this state of emergency will not become permanent, as in the Soviet Union and China, where the restrictions on individual freedom are no longer voluntary but are simply imposed by the state as a matter of course.

Fidel Castro is sincerely convinced that in Communism lies the ultimate salvation of Cuba. My own view is that this is possible only to the extent that Castro will be able and willing to depart from the old models and develop a new variant of Communism, to reinterpret Marx more flexibly and more creatively than has ever yet been done. "Every people has the right to its own ideology," said Fidel in May, 1959, long before becoming a Communist. "The Cuban revolution is as Cuban as our music." A Cuban form of Marxism created in this

---

* Actually, the missiles were always under Russian control.

spirit, one that would avoid dogma and allow its citizens more individual liberty and a freer role in their own government than other Communist states have been able to achieve, might succeed.

It would be very difficult. There has not been a major new development in Communist theory in forty-five years. In the early years following his announcement of his conversion, Fidel exhibited an alarming tendency to treat Marxism-Leninism as an infallible science whose theorems could be applied like the laws of physics. More recently, he has evidenced a willingness to strike out on his own ideological path.* Intellectual boldness and originality of imagination are two important requisites for such a task. Castro possesses these in abundance, as well as the ambition to be remembered in history as a seminal innovator in the development of Communist theory. The future of Cuba may very well depend on the degree to which Castro, in striving to evolve a "revolution as Cuban as our music," will be able to utilize the teachings of Marx and Lenin less as textbooks than as reference material.

Once, in the summer of 1964, when I was on a trip with Castro, Pedro Miret, a jovial young *comandante* with a bullet crease in his scalp from the original attack on the Moncada Barracks, told me an illuminating anecdote about what life was like with Fidel in the Sierra Maestra. We were in a hotel at Varadero Beach. It was after 3 A.M. Fidel, after a full day of traveling and work, was still going strong, playing a murderous game of ping-pong and simultaneously lecturing his exhausted audience about crop fertilizers.

"Look at him. He will be talking until six o'clock," Miret said with rueful admiration. "He is just the same now as he was in the Sierra Maestra. The only difference is that in the Sierra he would have looked at his watch and said, 'Well, only 3 A.M.—we still have time to

---

* In an important speech delivered on May Day, 1966, Castro indicated publicly that a certain amount of ideological rethinking is in progress. Some excerpts:

". . . no formula is always applicable to the letter, and in general, in political and social matters, formulas are always bad.

". . . We hear formulas and read manuals, but nothing teaches better than a revolution that, while we must appreciate and evaluate the importance of the experience of other peoples, each country must make an effort not to copy, but to contribute to [the] underdeveloped sciences, the political and social sciences." (Prolonged applause.)

". . . We are developing our ideas. We understand that Marxist-Leninist thought requires unceasing development; we understand that some stagnation has taken place in this field, and we even see that formulas that can, in our opinion, lead to deviation from the essence of Marxism-Leninism, are widely accepted.

". . . the worst of sacrileges is stagnation in thinking. Thinking that stagnates is thinking that rots." (Applause.)

walk to the next mountain!' Sometimes in the Sierra it got so bad we had to put Fidel on a mule. Only because the mule walked slower than Fidel!'"

In Communism, Castro has finally found a mule that he is able to ride. A mule, however, can be a balky animal. Often, it goes too slow. Sometimes it stubbornly goes its own way. For the rider, there is always the possibility that he may have to get down and walk a little faster, or even in a different direction.

But these are essentially long-range considerations, and highly speculative ones. A true revolution such as that which is taking place in Cuba is a dynamic process which to a large extent makes its own laws as it moves along. An outsider who devotes all of his attention to analyzing texts and constructing theories runs the risk of failing to understand its essential values, which are human and organic, and, being in flux, tend to resist intellectualizing. It is almost mandatory to go to Cuba and see for oneself to truly understand this. There is in Cuba today much of the same spirit of excitement, of a sense of purpose, of a moral momentum, of a people making their own destiny, that charged the air when Castro's Revolution swept into power seven years ago. The fact that this spirit, this *élan vital*, has been preserved through all the years of difficulties is one of the surest signs of the Revolution's health.

Lamentably, little of this reality is being communicated to us by the American press, which in its coverage of Cuba has been, to use the kindest words possible, woefully inadequate. In general it reports only the negative aspects—the economic difficulties, the purges of individuals from the government, the exodus of Cubans to the United States —and remains silent about everything else. It ridicules Castro's speeches and reduces him personally to a Hitleresque caricature. It consistently publishes as unchallenged fact the most absurd rumors that emanate daily from the embittered Cuban exile community. The net result to the American reader is an image of a Cuba troubled and torn and of a government on the brink of momentary collapse. The almost unrelieved bias with which our news media have approached the problem of Cuba lends little credit to the American tradition of editorial objectivity. More importantly, all of us may someday have to pay the costs of this misinformation and distortion and our consequent lack of understanding.

Perhaps we might begin by thinking not only of the two hundred thousand Cubans who are fleeing the harsh exigencies of the new social order but also of the seven million who are staying behind, willingly, to support Fidel Castro and to work for their own future. The fact is that Castro's Revolution is not moribund; today it is morally healthy, vital, and moving forward. It has demonstrated to the world that it possesses the ability both to survive its own mistakes and profit from them, and to withstand the severest pressures the United States has been able to bring to bear. In the process, the people of Cuba have transformed themselves from an apolitical, superficial people, fond of frivolity, into a nation of proud, dedicated, and militant revolutionaries capable of extraordinary sacrifice. This is surely one of Castro's greatest achievements. With unrelenting persuasion, he has turned every crisis into an advantage, has made of each adversity a forge upon which the revolutionary conscience of the people has been hammered each time a little finer. Unquestionably, all our belligerent moves against Castro, launched with the purpose of uniting the Cubans against him, have had exactly the opposite effect. They have provided him with the catalyst by which he has been able to consolidate and fuse their support, as well as with a foil against which to focus the thrust of his Revolution. Indeed, it is not far-fetched to conclude that Castro has derived much more benefit from the implacable enmity of the United States than he has suffered from it. As a master political tactician, Fidel fully understands the value of maintaining this tension. For that reason, it is unlikely that Cuba will show any interest in promoting a *rapprochement* with the United States within the foreseeable future.

For the time being, at least, difficulties still remain. One problem yet to be solved is Cuba's deep economic involvement with the U.S.S.R., which is not an unmitigated blessing, inevitably carrying with it a tacit pressure toward ideological homogeneity with the Soviet line. Nonetheless, both the Soviets and the Cuban people are equally aware that Cuba is not in any sense a satellite of the Soviet Union. Grateful as Fidel is for Russian support, he has on several occasions served notice that Cuba's goal is complete independence from all nations, not only economic but political independence as well.

The key to this independence is the health of the Cuban economy, which is to say, its agriculture. Here the prospect is surprisingly hopeful. In 1965, after six years of poor planning and chaotic mismanagement, Castro took charge of the agricultural program. Primarily as a result of his personal efforts, things have finally gotten organized for the first time since 1959. One has only to travel around the island and observe the quantity and the variety of agricultural production under way and the hundreds of thousands of acres newly under cultivation to convince himself of this fact. The 1965 sugar harvest was the third largest in Cuba's history. Although the 1966 *zafra* was a poor one, owing mainly to the severe drought of the year before, the prospects of 1967 and onward are for a succession of record harvests, and

Castro's announced goal of ten million tons by 1970 seems within reach.

Though sugar is still the staple, Cuba is diversifying its agriculture on a large scale to include cattle, citrus fruits, winter vegetables, coffee, and many other products (including, of course, tobacco). It is exporting increasing quantities of these each year to countries of the capitalist West, in spite of the blockade, in return for dollars. The program of cattle production, instituted on a crash basis in 1964, has been extremely well organized, and meat is about to become the second "crop." It may ultimately become Cuba's most dependable source of hard currency, since beef, unlike sugar, is always in demand on the world market and generally brings a high price.

Thus Cuba, already militarily and politically strong, seems to be, given a moderate amount of good luck, only a few short years away from achieving economic stability. It would be a bitter draught for the United States, after having gone to war against Communism around the world, to find it thriving in a small nation ninety miles from its coastline. And for Castro to have made a success of his Revolution in the face of United States opposition could have endless ramifications throughout Latin America, where several other countries seem to be on the verge of undergoing revolutions of their own.

Although serious problems remain, the crisis is over in Cuba, and it is now apparent that Fidel Castro and his Revolution are likely to remain a part of our world for some time to come. Unhappily, the United States Government is not willing to accept this reality. Our Cuban policy continues to be one of adamant opposition to Castro's regime. By flexing our hemispheric muscle, we keep Cuba isolated from the rest of Latin America. (With the exception of Mexico, no Latin American nation maintains diplomatic or trade relations with Cuba today.) By exercising leverage through our foreign aid program, we further restrict commerce between Cuba and other Western nations. Meanwhile, our naval ships still patrol outside Cuban waters, maintaining an informal but largely effective blockade on shipping to and from the island, while another branch of our government continues to train and infiltrate Cuban exiles as agents for subversive and paramilitary operations in Cuba.

It is time for the United States to re-examine its Cuban policy, on both ethical and practical grounds. Cuba is, after all, a sovereign nation, with all the international rights which that phrase implies. Moreover, its established government—unlike the regimes of certain right-wing dictatorships elsewhere in Latin America which we sanguinely support—has the demonstrable backing of the majority of its populace. The mere fact that its system of government is a Communist one is not in itself justification for our intransigent opposition to it. Communism, whatever we don't like about it, is a reality with which we must learn to live. Our continuing effort to keep Cuba isolated has caused and continues to cause considerable deprivation to the Cuban people, who, being an unindustrialized island society, must depend upon outside trade to raise their standard of living. We must ask ourselves seriously whether the suffering which we are causing seven million people because they support a regime which we dislike is morally justifiable.

There are also cogent practical reasons why we ought to re-evaluate our Cuban policy at this time. Why do we fear Castro? If Cuba were today a military base for the Soviet Union or even a Soviet satellite, located so close to our shores, we would indeed have cause for genuine concern. But it is neither. Castro did in fact have one brief flirtation with Soviet military hegemony in 1962, which culminated in the Missile Crisis, and our response was swift and unequivocal. It was a grave error for Castro for which he got badly stung. Since then, Cuba has moved steadily away from any such military or political dependence and increasingly toward a posture of autonomy and self-determination within the Socialist camp. This is an event of no little significance, of which our State Department has, perhaps, not taken sufficient cognizance.

From the standpoint of United States interests, the Cuban Revolution has today, after seven years, reached its most crucial point. Castro, having "won" the Revolution, having consolidated his own power, institutionalized his reforms, and gotten his economy organized on a basis that offers the prospect, at least, of a secure future, is now occupied with the task of giving the Revolution its ideology. As I have said, and as Castro himself indicates in the interview, his desire is for a broad application of Marxism attuned to the specific requirements of the Cuban people, one which would allow the greatest possible individual human liberty within the system. Whether or not he can achieve this new and liberal interpretation of Marxism is, of course, questionable, but it is unquestionable that the United States can play an indirect role in his success or failure. Castro has already been reviled by the Chinese Communists as a "revisionist" for certain liberalist ideological tendencies which he has enunciated. Moreover, just as in other Communist nations, there is among his own revolutionary cadre a strong element that exerts steady pressure on him to take a more radical, uncompromising position. The intransigence of the United States in continuing its efforts to destroy the Cuban Revolution is the single most compelling justification that this element has for pushing Castro toward a harder ideological line. Conversely, any efforts the United States could make in good faith to reduce the sources of tension between the United States and Cuba would undoubtedly give Castro more freedom in which to operate, and might result, in the long run, in considerable benefits for the Cuban people.

The United States Government also professes deep concern over Castro's stated policy of giving aid to other revolutionary movements in Latin America. I suggest that Cuba's ability to do this on any scale—even without the United States' economic pressure—has been and will continue to be extremely limited, not only because of her own internal necessities, which come first, but also because of a certain lack of receptivity on the part of those revolutionary movements to help from the outside, especially Cuban help.

Fidel Castro is an extraordinary man who has created an extraordinary revolution. It is time for us to accept the Cuban Revolution as a *fait accompli* and to begin to deal with it in a way which does us more credit as a democratic people. At a minimum, we ought to cease our efforts to bring down the Castro regime. The clock cannot be turned back on the Cuban Revolution whether Castro lives or dies—and if he were to be assassinated, who could be sanguine about the alternative that might succeed him? Secondly, for reasons both moral and practical, we should relax our pressures on other nations not to trade with Cuba; in the long run, we cannot prevent it anyhow. And, finally, we ourselves should try to exercise more understanding about what is going on in Cuba. The best way to do that is to allow every American citizen to go there and see for himself. Students and other young people especially, instead of having their passports confiscated, should be encouraged to visit Cuba as part of their education. The Cuban Revolution is a fascinating and exciting phenomenon. It is undoubtedly part of the wave of the future. Moreover, that future may be upon us sooner than we think.

ten: appendix

Che Guevara's disappearance

The quiet disappearance of Comandante Ernesto Che Guevara from the Cuban scene has provided a most intriguing mystery. Guevara, an Argentine by birth and a leftist by temperament, joined Castro's cause in Mexico. He sailed with him to Cuba aboard the yacht *Granma*, and was one of only thirteen of the original eighty-two revolutionaries who survived the landing in the Sierra Maestra in December, 1956. After the triumph of the Revolution, Guevara rapidly became, in importance and popularity, the number-two man of Cuba, serving under Castro in a number of different capacities, including that of President of the National Bank, Minister of Industries, and Cuba's major foreign policy spokesman and roving world ambassador.

In April, 1965, following a trip to the U.S., the U.S.S.R., and Africa, during which he leveled outspoken criticisms against the Soviet Union and China for their economic exploitation of the smaller, underdeveloped nations of the Socialist camp, Che suddenly dropped from sight. At first the word was given out that he was "cutting sugar cane in the fields of Oriente Province" and did not wish to be disturbed. But as the months went by and the usually vocal Che failed to be heard from, it became obvious that something else was afoot, known only to Castro and his inner circle.

During my interview with Castro, I asked him a series of questions about Che's disappearance and met with frustration. Here is the main portion of our exchange:

LOCKWOOD: What role will Che Guevara play in the future administration of the country?

CASTRO: You know that there have been many rumors about Che Guevara, many speculations. I spoke publicly about this and said that at a certain given moment we would inform the people about what relates to him. Actually and with good reason we have taken importance away from the speculations, and it is still not the proper moment to respond to that question, otherwise I would be glad to talk just as I have talked to you about all the other questions, but at the present time I cannot answer that interrogation. What I can tell you is that there has been absolutely no problem in the relations of friendship and the fraternal relations, the identification that has always existed between him and us. I can affirm that categorically.

LOCKWOOD: Che has been one of the most important leaders of the Revolution, one of those whom you relied on most to take responsibility. He even took on jobs which he didn't especially like and for which he had no real experience—

CASTRO: Really, none of us had any experience. We were all inexperienced.

LOCKWOOD: He had no experience as a banker, yet he was President of the National Bank of Cuba—

CASTRO: He played a great role defending the hard currency reserves of the National Bank. He was not a banker, but he knew how to defend the hard currency reserves.

LOCKWOOD: So it seems obvious to me that Che must go on playing an important role in the Revolution, that right now you need his leadership and responsibility more than ever. I don't see how you can do without him.

CASTRO: Well, but if I answered that we would enter into the essence of the question and we would be digging up the mystery. Don't take it in any way as a discourtesy on my part.

Throughout most of the year Castro continued silent about Guevara, and the growing mystery began to excite the Cuban populace almost as much as the foreign press. Finally, on October 3, 1965, on the occasion of the public assembly which introduced the new Cuban Communist Party, Castro read the following letter, purportedly written to him by Guevara at the time of his departure from Cuba six months earlier:

Che Guevara's Letter*

CASTRO: . . . I am going to read a letter, handwritten and later typed, from Comrade Ernesto Guevara [applause] which is self-explanatory. I was wondering whether I needed to tell of our friendship and comradeship, how and under what conditions it began and developed. But it is not necessary. I will limit myself to reading the letter.

. . . It has no date, as the letter was to have been read at the most opportune moment, but was actually delivered on April first of this year—exactly six months and two days ago. It says:

* Excerpt from Fidel Castro's speech at the closing ceremony of the presentation of the Central Committee of the Communist Party of Cuba, Havana, October 3, 1965. (Translated by the author.)

"Fidel:

"At this moment I remember many things—when I met you in María Antonia's house, when you suggested my coming, all the tensions involved in the preparations.

"One day they asked who should be notified in case of death, and the real possibility of the fact affected us all. Later we knew that it was true, that in revolution one wins or dies (if it is a real one). Many comrades fell along the way to victory.

"Today everything is less dramatic because we are more mature. But the fact is repeated. I feel that I have fulfilled the part of my duty that tied me to the Cuban Revolution in its territory, and I say goodby to you, to my *compañeros*, your people, who are now mine.

"I formally resign my positions in the national leadership of the party, my post as minister, my rank of major, and my Cuban citizenship. Nothing legal binds me to Cuba. The only ties are of another nature: those which cannot be broken as appointments can.

"Recalling my past life, I believe I have worked with sufficient honor and dedication to consolidate the revolutionary triumph. My only serious failing was not having trusted you more from the first moments in the Sierra Maestra, and not having understood quickly enough your qualities as a leader and a revolutionary.

"I have lived magnificent days, and felt, at your side, the pride of belonging to our people in the brilliant yet sad days of the Caribbean [Missile] Crisis.

"Seldom has a statesman been more brilliant than you in those days. I am also proud of having followed you without hesitation, identifying with your way of thinking and of appraising dangers and principles.

"Other nations of the world call for my modest efforts. I can do that which is denied you because of your responsibilities at the helm of Cuba, and the time has come for us to part.

"Let it be known that I do so with mixed feelings of joy and sorrow: I leave here the purest of my hopes as a builder, and the dearest of those I love. And I leave a people that received me as a son. That wounds me deeply. I carry to new battlefields the faith that you taught me, the revolutionary spirit of my people, the feeling of fulfilling the most sacred of duties: to fight against imperialism wherever I may be. This comforts and heals the deepest wounds.

"I state once more that I free Cuba from any responsibility, except that which stems from its example. If my final hour finds me under other skies, my last thought will be of this people and especially of you. I am thankful for your teaching, your example, and I will try to

be faithful to the final consequences of my acts. I have always been identified with the foreign policy of our Revolution, and I will continue to be. Wherever I am, I will feel the responsibility of being a Cuban revolutionary, and as such I shall behave. I am not sorry that I leave my children and my wife nothing material. I am happy it is that way. I ask nothing for them, as I know the State will provide enough for their expenses and education.

"I would like to say much to you and to our people, but I feel it is not necessary. Words cannot express what I would want them to, and I don't think it's worth while to banter phrases.

"Ever onward to victory. Fatherland or death. I embrace you with all my revolutionary fervor.

Che."

(Prolonged Applause.)

The last time I was in Cuba, shortly before this book went to press,* I again invited Castro to dispel the mystery. Again, he declined. He would say only the following:

"Che is alive. He is very well. I and his family and his friends receive letters from him often."

I remarked that this was news, since there had been reports in several newspapers and magazines that Che was dead, some even alleging that he had been "liquidated" by Castro.

"Those people who write such stories will have to square their accounts with history," Castro replied scornfully. "We do not have anything to say about Che at this time because it would be unwise, possibly unsafe for him. When he is ready and wants it to be known where he is, we will tell it to the Cuban people first, who have the right to know. Until then, there is nothing to be said."

Thus, the mystery remains a mystery. My personal belief is that Che's letter is genuine, that he really did leave Cuba voluntarily, not as the result of any falling out with Castro, and that he is alive today and working in another revolutionary movement somewhere in Latin America, probably in the Andes Mountains. Guevara is that rarest type of man, the pure revolutionary. He has no nationalistic allegiance. He is absolutely disinterested in personal power or wealth or glory. Che's one abiding interest is revolution: the emancipation of the exploited by the overthrow of their colonialist masters, wherever it can be accomplished. He has many times placed his life in jeopardy for that ideal, and there is little reason to doubt that he is doing so once again at this very moment.

---

* *In May, 1966.*

eleven: afterword

This year is the tenth anniversary of the accession to power of the Cuban Revolution, a milestone which the United States has done its best to ensure would never be celebrated. Three years have also passed since the author's interview with Castro on the Isle of Pines, an insignificant amount of time for an established nation, but nearly one-third of the history of revolutionary Cuba. During that period, a multitude of changes have occurred in Cuba, as one should expect from a revolution still in transformation. And yet, *plus ça change, plus c'est la même chose.* Looking back, whether over three years or ten, one finds that the Revolution has been characterized less by erratic movement than by a remarkable consistency of principle and direction. Every new change has seemed to reveal a little more clearly the true identity of the Revolution, as each stroke of a sculptor's mallet can be thought of as chipping away a little more of the superfluous material that masks the finished form beneath.

"The Revolution is an art. . . . We love it just as a painter, a sculptor, or a writer loves his work," Fidel said in 1965. And like an artist, the leader of a revolution, no matter how extensive his control or how great his power, cannot wholly predict the ultimate form that his creation will take. He can direct it, but he can never fully master it. It is inevitable, therefore, that some of Castro's confident predictions in our 1965 interview have fallen short of achievement, while there have been other developments that were not anticipated three years ago.

In the field of agriculture, upon which Cuba's economy almost totally depends, many of Castro's promises have been fulfilled and even surpassed. In the cattle industry, for example, Fidel predicted that seven hundred thousand cows would be under artificial insemination by the end of 1965. By the end of 1968, more than four hundred thousand cattle had been born and the number of cows under insemination had grown to one million five hundred thousand.* In a sensible effort to build up the herds, slaughtering is being kept to an absolute minimum at least through 1970.

---

* *Cuba had always raised cattle, but these were Zebú, which produce good meat but a low yield of milk (the meat was exported to the U.S.). Castro's insemination plan crossbreeds the Zebú with Holstein and Brown Swiss, traditional dairy cows, in an attempt to produce cattle which give both meat and milk in equal abundance.*

In addition to the crops mentioned by Castro in the interview, ambitious new plans have since been launched for the cultivation of rice, coffee, winter vegetables and other crops. Enormous areas of hitherto untilled land have been cleared by brigades of youths manning bulldozers, and planted by volunteer workers from the cities. The entire Isle of Pines (where our interview took place) has been swept clean of political prisoners and turned into a kind of victory garden for Cuba's youth, who have gone there to live and work at farming by the tens of thousands.

With the exaggerated emphasis that is typical of Castro and his revolution, agriculture has become the number one preoccupation of the entire country. Since agriculture is the ultimate key to Cuba's economic independence and survival, the "battle of the agriculture" is for Cubans not only a matter of economics but an ideological struggle in which all must participate, an essential part of the dialectics of the fight-to-the-death against Yankee imperialism. In a plan called "the Green Belt of Havana," a sweeping arc of land around the city of Havana—hundreds of thousands of acres—has been cleared, tilled and planted in the space of six months. In the spring of 1968, tens of thousands of "volunteer" factory workers, office workers, intellectuals, housewives, taxi drivers, and people of all other sectors of the city planted more than one hundred ten million coffee seedlings in the Green Belt. A "rice belt," a "dairy belt," and a "vegetable belt" are now being developed. By having the people of Havana produce much of their own food, Castro hopes finally to eliminate the recurrent shortages that have plagued the city persistently since 1959—shortages that have resulted in large part from inadequate means of transport and poorly organized distribution.*

Better planning and better organization are the most encouraging innovations in Cuba's agricultural program, which is still under Fidel Castro's personal direction. Important advances have been made in the use of fertilizers and irrigation throughout the island, and the need for agricultural technicians is at last beginning to be satisfied by thousands of young men and women who are graduating from the new technological institutes.

While long-range prospects for Cuban agriculture look better than ever, sugar, still Cuba's main crop, continues to be a serious problem. In 1965, flushed with the success of a sugar harvest of just over six million tons, Castro outlined to the author a five-year program for incremental increases that would culminate with ten million tons in

---

* Food rationing, which Castro predicted would end by 1966, is still in stringent effect. Moreover, many items on the ration book are available in insufficient quantities or are unavailable altogether. Cigars and even sugar are new ration items.

1970. Thus far, the difference between prediction and reality has verged on disaster:

	Predicted Yield	Actual Yield
1966	6.5 Million	4.5 Million
1967	7.5 Million	6.2 Million
1968	8.0 Million	5.2 Million
1969	9.0 Million	5.5 Million (est.)
1970	10.0 Million	?

Castro puts most of the blame for the reduced harvests on the weather. It is true that in 1965 and again in 1967 Cuba experienced the two worst droughts in her recorded history, severely curtailing the *zafras* of '66 and '68, and, furthermore, that torrential rains which fell in the spring and fall of 1967 also affected the '67 harvest and added to the sugar woes of '68. Nevertheless, it seems unlikely that bad weather alone could be held accountable for Cuba's consistent underfulfillment of her sugar goals in each of the first four years of her five-year plan to the extent that, out of a planned total of thirty-one million tons, production fell short by some ten million (an amount equal to the entire goal for the 1970 harvest!). Problems of labor mobilization, of transporting cut cane to the mills in time, and of the equipment in the mills also contributed. Apparently, much has already been done to rectify these conditions; certainly everything will have to be functioning perfectly in 1970 if the ten million ton harvest goal is to be achieved.*

Yet, repeated setbacks seem only to have hardened Castro's resolve to achieve a ten million ton *zafra* in 1970. Though it will require the formidable feat of doubling Cuba's 1968 production within only two years, ten million tons is no longer merely the end point of a five-year agricultural plan; it is now, in Fidel's own words, "a point of honor for the Revolution," a promise to the world which Cubans must fulfill in order to prove their revolutionary mettle.†

---

* *In a recent conversation with the author (June, 1968) Castro exhibited his usual optimism. "Be assured that we will produce ten million tons. If we couldn't produce ten million tons, the Revolution would be lost, without value. We will do it." He then spent a half-hour explaining why it will be impossible, drought or no drought, for Cuba not to reach ten million. He listed a series of eight or nine reasons why the yield would increase: so many hundred thousand tons from using more fertilizer, so much from better planting, so much from irrigation, so much from new fields, etc. He totaled up all the increases and added them to the 5.2 million tons of 1968 and arrived at a figure of just over eleven million tons. "You see!" he exclaimed. "I could be off in my calculations by a million tons and we'll still have ten million in 1970!"*

† *Sugar-cane harvesting is almost impossible to mechanize. For several years*

Even assuming that this enormous quantity of sugar can be produced (never bet against Fidel) and sold at a reasonable price (Castro is positive that it can), the pertinent question remains whether it is really worth the effort. In Cuba, as in most of the world, sugar cane must be harvested by hand, that is, by machete. It is arduous, grueling, backbreaking work, and it must be done properly to ensure the best yield and to protect the next year's crop. In 1968, in order to harvest five million tons, Castro mobilized many thousands of volunteer workers from the cities and the armed forces to augment the force of professional *macheteros*. They spent anywhere from two weeks to five months in the cane fields. For the 1970 harvest, even with improved efficiency and planning, it is possible that nearly every man, woman and student healthy enough to wield a machete will be required to spend several months in the *zafra*. This wholesale transferral of personnel is bound to disrupt food supply, bureaucratic functions, public services and day-to-day life of the nation in general, not to mention the other ambitious agricultural efforts under way which also require a considerable amount of volunteer labor from the cities.

Another subject that Castro discussed extensively in our 1965 interview is the question of the political institutionalization of the Revolution.

Castro agreed that the excessive concentration of power in one man (himself) was far from ideal, but he pointed to the formation of the party (which had already begun) and the imminent presentation of the Socialist constitution as the kinds of institutional guarantees of collective leadership that would assure the future of the Revolution.

It must be said that the organization of the Communist Party has made great progress in the last three years, if not at the hoped-for speed, at all levels of Cuban society. Though there is usually no more than one slate of "candidates" for admission in each political unit, the elections are democratic to the extent that the candidates must appear before popular assemblies of their fellow workers, where they are subjected to pointed questioning and, often, outspoken criticism. The criteria for party admission are high; there is demanded of each individual not only ideological rectitude, but intelligence, motivation, impeccable character and a personality which is, at the minimum,

---

Cuba, in conjunction with the Soviet Union, Czechoslovakia and other countries, has experimented in developing a harvesting combine. In 1968 Castro announced that a prototype combine designed by Cuban technicians had been successfully tested on a variety of terrains. Even if the machines work as well as reported, the transition from prototypes to production units will take time. Cuba's Minister of Sugar, Orlando Borrego, told the author in 1968 that at best only five percent of the 1970 zafra could be mechanized. (Shortly thereafter, Borrego was ousted from his ministry.)

fraternally oriented toward one's fellow citizens. Thus, the quality of the new party cadre is almost uniformly impressive, particularly on the lower rungs of authority, for example, those who are local party officials in rural towns or villages or in factories; in other words, those at the furthest remove from the Charybdian maw of party bureaucracy.

The very fact that an institutional structure has been created according to high standards is encouraging, certainly. Nonetheless, it is only a first step toward collective (i.e., "democratic") leadership, not the embodiment of it. At the top of the pyramid, Castro's power remains undisturbedly supreme. Though he promised that the first party congress would be held "by the end of 1967," and that the Socialist constitution would be promulgated "long before 1970," * neither of these fundamentally important events has yet taken place or shows signs of doing so in the near future. Nor, moreover, has there yet been held a national congress of "decentralized local institutions" (*Poder Local*) which Fidel had expected to take place late in 1966. The fact is that Fidel Castro, after ten years of power, is more than ever the indispensable man of the Cuban Revolution. There has been little diminution since 1965 either of his authority or of his popular support, and the likelihood that he will retire "at an early age" ("We propose this not only as a right, but as a duty") now seems as remote as ever.†

Unquestionably, the most significant new developments of the last three years in Cuba have been in two related areas of foreign affairs: her relations with the Soviet Union, and her involvement in the fomentation of new revolutions in Latin America.

In our 1965 interview, Castro said that Cuba's relations with the U.S.S.R. had recovered from the missile crisis and were at that time "better than ever." On the subject of aiding Latin American guerrilla movements he spoke theoretically and with some reticence. When asked which countries seemed susceptible to revolutions in the near future, he mentioned Brazil, Peru, Ecuador, Colombia, and Venezuela, but not Bolivia, where Che Guevara and several other Cubans were to give their lives only two years later in the attempt to create a continental revolutionary movement. In all probability, at the time of our talk in 1965 Castro still had not yet decided upon a Latin American adventure.

The Cuban Revolution has always suffered from an unresolvable dilemma: Cuba's geographical location. In 1960, Castro traded eco-

---

* Castro has been talking about "a new Socialist constitution" since May 1, 1961.

† He recently remarked to the author that he is working harder this year (1968) than at any other time since coming to power.

nomic dependence on the U.S. for economic and military dependence on the Soviet Union, naïvely believing that Russia's aid was being extended without any strings attached, in the pure spirit of "proletarian solidarity," from one Socialist people to another. The events that ensued taught him otherwise; Nikita Khrushchev's unilateral negotiations with John Kennedy to end the missile crisis of 1962 provided the object lesson that Cuba was after all only a pawn in the global chess game between East and West,* that to protect her sovereignty she must look outside the two great power blocs for alliances. Since Khrushchev's ouster from the Soviet leadership, as the U.S.S.R. has put increasing emphasis on "peaceful coexistence" with the capitalist world, Cuba's reaction to this policy has gradually moved from *sub rosa* quiet criticism to open and sharp attack. Simultaneously, her ideological position has become more radical and, significantly, has bridged the gap between theory and practical application. The man most instrumental in both changes was Ernesto Che Guevara.†

Guevara left Cuba secretly for the Congo toward the end of 1965, where it was his intention to remain for several years, helping the Congolese and other African peoples to organize revolutionary struggles against colonialism and imperialism. In apparent coordination with his mission, the First Tricontinental Congress was held in Havana in January, 1966, a meeting of representatives of the undeveloped countries of Asia, Africa, and Latin America. Many of these who attended the Tricontinental were *guerrilleros* or would-be revolutionaries traveling in disguise. The object of the congress was coordinate support for revolutionary wars of liberation throughout the colonialized world. Though the practical achievements of the meeting were small (in terms of results), it did bring about a direct though behind-the-scenes confrontation between Castro and the Soviet Union on the question of peaceful coexistence versus revolutionary war.

Fidel Castro—and his adherents—have always believed that their revolution is a transcendent event in world history, a model for self-

* The lesson taught by the missile crisis has never been forgotten by Castro, as illustrated by his reaction to the Soviet occupation of Czechoslovakia in August, 1968. While proclaiming his equivocal support of the Soviet action as a political necessity, he immediately called for the mobilization of Cuba's armed forces, figuring that under the unwritten conventions of the balance of power, if the U.S. was willing to allow the U.S.S.R. to invade Czechoslovakia with impunity, the Soviet Union might just as easily permit the United States to attack Cuba in retaliation.

† Guevara was in many ways the moral conscience of the Cuban Revolution (and is today). In the important area of ideology, Che's position was invariably to the left of Fidel's and in almost every case Castro himself ultimately came to take Che's position (e.g., intransigence toward the United States, moral vs. material incentives for workers, and, most important of all, the principle of armed struggle as the only road to revolution).

liberation of all colonialized peoples, especially in Latin America, and that Cuba should give aid to such liberation movements, within her means, wherever they occur. Since 1959, Cuban nationals have been involved in at least a dozen attempts at subversion in Latin America alone (not all of them supported by the Cuban government). As a convert to Communism, Castro has found ideological confirmation of this principle in the pre-Leninist concept of "proletarian internationalism," which he interprets to mean that every country that has had a revolution has the moral duty to give priority to the international struggle against imperialism, at no matter what sacrifice, rather than "building socialism in one country." *

Sometime in the first half of 1966 Che Guevara abandoned his effort to reorganize the remnants of Patrice Lumumba's Katangese rebels, frustrated by their lack of combative spirit, and he returned secretly to Cuba. By now the rift with the Soviet Union over the principle of armed struggle had widened to such an extent that Castro, fearing eventual total isolation and strongly motivated to prove the correctness of his position to the Soviets and the rest of the world (and also seeking to take advantage of the United States' accelerating military commitment in Vietnam), planned with Che the inauguration of a guerrilla *foco* in northwestern Bolivia which would ultimately serve as the training ground and command post for a continent-wide war for the liberation of South America. Guevara departed for Bolivia in November, 1966. In July, 1967, Castro convened the first congress of the new, Havana-based Organization of Latin American Solidarity (OLAS), attended by Communists and non-Communist revolutionaries from every country of Latin America. Conducted with an exaggerated lavishness in startling contrast to the rigorous ambience of guerrilla warfare, in the invited presence of hundreds of newsmen from the Communist, capitalist, and third worlds, the conference was clearly intended as a propaganda send-off for a new "international" of Latin American revolution. It began with the display of a huge portrait of Simón Bolívar as the backdrop and closed with a mural-sized portrait of Che Guevara, who was openly proclaimed leader of the guerrilla movement. In unequivocal language it ratified Fidel Castro's thesis that the armed struggle (*la lucha armada*) is the only road to self-determination for the peoples of Latin America, and it officially condemned the Soviet Union for her opposition to, and even

* *This, of course, bears great similarity to the line taken by the Chinese in the Sino-Soviet dispute. Cuba also shares China's anxieties over the possibility of eventual "encirclement" by the two great powers.*

It is one of the ironies of history, and probably more the result of ethnic and cultural differences than theoretical distinctions, that in spite of her obvious ideological affinity to China, Cuba's relations with that country today are much colder than with the Soviet Union, with whom she has deep polemical differences.

subversion of, the guerrilla movements already existing in Latin America through her influence over the established Communist parties and her policy of entering into commercial agreements with the oligarchies of various South American nations.

The failure of the Bolivian adventure, culminating in Che Guevara's death, is too recent an event for its full effects on Cuban policy to be known. What is clear is that it represents a severe setback to the revolutionary guerrilla movement in Latin America. As a defeat, but still more as an irreplaceable personal loss, it has left Fidel Castro and his close supporters in a semi-traumatic state from which they are still recovering.

Though Castro's ideological commitment to armed struggle remains as firm as ever, there is evidence that the circumstances of Che's failure have prompted a good deal of rethinking as to the ways and means by which it should be carried out. Meanwhile, since the death of Guevara, there has been in Cuba a decided shift in the focus of national attention away from international issues and toward more domestic concerns—as expressed by Castro's determination to make Cuba economically self-sufficient by 1970 through agriculture.* The burden of possibility for this achievement lies squarely on the shoulders of the Cuban people; the government, in calling on its citizens for ever more hard work and sacrifice, is invoking the spirit of Che Guevara. The "revolutionary offensive" announced by Castro early this year is at once a memorial to Che and a rededication of the Cuban people to the sacrificial and rigor-enduring spirit of the Sierra Maestra (in principle, at least, not unlike the cultural revolution in China). Individuals are asked to purge themselves of "egoistic" concerns about their material welfare and join in the great agricultural battle for economic survival. In line with the revolutionary offensive, bars and night clubs have been closed down, and all remaining small businesses have been nationalized, thus bringing to near completion the socialization of the Cuban economy.†

On the whole, although as Castro himself noted there has been a tangible increase in "inquietude and uncertainty" within the country, Cubans of all classes have responded to the Spartan demands with patience and dedication. This seems remarkable, since Cubans have experienced little more than sacrifice and hardship for ten years. How-

---

* Significantly, Castro's speech of January 2, 1969, celebrating the tenth anniversary in power, concentrated on agricultural matters and omitted any reference to Che Guevara or Latin American revolutions—an exclusion that even astonished many Cubans.

† Except for the holdings of one hundred fifty thousand small farmers, which are protected under the Second Agrarian Reform, but gradually being phased out as the farmers die off or retire and their lands are ceded or sold to the state.

ever as the "older generation," those who made the Revolution, are beginning to show signs of wear, it is the youth who are carrying that revolution forward. Their energy is kinetic, and their enthusiasm for the task is nothing short of exalted.

As 1968, "the year of the heroic guerrilla," draws to a close and the Revolution prepares to celebrate its first decade of power, what are its perspectives for the future? Castro's internal support, though somewhat diminished during the last three years (if one can measure such things without conducting polls or holding elections) is still strong. Although shortages continue and the sugar crop is well below expectations, Cuba's long-run economic prospects appear healthy as agriculture becomes more diversified and better organized.

Politically, however, Cuba today is more isolated than at any other time since 1959. With the exception of Canada and Mexico, she is treated as an untouchable by all the nations of her own hemisphere. (Whatever desires the former may have for increased ties with Cuba are easily held in check by the U.S.) The American economic blockade continues, with great (though far from total) effectiveness. Cuba still relies on the Soviet Union, ten thousand miles away, for economic survival and military protection. While it is not likely that the U.S.S.R. would willingly withdraw her support from the only Socialist nation in the Western Hemisphere, if Castro, as a matter of principle, persists in his virulent ideological attacks on Moscow, he may eventually succeed in forcing a rupture that Russia's leaders do not desire.

Those of Castro's enemies who long have characterized him as a base opportunist who "turned" Communist and took Cuba into the Socialist camp for reasons of expediency rather than conviction must now be sorely puzzled by the fact that Fidel has chosen precisely that moment in history when he is irreconcilably alienated from the United States and hardly on speaking terms with China, to embark Cuba upon an ideological collision course with the Soviet Union. Obviously, it would be much more in Castro's material interests to cooperate with the Soviets than to attack them. Moreover, the Soviets would be willing to accept ideological disagreement as long as it were kept on the level of intra-party conversation and debate; what they cannot accept is that Castro has determinedly transformed what ought (in their eyes) to be a private discussion into a public polemic.*

---

* *Castro's ideological independence is illustrated by his television speech of August 23, 1968, to the Cuban people about the invasion of Czechoslovakia by the Soviet Union and other Warsaw Pact nations a few days earlier. After warning that what he is about to say "may in some cases . . . be in contradiction with the emotions of many; in other cases, in contradiction with our own interests; and in others . . . will constitute serious risks for our country," Castro first seems to side with the Soviet action on the grounds that "something had to*

In fact, one of the most exciting attributes of the Cuban Revolution is the fact that the very combination of uncompromising idealism and unfaltering courage which characterized Castro's first attack on the Moncada Barracks in 1953, which sustained his guerrilla war in the mountains, and which brought him to victory in 1959 are still dominant today, after ten years in power. Although his programs have undergone significant transformations, his ideals, the ideals of his Revolution, have not. Despite formidable temptations and pressures from both within the society and from abroad, the Cuban Revolution has consistently, throughout a decade of adversity, refused to sacrifice principle to expediency. Today, Cuba, with all her imperfections, represents the only attempt in the entire world to test the proposition that it is possible to construct a society and to conduct foreign relations by placing ethical values first and practical considerations—up to and including survival—second. Undoubtedly this is why Cuba's Revolution continues to appeal to so many outsiders of all classes, cultures and ideologies, especially to young people in search of values everywhere.

In spite of the fact that the Cuban example has not been successfully emulated in the ten years since Castro took power, in spite of the chilling setback to Che Guevara's effort in Bolivia, Castro and his followers remain dedicated to the spread of the revolutionary movement by means of armed struggle throughout the colonialized world. To achieve this end they must contend not only with the implacable resistance of American imperialism but also with the intransigent opposition of the Soviet Union and of most of the Communist parties of the third world, over whom Russia holds sway. Today, Fidel Castro stands like an angry prophet nearly alone in a venal world that is weary of violence and would rather live in compromise than die for an ideal. Ten years after coming down from the mountains, Fidel seeks to make Cuba the Sierra Maestra of the globe and the Cuban Revolution its guerrilla *foco:* "the small motor which gets the big motor started." Once again, Castro is leading a guerrilla war against impossible odds, isolated, but with conviction firm, striving to strike the spark that will ignite the world into another, grander, ultimate revolution. The process does not end, it merely enters a new phase.

---

be done at all costs" to stop the "inexorable march" of Czechoslovakia toward capitalism and the West. He then devotes most of his speech to a scathing attack on the U.S.S.R. for the "illegality" of the invasion and for her hypocrisy in accusing the Czechs of instituting "neo-capitalist" economic reforms when, in fact, the Soviet Union was experimenting with similar departures from orthodox Marxist economics.

A Selected Bibliography
of Books About Cuba

ABEL, ELIE. *The Missile Crisis*. New York: Bantam Books Inc., 1966 and J. B. Lippincott Co., 1966.

ARNAULT, JACQUES. *Cuba et le Marxisme*. Paris: Les Editions Sociales, 1962.

BARNET, MIGUEL, ed. *The Autobiography of a Slave*. New York: Pantheon Books, 1968.

BOORSTEIN, EDWARD. *The Economic Transformation of Cuba*. New York: Monthly Review Press, 1968.

CASTRO, FIDEL. *History Will Absolve Me*. New York: Liberal Press, 1959.

CASUSO, TERESA. *Cuba and Castro*. New York: Random House, 1961.

CUBAN ECONOMIC RESEARCH PROJECT. *A Study on Cuba*. Miami, Fla.: University of Miami Press, 1965.

DEBRAY, RÉGIS. *Revolution in the Revolution?* New York: Monthly Review Press, 1967.

DESNOES, EDMUNDO. *Inconsolable Memories*. New York: New American Library, 1967.

DRAPER, THEODORE. *Castroism: Theory and Practice*. New York: Frederick A. Praeger, 1965.

———. *Castro's Revolution: Myths and Realities*. New York: Frederick A. Praeger, 1962.

FAGEN, RICHARD R., BRODY, RICHARD A., and O'LEARY, THOMAS J. *Cubans In Exile: Disaffection and the Revolution*. Stanford: Stanford University Press, 1968.

GERASSI, JOHN, ed. *Venceremos! The Speeches and Writings of Che Guevara*. New York: The Macmillan Co., 1964.

GOLDENBERG, BORIS. *The Cuban Revolution and Latin America*. New York: Frederick A. Praeger, 1965.

GUEVARA, CHE. *Reminiscences of the Revolutionary War*. New York: Monthly Review Press, 1968.

———. *The Diary of Che Guevara*. Ed. Robert Scheer. New York: Bantam Books, 1968.

———. *The Complete Bolivian Diaries of Che Guevara and Other Captured Documents*. Ed. Daniel James. New York: Stein & Day, 1968.

GUEVARA, ERNESTO "CHE." *Obra Revolucionaria*, Roberto F. Retamar, ed. Mexico City: Ediciones ERA, S.A., 1967.

HUBERMAN, LEO and SWEEZY, PAUL M. *Cuba, Anatomy of a Revolution*. New York: Monthly Review Press, 1961.

———. *Socialism in Cuba*. New York: Monthly Review Press, 1969.

JULIEN, CLAUDE. *La Révolution Cubaine*. Paris: René Julliard, 1961.

LÓPEZ-FRESQUET, RUFO. *My Fourteen Months with Castro*. Cleveland, Ohio: World Publishing Co., 1966.

MACGAFFEY, WYATT and BARNETT, CLIFFORD R. *Twentieth Century Cuba: The Background of the Castro Revolution*. Garden City, N.Y.: Anchor Books, 1965.

MATTHEWS, HERBERT L. *The Cuban Story*. New York: George Braziller, 1961.

———. *Fidel Castro*. New York: Simon and Schuster, 1969.

MILLER, WARREN. *Ninety Miles from Home*. Boston: Little Brown, 1961.

MILLS, C. WRIGHT. *Listen Yankee*. New York: McGraw-Hill, 1960.

PLANK, JOHN, ed. *Cuba and the United States: Long-Range Perspectives*. Washington, D.C.: The Brookings Institution, 1967.

RUIZ, RAMON EDUARDO. *Cuba. The Making of a Revolution*. Amherst, Massachusetts: University of Massachusetts Press, 1968.

SCHEER, ROBERT and ZEITLIN, MAURICE. *Cuba: An American Tragedy*. New York: Grove Press, 1963 and London: Penguin Books, 1964 (revised edition).

SEERS, DUDLEY, ed. *Cuba: The Economic and Social Revolution*. Durham, N.C.: University of North Carolina Press, 1964.

SOBEL, LESTER A., ed. *Cuba, the U.S. and Russia: 1960–63*. New York: Facts on File Interim History, 1964.

SUÁREZ, ANDRÉS. *Cuba: Castroism and Communism, 1959–1966*. Cambridge, Mass.: The M.I.T. Press, 1967.

SUTHERLAND, ELIZABETH. *Cuba Now!* New York: Dial Press, 1968.

TABER, ROBERT. *M-26: Biography of a Revolution*. New York: Lyle Stuart, 1961.

URRUTIA LLEO, MANUEL. *Fidel Castro and Co., Inc.: Communist Tyranny in Cuba*. New York, Praeger, 1964.

YGLESIAS, JOSÉ. *In the Fist of the Revolution: Life in a Cuban Country Town*. New York: Pantheon, 1968 and Vintage Books, 1969.

ZEITLIN, MAURICE. *Revolutionary Politics and the Cuban Working Class*. Princeton, N.J.: Princeton University Press, 1967.

index

Acosta, Armando, 21
Africa, 77, 354–355
Agrarian Reform, 88, 89, 96, 152, 333, 337; Institute of (INRA), 176
Agrarian Reform Law, first, 164; second, 99
agriculture, 87*ff.*, 188, 337–338, 349–352, 356
agricultural technicians, training of, 108–109, 233
airlift to the U.S., 290
art and art criticism, 111*ff.*, 136
artificial insemination of livestock, 93, 349–350
Associated Press (AP), 18, 27, 57

baseball, 289
Batista, Fulgencio, xi, 156, 165–169, 332
Bay of Pigs, 103, 218, 231, 248, 252, 333
blockade, xv, 227
Bolivia, 355–356
Bonsal, Philip (U.S. Ambassador to Cuba), 159
book publishing, 112, 136, 234
Bundy, McGeorge, 26
bureaucracy, 94

Camarioca exodus, 283*ff.*
campesinos, 13–17, 28, 184, 248, 252–253; special rehabilitation plan for, 261*ff.*
capitalism, 215*ff.*
Carpentier, Alejo, 136
Castro, Fidel, *passim.* On sugar, 62; personal portrait, 71–74; on study, 88, 188; on terror, 102–104, 165; on personal power, 147*ff.*, 175*ff.*, 352–353; political autobiography, 155–160; importance as leader of Revolution, 169–173, 328*ff.*; oratory, theory and method of, 184–186; on athletics, 188–190; on political and social character of U.S., 191, 211–212, 215–220
Castro, Raúl, 8, 11, 16–17, 163, 170, 176
cattle, 97, 338, 349

censorship, 111*ff.*, 330–331
Central Intelligence Agency (CIA), 75, 103, 190, 227, 231, 253, 333
centralization of power, 152, 180
Chibás, Eduardo, 157
China, People's Republic of, 92, 226, 251, 339, 342, 355n.
class struggle, 216, 325–329
class systems, 114, 147–148, 165
collectivization of agriculture, 96–99
Communism, 102, 153n., 160*ff.*, 217, 294, 334–336
Communist Party (pre-Castro), 151n., 166n., 328, 352–353
Communist Party of Cuba (PCC), 148, 153–154, 182, 329
Congo, 354–355
Constitution (1940), 164
Constitution (Socialist), 153, 187, 353
cooperatives, agricultural, 97–99
counterrevolution, 101–103, 172, 190, 191, 231, 291
criticism of government, 114–116, 147–148, 330
Cuban Revolution, see "Revolution, Cuban"
cult of the individual, 182–183
Czechoslovakia, Soviet invasion of, 354n., 357n.

DeGaulle, Charles, 171
democracy, 187
Desnoes, Edmundo, 136
Dominican Republic, 9, 25, 26, 27, 218, 220, 221
Donovan, James B., 232n.
Dorticós, Osvaldo, 30–31, 175, 177, 283

education, 107*ff.*, 116–117, 126, 249, 333
eggs, 99
egotism, 186
Engels, Friedrich, 163, 250
Escalante, Aníbal, 151–152, 173
exiles, xiv, 173–174, 291–293

Federation of Cuban Women, 261–263
food, scarcity of, 91, 350n.

García, Guillermo (army commander), 21, 22–24
Germany, Nazi, 186
granjas (people's farms), 96–97
Granma (party newspaper), 252
Granma (ship), 5, 19, 163, 178, 342
Green Belt of Havana, 350
Gromyko, Andrei, 285
Guantánamo naval base, 228
Guardián, 60, 61
guerrilla warfare, 169, 354–356
Guevara, Ernesto "Che," 5–8, 136, 149, 150, 162–163, 329, 342*ff*., 354–356
gusanos, 31

Harvard University, 26
Havana, 94, 104
Herter, Christian, 212
History Will Absolve Me (Moncada defense speech), 159, 162
homosexuality, 106–107

ICAIC (Cuban Film Institute), 136
imperialism, 155, 159
individuals, role of in history, 179*ff*.
industrialization, 95–96
institutionalization, 55, 180, 352–353
Interior, Ministry of, 178n., 253, 285
Isle of Pines, 55*ff*., 259, 350

Johnson, Lyndon, 18, 25–26, 170
journalism, 117

Kennedy, John F., 170, 191, 354
Korda, Alberto, 1–3, 20, 30–31, 57
Khrushchev, Nikita, 25, 225–226, 333–334, 354

labor movement, 328
land reform, see "agrarian reform"
Latin America, 155, 212, 221–223, 250, 291, 334, 338, 353–357
Lenin, Vladimir Ilyich, 163, 179, 250, 329, 335n.
Lincoln, Abraham, 161, 216
literature, 111–112, 136
local power (*"poder local"*), 153, 353

March 10, 1952 (Batista *coup*), 156, 158
Martínez, Raúl, 136
Marx, Karl, 155, 163, 250, 329
Marxism, 114, 147–148, 159, 162, 216, 292, 335; in art, 111; adaptation to Cuban society, 188, 339; concept of man, 215; Castro's use of, 325
masses, 184*ff*., 332, 333; attitude toward leaders, 149–150, 172; role in social change, 216
mechanization, 98, 351–352n.
Mexico, 222, 338
middle class (Cuban), 165–167, 328–329; in general, 155
Mikoyan, Sergo, 17
militia, 102
Minas del Frío, 108, 126
Miret, Pedro, 335
Miró Cardona, José, 181
missile crisis, 25, 223*ff*., 290, 292, 344, 354
missiles, atomic, 225
Moncada attack, 163, 178
Moncada program, 159, 160, 164–165

Naranjo, Pepín, 21, 27, 28
nationalization, 212, 356
Nixon, Richard, 211–212
nuclear equilibrium, 221, 224

OLAS, 355–356
Organization of American States (OAS), 25
Ortodoxo Party, 156–157
Otero, Lisandro, 136

Padilla, Heberto, 136
party, see "Communist Party of Cuba"
personal power, 329, 331, 352–353; see also subheading under "Castro, Fidel"
Piñeiro, Manuel, 75–76
political indoctrination, 110–111, 233–253
political prisoners, see "prisoners, political"
Portocarrero, René, 136
posadas, 105–106
Prensa Latina, 27

press, American, see subheading under "United States"
press, Cuban, 113–115, 252
Prime Ministry, office of, 174–175, 180–181
prisoners, political, 172, 230–264
private farming, 99–101
prostitution, 106

racial discrimination, 114, 216, 333
rationing, 91, 350n.
rehabilitation plan, see *"campesinos"* and "prisoners, political"
Retamar, Roberto Fernández, 136
revolution, 231; in underdeveloped countries, 219–220; Cuban aid to, 220–221, 325, 353–356
Revolution, Chinese, 251
Revolution, Cuban, character of, xiv, 186, 349; achievements and limitations of, 325*ff.*
Revolution, French, 164
Revolution, Russian, 164, 251
Revolutionary War, 164–169, 325–328
Rodríguez, Carlos Rafael, 176–177

Sánchez, Celia, 55–56, 74–75
Second Front of Escambray, 101, 102
sectarianism, 151–152, 173, 182
sexual customs, 105–106
Sierra Maestra, 24
small farmers, see "private farming"
socialism, 112, 164–165, 219, 233, 251
socialist realism, 136
Soviet Union, relations with, 223*ff.*, 325, 337, 354–356, 357, 358; trade with, 92–93, 212–214, 333, 337
Stadelhofer, Ernst, 283, 287–288, 293
Stalin, Josef, 24–25, 179
sugar, cultivation of, 62, 87–88, 89, 92, 350–352; U.S. import quota, 89, 213, 333
Swiss ambassador, see "Stadelhofer, Ernst"

Tamargo, Orlando, 70
Tarzan, 234
teacher training, 108, 126

technology, agricultural, 88, 350
television, 332
Topes de Collantes, 126
trade, with U.S., 89–90, 95; with Socialist bloc, 92–93; with U.S.S.R., 92–93, 212–214
Tricontinental Congress, 354

unemployment, 94
Union of Soviet Socialist Republics, see "Soviet Union"
United Fruit Co., 98
United Press International (UPI), 18, 27, 57
United States, economic blockade of Cuba, 227; foreign policy of, 9, 18, 25–26, 95, 155, 167, 216–219, 224; internal character of, 113–114, 147–149, 168, 191, 215, 220; invasion of Cuba, 103, 218, 228, 229, 231, 333; investments in Cuba, 98, 174; official Cuban view of, 114–117; press coverage of Cuba, xv, 336; relations with Cuba, xiv–xv, 9, 95, 103, 113, 159, 161, 211–212, 218, 224, 227–230, 231, 290–292, 339–340; and Dominican Republic, 9, 25, 26, 27, 218, 220, 221; Vietnam war, 9, 18, 25, 57, 216, 229
Urban Reform Law of 1960, 105, 333
Urrutia, Manuel, 175, 181
Uruguay, 222
U-2 flights, 230
Uvero, 5–8

Valdez, Ramiro, 289
Vallejo, René, 55–61, 65–66, 68–71, 74, 77, 283–284
Venezuela, 216, 222–223
Vietnam, 9, 18, 57, 218, 221, 229
voluntary work, 248–249

Women, see "Federation of Cuban Women"
work, social value of, 24

Young Communists, Cuban Union of, 286

LEE LOCKWOOD was born in New York in 1932, attended Yale, Boston University and Columbia University. He is a photo-journalist with the Black Star Photo Agency. His photographs and articles have appeared in leading magazines in the U.S. and abroad. He was present in Cuba on January 1, 1959, when Fidel Castro came to power, and has made more than a dozen trips to Cuba since then. *Castro's Cuba, Cuba's Fidel* received the 1967 Overseas Press Club award for best foreign reporting. Mr. Lockwood is the author of a forthcoming Random House/Vintage introduction to Fidel Castro's thought. Mr. Lockwood has received a Rockefeller Foundation grant for 1967–68 to experiment in educational television at WGBH–TV, Boston.